D1825741

THE LINGO

Graham Seal teaches Australian Studies at Curtin University in Western Australia. His commentary on language and culture is recognised both in Australia and internationally. Among the several books he has written or edited are *The Outlaw Legend: A Cultural Tradition in Britain, America and Australia* (1995) and *The Hidden Culture: Folklore in Australian Society* (first published 1989; second edition 1998).

2746

424.994

Colchester VI Form College WITHDRAWN

00002746

THE
LINGO

LISTENING TO
AUSTRALIAN ENGLISH

Graham Seal

UNSW PRESS

To the memories of Jack and Des—great Lingoists.

Think with the wise
but talk with the vulgar.

GERMAN PROVERB

A UNSW Press book

Published in Australia by
University of New South Wales Press Ltd
University of New South Wales
Sydney 2052 Australia

© Graham Seal 1999
First published 1999

This book is copyright. Apart from any fair dealing
for the purpose of private study, research, criticism
or review, as permitted under the Copyright Act,
no part may be reproduced by any process without
written permission. Inquiries should be addressed to
the publisher.

National Library of Australia
Cataloguing-in-Publication entry:

  Seal, Graham, 1950– .
  The lingo: listening to Australian English.

  ISBN 086840 680 5.

  1. Australianisms. I. Title.

  427.994

Printed by Griffin Press, Adelaide

CONTENTS

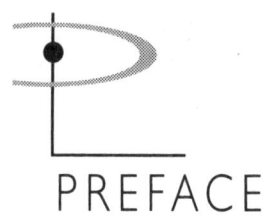

PREFACE

From the late 1940s Australians began to fear the great numbers of NEW AUSTRALIANS bustling down the gangways of migrant ships. This was the era of politician Arthur Calwell's now-notorious pronouncement, 'two Wongs don't make a white', and a time when Australians had begun to assert their own ideas of cultural identity. The key official words applied to migrants were 'integration' and 'assimilation'. We wanted migrants to become as much like us as possible, as quickly as possible.

One minor but revealing response to this incursion of foreignness was the development of a slang test. A group of social psychologists searching for ways of measuring the Australianness of new migrants invented a quiz of Australian slang for this purpose. After some time living here, new migrants would take the test and their score would indicate the extent to which they had become Australian; in short, how well they had 'learnt the Lingo'.

This slang test, discussed in a little more detail in chapter 2 was, fortunately, never used. Its invention though, indicates two things: one was, as it turned out, the transitory importance of the assimilationist ethic during the immediate post-World War II years; the other was the singular extent to which Australians have continued to regard their vernacular as a significant indicator of national identity. While the existence of colloquial language is not unique to this country, our emotional attachment to the Lingo is an Australian peculiarity, one that both reveals and hides much about ourselves. The causes of this colloquial dependence can be traced to the earliest settlement of English speakers on these shores, through the 19th and 20th centuries, into the uncertainties that have again thrown questions of cultural identity into sharp relief.

The Lingo is about the development and power of that Australian vernacular. It is in part a history, in part an investigation and analysis of what is arguably our single most important signifier of cultural identity. It is also a celebration — though not an uncritical one — of the colour, cleverness and sheer vitality of the many linguistic forms that make up our Lingo. These include slang, insults, derogations, colloquialisms, similes and traditional wisdom, rhyming slang, the naming of places, houses, PUBS, body parts, nicknames, BARRACKING, folk names for flora, fauna and natural features, and many other informal uses of language. These forms of popular parlance are heard throughout an impressive range of everyday experiences, including working, relaxing, playing, growing up, gambling, drinking, family life, sport, crime, war, politics, and sexual relations.

In addition to this great well of colloquial speech that, to a greater or lesser extent, all Australians have in common, there are what are called here the 'little lingoes' of Australia. These are the more restricted jargons, argots, naming practices and speech oddities that give different social groups — ethnic, occupational, regional, special interest — their sense of identity. There has been, and is, a surprising amount of crossover between these restricted speech communities and those of the broader Australian Lingo. This interplay contributes to the strong sense of nation that most Australians hear in our speech. These aspects of the vernacular are also treated, necessarily selectively, in this book.

Listening to Australia's many lingoes provides a way of looking at certain aspects of our past and present, our folklore and many of our national mythologies. The Lingo reveals a good deal about some of our most cherished self-perceptions, especially those about our ongoing romance with the bush, our casual attitudes to officialdom, to work, to leisure, to interpersonal and gender relations and, increasingly, our interactions with others — those non-Australians who have both attracted us and repelled us, often at the same time.

Because we have these various notions about ourselves, and express them through our vernacular, does not mean they are necessarily true. Eavesdropping on the Lingo demonstrates that we have as great a capacity for self-delusion as any other national group. Nowhere else can our inconsistencies and ambivalences be more clearly observed than in what we say, the way we say it, or what and about whom we say it. Our Lingo carries and perpetuates prejudices of race, ethnicity, gender, and belief. It is a mire of malevolence and insult of an especially creative kind and it carries a large baggage of negativity, paranoia, and cultural loathing. It also carries our more cherished ideals of egalitarianism and anti-authoritarianism, sympathy for the SMALL CAPS BATTLER and the persistent yearning for a FAIR GO. Always it is witty, colourful, and playful, often most so when most abrasive. The faint-hearted should take note that no punches are pulled; the Australian vernacular is presented in all its colour, vulgarity, and offensiveness.

Ultimately, this book is about the peculiar power the Lingo has over the way we Australians see the world and our place in it. The colloquial past and present of Australia reveals much about the self-image of its people. Not all that is seen and heard is pleasant. But it is not all bad, either.

• • •

The fine distinctions necessarily made by linguists and lexicographers for slang, argot, jargon, and so on, are not generally followed in this book. All forms of unofficial Australian English have been labelled L/lingo in order to discuss them and their significance in a non-technical, but useful, way. All such L/lingo forms that appear have been typeset in SMALL CAPITALS while those words that are British dialect (the origin of much of our L/lingo) are enclosed in 'quotation marks'. The convention of *italicising* non-English, including Aboriginal words, has been followed. In matters of spelling *The Macquarie Dictionary* has been used as the authority, except in a few cases where the regional spelling and/or pronunciation dictates otherwise.

1

HEARING THE COLLOQUIAL COMMONWEALTH

...the Australian interlards his conversation with large quantities
of slang...This use of slang is so common that the public memory forgets that it is slang, and it finds its way into the most
unexpected places. Chief Justices on their benches, leading
newspapers in their editorials, statesmen — such as Australia
boasts — all disfigure their utterances by jarring slang terms
and phrases...drawn from the lowliest sources — the racecourse, the football match, and the prize ring...

VALERIE DESMOND, THE AWFUL AUSTRALIAN (1911)

It was a moonless night in France during World War I. A British
officer was sent to locate a troop of Australians lost somewhere in
the labyrinth of muddy trenches known as the front line. The officer
stumbled and crawled into a number of dugouts and firing positions,
inquiring if the occupants were Australians or not. No, they were
British or French. Eventually the officer came to a group of soldiers
occupying a forward trench. It was still too dark to see what uniform
the soldiers were wearing so he asked politely if they were Australians or not. 'Who the bloody hell wants to know?' came the belligerent reply. 'Oh', said the British officer, relieved: 'I've found you
Australians at last.'

This yarn, one of a number dealing with DIGGER bad language,
suggests how important the vernacular is for our sense of self. Not
only is the belligerent bad language characteristic of what many con-
sider to be the typical and authentic Australian character, but the
British officer mildly identifies the soldiers as Australian by their not-
very-mild language. What they say and the way they say it is their

badge of identity. The story at once highlights our view of ourselves and marks us off as different from the British.

That 'bad' language is the Australian vernacular, or Lingo. It is the language that many, perhaps most, Australians use in factories, shops, offices, schools, on building sites, on the road, at home, in the pub and wherever Australian is spoken. And it has been much the same story since the first days of European colonisation. Although one of the youngest nations, Australia was remarkably quick to develop its own version of English. Even more remarkable is the affection we have for our Lingo as an essential component of Australianness. Perhaps more than anything else, more than swagmen and blackened billies, Ned Kelly, Gallipoli, and our many other icons, colloquial speech is our most cherished indicator of cultural distinctiveness. Bound up with what we say and the way we say it are some of our fundamental, and sometimes inaccurate, ideas about ourselves as a nation and as a people.

Although mostly taken for granted, the importance of the vernacular in everyday life is apparent from the number of Lingoisms describing or referring to it. CHINWAG; GASBAG; HAVE A YARN; BEND YOUR EAR; COP AN EARFUL; EARBASHING; YABBER; YACKING; VERBAL DIARRHOEA; TO BULLSHIT; TO GO ON; TO TALK UNDERWATER WITH A MOUTHFUL OF BREAD; WINDBAG; HAVE A CHAT; CHATTER; gossip (now often shortened to GOSS, as in GIVE US THE GOSS); STIR; SKITE; A MOUTH LIKE A SEWER; SPIELER; CHIACK; BARRACK; SLEDGE; SPITTING CHIPS, MAGGING..., and so on. Lingo has always played a central, if taken-for-granted, role in the life of the nation.

Lingo is made up of words, phrases, and expressions that are mostly not found in any dictionary of standard English or even Australian English. Many use these speech forms as a matter of course, all day and every day without ever thinking about it. The colloquialisms that make up this unique language identify us to ourselves, and to others, as speakers of Australian English, rather than of American English, or Canadian English, even of English English. This distinctiveness of Australian everyday speech has long been commented upon — often unfavourably as in the epigraph to this and some later chapters. As well as being 'low' in character, according to some at least, Lingo is a particularly colourful, creative and vibrant variant of the English language. To decode phrases like FLAT TO THE BOARDS LIKE A LIZARD DRINKING, LOOKS AS THOUGH THEY MIGHT CUT UP RUSTY (OR ROUGH) or IT'S CRACKING HARDY TODAY..., the listener needs to be a member of the group that habitually utters such oddities.

This book documents some aspects of this Australian, mentions some of its many interesting characteristics and uses, provides some translations of the more obscure items, and speculates on what the Lingo might reveal about our perceptions of ourselves and others. A fair bit of space is taken up with looking at and listening to those aspects of Lingo, great and small, that have affected our ideas of ourselves as a nation. The speech of convicts, LARRIKINS, DIGGERS, shearers, punters, and many other groups, legendary and little-known, is discussed along with a smattering of the ballads, jokes, rhymes and yarns by which a good deal of our popular tongue is carried. As well as colloquialisms, slang and other aspects of everyday verbal communication, this book looks at naming practices, specifically those related to naming towns, places, houses and certain public buildings, including the PUB. It also deals with the private languages, or little lingoes, of various social, occupational, age and gender groups and with State and regional vocabularies.

While Lingo is a term widely used in Australia to denote these sorts of unofficial speech, the word is not itself an Australianism. Lingo is variously said to be derived from Portuguese *lingoa*, via the Latin *lingua* for tongue or, according to some sources, from an in-group language or argot called Polari, a lingua franca dating from the 11th century and still used by circus people and other travelling entertainers (see chapter 9). This venerable term continues to have much the same meanings in Britain and the USA, a fact that is especially appropriate as a sizeable segment of Australian Lingo, past and present, derives from the slang of these other two countries. The implications of this are discussed later. The point will be made here for the first, if not the last time, that it is not the origin of the terms that gives them their Australian flavour, but the use of those terms in the mouths of Australians, together with the overall sense of belonging that knowledge of the Lingo imparts.

THE COLLOQUIAL COMMONWEALTH

Australian vernacular speech is a colloquial commonwealth that acknowledges no boundaries or borders of class, nationality or race. Lingo takes what is useful and appropriate from wherever it comes, altering and adapting to whatever communicative necessities prevail at a given time and place. Lingo is the unfettered expression of the popular or the folk. It is, and always has been, crude, vulgar, colourful and alive on the tongues of everyday Australians. For many, colloquial speech is the signifier of Australianness, cherished by most and disapproved of by a few WET BLANKETS and MISERYGUTSES.

The use of colloquial speech at all levels of society has long been a characteristic of Australian English. Few English-speaking (or probably many other) nations would tolerate the degree of Lingo spoken

by Australians of all social statuses and in all sorts of situations, rang-
ing from the weekend BARBIE to Federal parliament. A prime minister can refer to employers as BUMS and their refusal to give workers a
holiday as A BASTARD ACT, as did then-prime minister Bob Hawke
(THE SILVER BODGIE, also dubbed THE SILVER BUDGIE by a political
opponent) on the occasion of Australia winning the America's Cup,
and use the term BULLSHIT on a major capital city radio show — all
without anyone lifting an eyebrow. When the same LARRIKIN prime
minister, already notorious as a user of colourful language by the
mid-1970s, called a Tasmanian pensioner 'a silly old bugger' it was
not his language that was the issue but the fact that he had been rash
enough to insult a senior citizen in public. Hawkie's eventual succes-
sor as prime minister, Paul Keating (nickname: MR CHEATING), was in
the habit of calling his parliamentary opponents 'scumbags' and
other honorifics during his reign as 'the world's greatest Treasurer'.
After his elevation to prime minister, Paul Keating continued to wield
the Lingo with usually wicked effect. And on the subject of politicians and Lingo, the founder of the Australian Democrats, Don
Chipp, is justly famous for his declaration that his party would 'keep
the bastards honest'. Even such a well-educated and articulate wielder of standard English as ALP politician Gareth Evans (nickname:
BIGGLES), peppers his responses to media questions with lingoisms
like SKERRICK, also used by the succeeding prime minister, John
Howard (nickname: LITTLE JOHNNY HOWARD), from time to time.
The representative of Her Majesty the Queen of (among other
places) Australia , Elizabeth II, is officially called the governor-gen-
eral. This is usually shortened to GG which, as Phillip Adams once
noted, makes him sound like an entrant in the Melbourne Cup.
Australians frequently refer to Elizabeth II as LIZ and her husband,
Prince Philip, the Duke of Edinburgh, as PHIL THE GREEK.

Not only is Lingo spoken throughout the Commonwealth of
Australia, it is itself a colloquial commonwealth. The ability to speak
the Lingo and to use it means that person is a member of a particular
linguistic community in which all speakers are, if not equal, at least
expected to appear so in everyday conversation and in their public
utterances. The democracy of slang, the vernacular republic that is 'the
Great Australian Lingo' reflects one of the greatest Australian myths,
that of egalitarianism. We fondly believe Australia to be the land where,
as Russel Ward put it so long ago in *The Australian Legend* '... Jack is
as good as his master, if not a good deal better.' We speak still of the
FAIR GO, of DOING THE RIGHT THING, of HAVING A FAIR SUCK OF THE
SAV or [SUCK OF] THE SAUCE BOTTLE. What degree of truth there might
be, or might have been, in this belief matters little. Enough people still

believe it to be true and speak accordingly, making a vernacular treasury that, for many, spells Australian.

One outstanding feature of the Lingo is that even its more offensive exclamations have increasingly become a part of accepted speech. There are various reasons for this. One is the continuing liberal influences of the 1960s leading to a freeing up of the airwaves, especially radio, where everyday speech is heard every day, even on the ABC. (Though the f-word seems to be mostly okay on ABC radio it is still often beeped out on ABC television — unless in drama shows where this venerable Anglo-Saxonism seems to benefit from a magical dispensation.) This word, and other four-letter taboo terms are as common as BLOODY in today's youthspeak, proving once again the generational amelioration of slang.

We will soon need to find new taboo words. Good candidates for this dubious honour are those derogatory terms used by earlier generations to describe migrants. So great has the weight of official censure against such words become since the early 1980s that they have been given the status of forbidden fruit. As moral attitudes have altered to give us a more relaxed attitude towards sexuality, and so to much of the vernacular describing it, so we have needed to find a new vocabulary of transgression. We seem to be finding it in those terms that once formed our linguistic defence against the incursions of post-World War II mass immigration and the consequent introduction of 'multiculturalism'. The dominant Anglo-centric culture of the 'old Australia' developed its epithets as a kind of compensation for invasion. Many Australians resent being coerced into giving up these ways of speaking, a resentment directly related to questions of what can be said and what cannot be said, by whom and about whom.

An enlightening exchange on the contemporary use and misuse of the term WOG, and so of attitudes towards the word and others like it, took place in the run-up to the 1996 Federal election campaign. In January that year the National Party candidate for the Queensland seat of Leichhardt, Mr Bob Burgess, a British child-migrant, described citizenship ceremonies as 'de-wogging ceremonies'. The leader of his party and of its ally, the Liberal Party, immediately repudiated Mr Burgess's remarks. Burgess defended himself, refusing to apologise and is quoted as saying of the word WOG: 'It is a flippant Australian colloquial remark, it isn't racist and it wasn't meant to be racist.' Electoral imperatives, presumably, forced Mr Burgess to later apologise if his remarks caused offence, but he persisted in his view that the term WOG, and variants, were simply part of everyday Australian speech and should not be interpreted as racist. He also made the point that the government had not objected to the title of the famous stage show *Wogs Out of Work*.

While Mr Burgess clearly believed that WOG was not offensive, the Liberal candidate for the same seat thought the word belonged in the 1960s. The reactions of many other public figures and much of the mainstream mass media suggested that WOG was not a proper term to use in public, unless in a theatrical context involving ethnic Australians using the term themselves to make satirical points about Australian culture. No-one mentioned in the course of this debate (or, if they did, it was not reported in the press) that the *Wogs Out of Work* show also used the term SKIPPY, referring to persons of Anglo-Celtic origins and intended to be equally as offensive as WOG.

That same Federal election also returned a first-time member of parliament to the House of Representatives for the Queensland seat of Oxley. The 'fish-and-chip-shop lady', the 'Oxley moron', Pauline Hanson, was given this shock victory, in part at least, by an electorate puzzled and smarting from years of being told what it could and could not say in everyday speech. Those who believed that this was simply a local aberration were quickly jarred into the realisation that the disenchantment was widespread. Within eighteen months of her election, Hanson had formed a new political party, 'One Nation', on a platform that promoted a regressive and aggressive nostalgia for an Australia that most thought was gone forever, if it ever existed at all. The thousands who initially flocked to support Hanson and her party presumably shared this pugnacious view of national identity, a view that is closely related to earlier ways of using the Lingo.

Australian language has even caused international incidents. In mid-1997 an international government conference, the Foreign and External Ministers' Meeting (FEMM) was held in Brisbane. Australia was host to the representatives of numerous Pacific Ocean neighbours. All was proceeding politely, as such diplomatic GABFESTS do, when a careless official of the Department of Foreign Affairs and Trade (DOFAT) left a copy of the briefing papers provided to the Foreign Minister, Alexander (nickname: TEDDY BEAR) Downer, and his OFFSIDERS. A journalist came upon the documents and was astounded to discover that they were confidential assessments of prominent public figures in the various nations of the region. Worse — or better, from the journalist's point of view — these assessments were most undiplomatically phrased, referring to certain government eminences as 'opportunists', 'alcoholics', and a number of other impolite things, often expressed in extremely blunt Australian. Needless to say, when these words were published, there was a furore and the Australian foreign minister had to spend the next few months travelling through the Pacific region apologising and MENDING THE BROKEN FENCES.

THE LITTLE LINGOES

To SPEAK THE LINGO is to become a member of a group that shares a sense of itself and expresses that sense in its own language. In the case of the Great Australian Lingo that group consists of all its speakers — most Australians, in fact. But there are also many other lingoes, past and present, that are and have been spoken in Australia by different groups, or speech communities as they are sometimes called. Sometimes, these are impenetrably bizarre terms and usages understandable only to those who have been initiated into the group and can prove their membership by speaking and understanding the restricted language of that particular collective. Groups with such distinctive argots and jargons have included convicts, DIGGERS, SURFIES, computer professionals, army cadets, goldminers, and other occupational groups, criminals, women, children, and an almost endless diversity of other speech communities, including generational groupings and those who live in different States, Territories, and regions. Some of these vocabularies have contributed words and phrases to the larger stock of Australian Lingo; many more remain, DOUBLE DUTCH or just GOBBLEDYGOOK to the rest of us.

What does the term TALK RIVER mean, for example? You almost certainly will not know unless you worked in or were close to the Murray River boat trade. In that speech community it means to talk about matters relating to the river, its people and its business. Unless you are involved with the welding trade you would be unlikely to know that STICK and TIC refer to different forms of welding — STICK is with flame heat and TIC with an electric arc. Nor would you know what a KROMER CAP is, or what it might signify to the initiates of the welding fraternity. In some parts of rural Western Australia snakes are known as YELVINS and unless you were a SHOWIE or pretty closely associated with members of the travelling show fraternity you would not have a clue what the strangely evocative term STILL-TOWN might mean. (It refers to a town where the vehicles and members of the show group rest between shows, a practice known as STILL-TOWN-ING.) As well as talking about the Great Australian Lingo that, in varying degrees most Australians speak or hear, this book also looks at a selection of our many little lingoes.

● ● ●

The beginning is a good place to mention what will not be considered to any great extent in the rest of this book — the Australian accent, or accents. This topic has been, like Lingo itself, the focus of fierce and mostly fruitless debate. Some people hold that there is no difference of accent between States, Territories, and regions of this vast country. Others will swear blind (or deaf) that there are detectable differences of pronunciation and speech pattern. Evidence for this is sometimes said to be in the slower speech of the BUSHIE (a term in use from at least the late 19th century) compared with that of those from the cities — TOWNIES (in Australians' mouths since at least the 1820s). A variant on this theme of presumed superiority is that West Australians, Queenslanders, TASWEGIANS, and other peripheral peoples also speak more slowly than those at the vital throbbing hub of things — invariably Sydney, Melbourne and Canberra. Like complaints about the nasal or other allegedly undesirable aspects of Australian speech monotonously made by supposedly better-spoken visitors, these comments generally reflect the prejudices of those who make them. While there are certainly identifiable differences among speakers of Australian in all its fascinating forms, these are only mentioned in passing. There are some exceptions to this for special and regional pronunciations, but this book concentrates on the shared speech communities of Australia, about the words, phrases, and the attitudes that they reveal, rather than about how they are, or are not, pronounced.

Largely ignoring accent also avoids the necessity of dealing further than this one paragraph with the mischief known as STRINE, the supposedly 'typical' pronunciation, or mispronunciation, of Australian English. The classic example of Strine is EMMA CHISIT, said to translate as 'how much is it'). While the 1960s obsession with Strine reflected an interest (largely elitist) in certain aspects of the Australian accent, the emphasis soon became tedious and led to excesses, such as ZARF TRAWL, supposed to be the Australian pronunciation of 'after all'. Journalists, academics, and speakers of everyday Australian, vied with each other to render words and phrases into increasingly unlikely forms of Strine — ILER CALF TRIM, for instance (you work it out). Apart from doing considerable injustice to the variety of speech in Australia, the Strine game very quickly becomes boring. The Lingo itself, the vernacular vocabulary, is far more interesting, colourful, and even arresting, especially in some of its more creative forms. This book is a journey into the past, the present, and perhaps the future, of the colloquial commonwealth and its Lingoes, large and little. Best of all, perhaps, this book does not propose any more theories about the origins of the term POMMY — FAIR DINKUM.

2

NATIVES,
NEW CHUMS
AND SEPTICS

All newcomers,
of course,
will have to learn
to speak Australian.

ARTHUR A. CALWELL, MINISTER FOR IMMIGRATION, 1945

NATIVES AND NEW CHUMS

On 29 April 1770, Captain James Cook gazed upon the inhabitants of the landmass that he claimed for Great Britain and named 'New South Wales'. He described the people he saw — and some of whose language he collected — as 'natives', the indigenous residents. This became the official term for the Aboriginal peoples of the continent, used in legislation and for official titles such as 'Protector of Natives'. A few years after European occupation in 1788, the increasing numbers of children born in the colony of New South Wales were also referred to as 'natives', confusing just about everybody. This confusion was one reason why the term 'currency' came into vogue from around, if not quite some time before, the 1820s to describe those born here who were not Aboriginal. Those who were not convicts and not native-born were called 'sterling', a discriminator that we have never quite gotten over. People who were both Aboriginal and native, inevitably were given what are now considered derogatory names like 'half-caste' and, later, may have been described in Lingo as having A TOUCH OF THE TARBRUSH. Equally unacceptable in today's formal discourse is the term 'native' for Aboriginal

Australians. Unfortunately far more derogatory expressions persist in Lingo, including NIGGER, BOONG, ABO (now often shortened to AB), COON AND GIN.

The extent to which these derogatory terms and the attitudes beneath them are still very much a part of popular Australian speech was demonstrated in the long-running furore over racist abuse in football and other sports that occupied the media and football administrators in 1994 and 1995. It was obvious that many football players, administrators and fans saw nothing wrong with using racist insults on the playing field while the 'national game' was being played. Similar controversies arose during the same period about the actions of Aboriginal runner Cathy Freeman at the Commonwealth Games in Canada where, after winning her race, she took a lap of honour clutching the Aboriginal, as well as the Australian, flag. Sporting official Arthur Tunstall, along with many others, criticised Cathy Freeman for this spontaneous and colourful action. The controversy that followed these criticisms had barely died away when, in mid-1995, the same official was reported to have told a racist joke involving a Lingo term for Aboriginal people. Again, opinions were heatedly expressed around the country. Some defended the right of the individual to tell such jokes, others condemned the practice. Regardless of the rights or wrongs of this and similar incidents it is clear that the way in which the language is used or abused is a matter of crucial importance to many Australians, especially when it is the language of prejudice.

As well as being the source and perpetuator of racist slurs against the indigenous people, Lingo has also been the first line of defence, and offence, against any of those settlers who came after the First Fleet. The currency population and those who had been here a little longer than the latest batch of migrants were very quick to label the migrating hopefuls with various names. NEW CHUM, originally noted by Vaux as a convict term for a just-landed transportee, continued through the 19th century to describe those newly arrived, if now mostly free settlers. A number of ballads and popular songs give a clear picture of the NEW CHUM, such as Charles Thatcher's 'The New Chum Swell' (1860s):

> *His dress was spicy as could be,*
> *His fingers hung with rings,*
> *White waistcoats, black silk pantaloons,*
> *And other stylish things...*

Later the NEW CHUM arrives on the goldfields to make his fortune, rather shocked to find that he will actually have to work for it. Not used to getting his hands dirty, the SWELL

...went and bought a shovel
And a pick and dish as well;
But to every ten minutes' work,
He took an hour's spell.
The skin from off his fair, white hands
In blisters peeled away
And thus he worked and sunk about
Twelve inches every day.

The usually derisive NEW CHUM is still heard occasionally (unlike another early synonym, GUMSUCKER) though it was more or less officially replaced in the 1950s by NEW AUSTRALIAN. This is a term that has now become politically incorrect but, in hindsight, seems to be one of the least value-laden of all terms used to describe migrants. It is certainly preferable to most of those still used in Lingo and which continue the long tradition, initiated by Cook, of pointing the linguistic finger at feared others.

Our ability to bend the Lingo to all manner of ethnic slurs has been taxed by the arrival of migrants from many parts in the waves of post-World War II migration. While it was difficult to impute negative ethnic traits to those who came from Britain to an overwhelmingly Anglo-Celtic country in the late 1940s and early 1950s, we did find a way to insult and stereotype these newcomers. They became WHINGEING POMMY BASTARDS, a reference to the alleged willingness and frequency of POMS to complain about Australia and Australians, and they became the butt of jokes about British Airways jets 'whining on the runway' and their towels being far too dry. Barely had we settled into this satisfying revival of name-calling than large numbers of migrants from southern Europe began bouncing down the gangways and into the hostels. We soon invented or appropriated Lingoisms for them. We came up first with REFFOS, a less-than-affectionate diminutive of 'refugees'. Then we resurrected borrowed terms like WOG and DAGO, generalised insults for anyone from southern Europe. We went on to be specifically derogatory with terms like BALT (arrivals from the 'Baltic' countries), EYTIE, DING (an Italian — mostly used in Western Australia) and LEBBO ('Lebanese'and LEBS). A few years later we had the opportunity to revive some of our mid-19th century gold-rush Lingoisms relating to our fear of THE YELLOW PERIL. CHINK was heard again in the land, followed in the next breath with SLOPE-HEAD (or just SLOPE), SLANT-EYE and many others. CHOGUE or CHOGIE was in vogue in Western Australia as a derogation for Asians in the mid-1990s, as was RAG-HEADS for Muslims. Not only were all these new people foreign, they did not SPEAK THE LINGO.

For decades we had successfully kept out the unwanted by manipulating various immigration filters. One of these was that essential apparatus of 'White Australia', the dictation test. Introduced originally as part of the *Immigration Restriction Act 1901*, the test consisted of being able to understand 50 words of any European language. Failure meant no entry. Four years later 'European language' was altered to 'prescribed language'. The dictation test was concerned with the correct speaking of a language, rather than with its unofficial forms. Its main purpose, as in the USA where a similar contrivance operated from 1917, was to keep undesirables out of the country. Almost always these were people of non-European backgrounds.

Once the lucky ones had been allowed in, though, there was the problem of assimilation, particularly for those whose first language was not English. We did not want them to keep up with their languages and traditions, we wanted them to become, as quickly and efficiently as possible, just like us. To test the degree to which migrants had been incorporated into the Australian community during the 1950s, some social psychologists developed a 'slang test' which they proposed should be taken by NEW AUSTRALIANS. Terms such as STOUSH, FAIR COW, BONZER and OFFSIDER were listed, each with four possible meanings. FAIR COW, for instance, had the following meanings: a pin-up girl, something very disagreeable, butterfat, or something valuable. The NEW AUSTRALIAN was to choose the correct translation — then indicate how often he or she employed this particular term — often, sometimes, or never? According to the creators of this test, how the hapless migrant scored would produce a measure of the extent to which the person tested had become Australianised. It is not known whether the slang test was ever applied, but its existence suggests the importance we attach to Lingo as an indicator of Australianness.

In these more enlightened times we have embraced the policy and, mostly, the spirit of multiculturalism. This policy encourages respect for the traditions and values of the numerous ethnic groups that now constitute Australian society. Some of the older ethnic slurs are sometimes heard from unreconstructed AUSSIES, but words like WOG and DAGO are no longer acceptable in polite conversation or even in some impolite conversations. Lingo has, however, outwitted the politically correct and the term ETHNIC has now become a generalised term of abuse, as in BLOODY ETHNICS. Even MULTI-CULTS or just MULTS are used in similar ways. And there are always subtle ways to express dislike of difference, as in the term ABBA HOUSES, a reference to a baroque style of housing favoured by some Mediterranean migrants and meaning all BLOODY balustrades and arches. Since the 1980s Australians of Anglo-Celtic extraction have been increasingly referred to by those of other ethnic backgrounds, usually disdainfully, as SKIPPIES, SKIPS, ANGLOS or *gubbahs*.

While this only goes to show that ethnic slurs are not restricted to any particular group, it also serves to highlight the differences and the distinctions among such groups and the ways in which they use informal language. The positive side of the numerous derogatory terms that have evolved in our Lingo is that they are a reflection of the multi-ethnic and poly-cultural diversity that has been a feature of 'the land DOWN-UNDER' since 1788. Some idea of this can be conveyed through listening to a little of the linguistic interaction between English and some of the many other languages spoken here.

INTERACTIONS AND TRANSFORMATIONS

An important and uniquely Australian aspect of Lingo is the use and misuse of indigenous terms. The consequences of this linguistic adaptation may often be absurdly humorous. A favourite example is *Moomba*, the supposedly indigenous word used for Melbourne's famous Moomba Festival. It seems that Moomba has no relation to anything at all festive but means BACKSIDE. While this may be a fitting piece of linguistic revenge, the other wrongs done to Aboriginal languages by Australian English are many. The wonderfully descriptive term MANGULATION comes to mind in this context, with such compounds as Wagga Wagga, all the 'ups' in Western Australian place names, the most amazing of many surely being Mandogalup, and the violence done to *warra* used as a suffix, including Karrawarra and Kemblawarra. The Aboriginal prefix *yarra*, common in New South Wales and Victoria (usually said to mean water) is another that has a good deal to answer for, including Yarramundi, Yarrawonga and Yarramalong, not to mention the Yarra River itself.

While these examples are not strictly Lingo, the process of their adaptation from indigenous languages is similar to that which takes place when Lingo terms are taken from Aboriginal languages. These include *munjong/munjon* (from Yinjibarndi, Fortescue River area, Western Australia) and meaning an Aborigine who has had little contact with Europeans, or an Aborigine who has been raised in white society and has consequently lost touch with traditional ways. Another term, used more in Aboriginal English, but also known in white speech in Western Australia is MONAYCH, used for a policeman, from the West Australian Nyungar group of languages' descriptor for a white cockatoo. More widely used is the term the GIBBER/GIBBA (a dry, stony and usually desolate area of land), from the Dharuk (Port Jackson area, New South Wales) language, also heard in combinations like GIBBER COUNTRY and GIBBER ROCKS.

An interesting recent development in adolescent folk speech has been the importation of words from various Aboriginal languages. In current Darwin youthspeak, the term BUJU is used by both black and white people to mean that the person so-described is sexually appealing, a usage that older Aborigines generally find outrageous. Younger people in Western Australia have incorporated some Aboriginal terms into their everyday speech, including UNNA, an interrogatory interjection that can be used in various ways, though always as an invitation to respond rather than as a request to do so, in accordance with direct questioning being considered rude in many forms of Aboriginal conversation. SOME OTHER TIME, UNNA? is a simple example where the placing and meaning of the term corresponds to ending an English sentence with 'a?' UNNA can be used in many more complex ways, as demonstrated in Archie Weller's novel *Day of the Dog* and in the numerous other forms of Aboriginal writing now available.

Another such term from a similar source is KWON meaning BACKSIDE or ARSE and borrowed from the Nyungar (south-west Western Australia) word *kwon* or *kwona*, meaning faeces. YAMMAGI spelt in various ways, is from the Watjari (Murchison region, Western Australia) language and is also used quite widely in Western Australia as a generic term for an Aboriginal man. This word has been in use since at least the early 20th century. A Nyungar word meaning spring festival or celebration was adopted in 1998 as the name for Curtin University's *Mundjah* Festival, held in October.

COOEE is derived from a Dharuk word *guwi*, for come here. Its use as a distress signal for those lost in the bush is well known, if overly romanticised. It is also heard in other forms, such as WITHIN COOEE, originally meaning within earshot though also used to indicate hopelessness, as in phrases like THEY WEREN'T WITHIN COOEE OF SCORING. NEVER-NEVER meaning the outback or some distant and desolate area (variously said to be derived from English or from an Aboriginal term, *nievah vah*, though it resonates strongly of the Western notion of a mysterious place, far beyond the boundaries of the everyday and has been traced to English origins). Corroboree comes from the Dharuk term *garaabara*, and means a ceremony involving the decoration of the body with coloured paints, dance, music and song. A corroboree may be religious and may relate to ritual and mythological aspects of Aboriginal belief (some corroborees take place at full moon, some only at night) or may be an informal meeting. Whether ceremonial or informal, the senses of meeting and communality are central to corroboree. In Lingo the term has come to mean a festive get-together, as in YOU COULD HEAR THE SHEARERS ALL CORROBOREEING THROUGH THE NIGHT.

Not surprisingly, many Aboriginal words appear, in one form or another, as the Lingo names for native plants and animals — BARRAMUNDI, NANNYGAI, WOBBEGONG — all fish; BRIGALOW, COOLIBAH, GIDGEE, JARRAH, KARRI, MULGA, all trees or tree-like plants. Other plant, bird and animal names include BINDI-EYE, CUNJEVOI, WARATAH, BROLGA, BUDGERIGAR, GALAH, KOOKABURRA, BILBY, KANGAROO, PADEMELON and WOMBAT, to name only some. The indigenous contribution to the Lingo is one of the elements that gives Australian colloquial speech its distinctiveness.

Not all Aboriginal-derived terms relate to real beings of the natural world. BUNYIP comes from the Wergaia dialect of the Wemba (Loddon and Glenelg districts, Victoria) language and means an inland water-dwelling monster. The word is known in this sense from at least the 1840s, since when the BUNYIP has been the focus of numerous Aboriginal and non-Aboriginal folktales and beliefs. In European–Australian folklore the BUNYIP is a kind of bogy-monster, not unlike the northern English Jenny (Ginny) Greenteeth who lives in waterholes and drags unwary passers-by to their deaths in the mysterious depths. In reminiscences of the 1890s by Eugenie McNeil titled *A Bunyip Close Behind Me* (1972), the author describes the monster:

> The bunyip lived in creeks and waterholes. His shape was a bit vague, but he was as big as the cow and covered with long, black hair, very curly. He had a nose like a mopoke, so was probably nocturnal...On the whole, the Bunyip was friendly, but there was a vague hint he might Come and Get Us if we were naughty...

It is likely that the BUNYIP is related to the widespread creature of Aboriginal mythology, the Rainbow Serpent, an important entity that goes by many different names, but which is usually associated with the creation of the landscape.

The term BUNYIP was also used in the early 1850s in a derogatory reference to early suggestions by W.C. Wentworth, explorer, journalist, poet and LEGAL EAGLE, that Australia should establish an hereditary peerage along British lines. As the Chair of a Select Committee given the job of drafting a Constitution for New South

Wales in 1853, Wentworth put forward this ill-starred idea. In the course of massive public opposition Daniel Deniehy made a speech in which he described Wentworth's suggestion as, among other things, 'this Bunyip Aristocracy'. The other things have long been forgotten, but the colourful and appropriately scornful phrase ridiculing the notion has stuck. The 'Bunyip Aristocracy' was never established, perhaps partly because of Deniehy's shrewd use of BUNYIP in this official political context. Interestingly, and obviously unknown to Wentworth, at this time in Sydney underworld parlance 'bunyip' meant an imposter or CON MAN. This usage is pretty well obsolete today, though BUNYIP ARISTOCRACY is still heard occasionally on the lips of New South Wales Labor politicians baying against their conservative opponents.

The YOWIE (from the Yuwaalaray–Lightning Ridge area, New South Wales — *yuwi*, meaning a dream spirit) is supposedly an ape-like monster found in various parts of eastern Australia. This creature has come to be identified with wilderness mystery monsters such as the yeti and has accreted similar 'sighting' tales. The YOWIE shares yarns of this type with strange 'tigers', such as the Tasmanian tiger (from the 1830s), the Tantanoola tiger of South Australia (from the late 1880s) and the Nannup tiger of Western Australia's south-west and other, as yet unproven, 'panthers' and similar fabled creatures that are the quarry of cryptozoologists. YOWIE does not seem to have been used in the mainstream Australian press until 1975 when it appeared in the *Bulletin* on 17 May. It seems, however, that at least one cryptozoologist with a long interest in such fabled creatures, Rex Gilroy, may have been using the term YOWIE earlier which suggests that it has had an extended, if mostly subterranean, existence in the language.

Another term with Aboriginal supernatural associations is the MIN-MIN LIGHTS or DEAD MEN'S CAMPFIRES. These are believed by some Aborigines and some non-Aborigines to be a form of ghostly apparition of dead souls, not unlike the British 'will-o'-the-wisp'. *Min-min* is thought to be derived from a Queensland Aboriginal language, the phenomenon appearing in European accounts from at least the 1830s. The lights are seen dancing across parts of northern Queensland on some nights and were described by writer Ernestine Hill as 'a luminous oval like a florescent football, floating a foot or two above the ground and always half a mile away'. The prosaic explanation for the MIN-MIN LIGHTS is that they are caused by the ignition of naturally occurring gases.

Lingo for a noisy nuisance is a YAHOO, also used as a verb in TO YAHOO. The term was used in *Gulliver's Travels*, published in 1726, but in its Australian usage is thought to come from a New South Wales Aboriginal language word for an owl or other bird, though it also referred to an evil spirit or monster, often with distorted human features. The monster so described, which is similar to the BUNYIP and YOWIE, seems to have been identified with those humans who made themselves monstrous by their anti-social and silly behaviour. In recent years the film-maker and actor Yahoo Serious has made good use of this term in his screen name and persona. Yahoos are also known in Britain and in the USA (where the term means a stupid person, or dope). In these places the word may also be used as a hailing term, from which application it has been adopted as the name of a well-known Internet search engine, though what that has to do with the Lingo is not clear.

Aboriginal adaptation of both the vocabulary and the spirit of the vernacular can be found in terms like GAMMON (GAMMIN) and FOOT-FALCON. The first has a complex etymology, being derived from colonial pioneering slang, by way of 18th-century Cockney and cant, and now commonly used in the Northern Territory to mean anything that is of dubious authenticity or truth. A FOOT-FALCON is a widespread indigenous Lingoism for travelling on foot, similar to SHANKS'S PONY. Terms such as DEADLY (a general adolescent term) and FLASH (an old colonialism) have also been incorporated into Aboriginal English where they are used to mean that something is good or positive in some way. As with all Lingoes, however, large and little, local knowledge is often needed. In current Sydney Aboriginal usage someone who speaks the FLASH LANGUAGE is one who is trying to sound like a speaker of mainstream Australian English and may be chastised for so speaking within the Aboriginal community. This means that an Aboriginal person often has to speak in a certain way at home and in another, more 'correct' way at school or elsewhere in the broader society. The ironies of the generic name for the speech of the earliest European inhabitants being preserved in a derogatory Aboriginal term for white talk are another indication of the cultural depths sounded in Lingo. FLASH, of course, is still heard quite commonly in general parlance as in VERY FLASH, meaning that someone or something is exceptionally well TURNED OUT, even approaching POSH.

An important example of Aboriginal lingo is the term *gubbah* and its variants — GUB, GUBBY, GUBBISE. GUBBAH is used by many Aboriginal people as a generic term for white people, often in a derogatory manner. The word encompasses all of those things associated by Aborigines with white Australia and is used with this sense in various ways. The origins of the word are unclear, though it may derive from the term GOVERNMENT BLANKET, widely pronounced by

Aborigines as GUBMENT BLANKET, sometimes GUBBY BLANKET. Such blankets were often identified with a red stripe or other device sewn along them. It is said that Aboriginal people would spend many hours unpicking these stitches and over the years this hated symbol of dependence on white handouts has been honed to its present usage.

In 1789, as modern Australia was being founded, Fletcher Christian and accomplices mutinied aboard HMS *Bounty*. They were, as every film-goer knows, reacting against the bullying and tyrannical nature of their commander, William Bligh, later to be a governor of New South Wales. The mutineers forced Bligh and those who remained loyal to him into an open boat and set them adrift. After an astounding trial of seamanship and survival, Captain Bligh and his much-reduced command made it to safety. Christian and the other mutineers, together with 19 Tahitian women and 6 Tahitian men, sailed to Pitcairn Island where, among many difficulties and considerable violence, they established a community that persisted until 1856 when the inhabitants were shipped to Norfolk Island.

In the intervening 70 or so years the mutineers developed their own language or *patois*, a mixture of Tahitian and 18th-century English. On Norfolk Island this language was known as 'Norfolk' and spoken alongside Australian English. A few examples of this language: *bout-yer-gwan* (where are you going?); *fus* (first); *gurret* (angry); *hupa* (bad); *lou-fee* (sick); *semithway* (odd) and *stolly* (a lie). Pitcairnese is probably the earliest ethnic language to develop in modern Australia. Those who still speak it on Norfolk Island claim that there are enough differences between the earlier Pitcairnese and the version they now speak as to constitute a distinctive dialect — 'Norfolkese'.

Although rarely having such colourful histories as Pitcairnese, the many other languages imported into Australia or adapted here, especially since the post-World War II era of mass migration, have had an incremental impact on both mainstream Australian (*felafel, smorgasbord, souvlakia, kebab*, and many other food names, for instance, some of which have localised pronunciations and spellings) and on the Lingo. Many of the accommodations and constructions that migrants have made between their own languages and what they heard on these shores have given us a rich variety of ethnic Lingoisms. These include such delights as SHEMOZZLE— Yiddish for disorder or disaster, the Italian for hello and goodbye, *Ciao, Skol* — a Danish drinking toast roughly equivalent to good health, and the Australian Italian term for a billycan — BILLICANO. DELICATESSEN, more usually DELI, is a Lingoisation of the German *Delikat Essen* for specialty foods that probably got underway in the German-speaking areas of South Australia's Barossa Valley. Similarly, BERLINER is a jam doughnut in the Barossa, from the original German *Berliner pfannkuchen*, an example of an entire little lingo amalgamated from English and Silesian and standard German known as BAROSSA DEUTSCHE. MILKBARAKI is Greek–Australian for a milk bar — literally a little milk bar. (Milk bar, despite being used extensively throughout the country is not an Australianism, it comes from the USA, but MILKO for the man — usually — who delivers the milk, was first recorded here in 1865 as the cry of the milk-deliverer). FARMISTA is Italian–Australian for a farmer while LA TICHETTO (ticket), and LA BICCIA (beach) are also Italianisations. KARO is Greek–Australian for car and DE SHOP is the Dutch–Australian version of the shop. PRAAM or PRAAM BOAT is a Murray River adaptation of a Dutch word meaning a flat-bottomed boat. In Dutch it is pronounced as a long 'a' while in Australia it rhymes with pram. Migrants from the Greek island of Kastellorizzo (from the Italian *Castello Rosso*, red castle), and their Australian-born descendants call themselves CASSIES (pronounced Cazzies). These are no more than a few of the many examples of ethnic Australian that might be given. Like Lingo of any kind, they are in a continual state of flux, adapting and re-adapting to social, economic and generational change.

An example of this process came about before the postwar mass migration programs. In one of the more bizarre incidents of World War II, a number of Jews who escaped Hitler's Germany were rounded up by the British authorities and despatched aboard a ship called the *Dunera* to an internment camp in New South Wales. Known as THE DUNERA BOYS, these latter-day transportees established their own society and cultural pursuits within the barbed-wire compound. They decided to print their own money and gave the denomination the odd title GOODONYA. Apparently they had heard their Australian guards habitually using GOOD ON YA to each other and, once they found out what it meant, concluded that this would be a good thing to name their notes.

SEPTIC TANKS DOWN-UNDER

Australians have long held contradictory attitudes towards another group of 'significant others'. Officially, the Americans are our allies, trading partners and cultural cousins; unofficially, they are YANKS, with whom we keep up an ongoing love–hate relationship. In Australia people admire the Americans for being how we like to see ourselves — as a frontier, independent society, a breakaway from the apron-strings of the Empire. At the same time we Australians are frequently appalled by the seemingly cloying patriotism, affluence, brashness, and apparent insensitivity to small friends displayed by Americans in various guises such as politicians, trading partners, and tourists.

This ambivalence is reflected closely in Lingo. On the one hand we have a considerable body of expression concerned to denigrate Americans in one way or another, including the term YANK and its rhyming slang equivalent SEPTIC TANK. But on the other hand we are continually taking into our vernacular American linguistic items of all kinds — GAS for petrol; BUCK for dollar, GUY for a male person, CATCH-22 for a no-win situation, among many others. This continuing contradiction between the official and the unofficial facets of our relationship with the USA and our deep-seated suspicions about SEPTIC TANKS goes back to at least the early years of the 20th century.

In 1917 it was widely believed that the brilliant middleweight and heavyweight boxer from Maitland (New South Wales), Les Darcy, was poisoned in Memphis, Tennessee, because the Americans feared his skill in the ring. As a parody of 'Way Down in Tennessee' usually called 'The Ballad of Les Darcy' put it:

> ...he gave up hope
> When he got that dope
> Way down in Tennessee.

In fact, Darcy died from septicaemia brought on by an untreated broken tooth, a ring injury he had sustained in Australia before leaving for the USA. Much the same thing happened again in 1932. Many Australians were, and still are, convinced that the great racehorse Phar Lap (whose name, intriguingly, is not a drollery on far lap but seems to be derived from the Thai for lightning — *phar laep*) had somehow been nobbled by the YANKS when this legendary winner of the Melbourne Cup and many other races died in California. During the depression years, when we were still nursing these dark suspicions about American sports, we began welcoming and nurturing more Americanisms. Under the growing influence of US films and the prominence given US country music on radio, US terms like BUM (in the American sense of a hobo) entered our language. Folk songs of the depression period were often peppered with importations like HANDOUT and US-sounding nicknames like Box-car Harry. Even our own country music performers sported American stage names, like Tex Morton (originally from New Zealand) and, slightly later and still famously with us, Slim Dusty.

At that time, apart from the influence of sound recordings and movies, very few Australians had any direct knowledge of, or contact with, the USA or Americans. The bombing of Pearl Harbor, followed in fewer than two months by the fall of Singapore in February 1942, rapidly changed this situation. During the following months, hundreds of thousands of American troops 'invaded' Australia under the command of General Douglas MacArthur. Although the Americans were on our side certain tensions quickly developed, solidifying our existing suspicions of the YANKS. The efficient, glowingly healthy (their teeth were noticeably better than Aussie dentures) and amazingly self-confident (COCKY to us) GIs (US soldiers) burst onto a sleepy nation still suffering chronic colonial cringe. American technologies, both of death and pleasure, matched their mostly male numbers in sophistication, sheen and finish. They had machines to do just about anything and an accompanying cultural baggage of popular music, film and dance that increased their cargo-cult impact. They were better fed, better dressed, better paid and, Australian males immediately feared, better catches than their local equivalents. In the famous phrase of the time, they were 'oversexed, overpaid and over here' (the American retort to which was, allegedly, that Australians were 'under-sexed, under-paid and under MacArthur').

Sexual jealousy generated many anti-USA ditties, like the parody of the popular song of the time 'When They Sound the Last All-Clear':

When they send the last Yank home,
How lonely some women will be.
When they turn out the lights
There'll be long, lonely nights,
All those good times a memory.
Evermore they'll be alone,
Those women no Aussie would own.
All they'll have are some clothes
And a kid who talks through its nose,
When they send the last Yank home.

When the YANKS did finally go home from 1945, large-scale contact ended for a generation or so. There were some consequences of their invasion, however, succinctly put in this parody of 'Count Your Blessings':

Count your children, count them one by one,
Count your children, count them one by one,
Count your children, count them one by one,
You will be surprised at what the Yanks have done.

By the time relationships reached that stage, most US servicemen would, presumably, have become more intimate than they had at first been with the Great Australian Lingo. In 1942 the Special Services Division of the US Army found it necessary to issue a *Pocket Guide to Australia* to their soldiers voyaging DOWN-UNDER. This compilation provided factual summaries and brief explanations of Australian values and attitudes, together with a good deal of propaganda about the close ties of Australia and the USA. After dismissing 'the 70 000 or so ABOS who roam the waste lands', the *Guide* pointed out that 'Australians are nearly 100 percent Anglo-Saxon stock' and 'an outdoors kind of people, breezy and democratic. They haven't much respect for stuffed shirts, their own or anyone else's.' Lingoisms revolving around Ned Kelly were explained by reference to Jesse James and the troops were assured that 'Of course, the best thing an Australian can say about you is that you're a "bloody fine barstud" [sic].' The author went on to give some specific examples of Australian slang, prefaced with the observation that 'When it comes to slang, the Australians can give us a head start and still win. Their everyday speech is just about the slangiest of all the brands of English.' Some of the carefully sanitised examples were less than accurate, with a DRONGO being described as a clumsy insect and COOEE as the equivalent of YOOHOO. The list, however, recognised such conversational essentials as SNINNY (a woman), SHIVOO (a party), SMOOGE (to flirt, or PITCH WOO as the translation into US Lingo had it) and WOULDN'T IT (pronounced woodnit), a popular term for any complaint; a contraction of WOULDN'T IT GIVE YOU A PAIN IN THE — .

American influences persisted in youth culture after World War II. The terms WOOLLOOMOOLOO YANK, GEORGE STREET YANK and FITZROY YANK arose to describe anyone pretending to be a YANK by sporting American clothes, haircut, and chewing gum. These apers of US fashion and music eventually turned into BODGIES and their girlfriends, WIDGIES (see chapter 6). All were strongly influenced by US popular culture imported by radio, record, cinema and, after 1956, through the TELLY.

It all happened again, if on a smaller scale, during the Vietnam War years of the mid-1960s to the early 1970s. The sons of some of the invading YANKS of World War II came to Australia for R AND R, Rest and Recreation. While Australia was a much-altered place in the late 1960s and 1970s our folk memories of the YANKS were awakened and the tradition of YANK-BASHING continued. Its most notable and persistent effect in Lingo was the development of the rhyming slang term SEPTIC TANK for YANK, a kind of double Lingoism of rhyming slang on slang. Usually in the shortened form of SEPTIC, with all the over- or under-tones of smelly toilets and festering sores, this term is still a cherished item of our vernacular. As well there are other Lingoisms such as YANK TANK for a petrol-guzzling car. But the YANKS are well ahead on points. Americanisms, old and new, are found throughout our folk speech, loudly lamented and decried by many, but there nevertheless.

THE LITTLE NATIONS

One of Australia's abiding national characteristics is the inability of the States and Territories to agree on almost anything. The result has been such notorious nuisances as different gauge railway lines across the country and a whole host of conflicting rules, regulations and laws on everything from driving a car to the requirements of the various education systems. While this determined difference is regularly lamented, especially by Federal politicians, it has hardly improved since Federation, with States' rights being vociferously defended and extended by State and Territory governments, despite the mid-1997 setback when the High Court ruled that most State taxes were illegal.

This territorial independence and diversity is not, paradoxically, recognised in Australian speech. There is a strong body of opinion that says Australian vocabulary and pronunciation are depressingly similar across the country. Observations of this kind are usually made by those who have negative views of Australian speech and who explicitly or implicitly contrast this situation with that of older more 'cultured' countries such as Britain and the USA where, in some places, a different dialect can be heard a few kilometres down the road.

Distinctive speech patterns include the upward interrogatory inflexion in sentences that are not questions, often said to be typical of Queenslanders and persons from northern New South Wales. There is a tendency in the eastern States especially, particularly among working-class girls and young women to end sentences with BUT, meaning roughly 'however' or 'though', as in I WANT TO GO TO THE MOVIES, BUT. This may sometimes be combined with the interrogative inflection to produce what, to the uninitiated, sounds like an unstable utterance that is at once a statement and a question, as in 'What's your favourite drink? Beer?' The autobiographical novel *Puberty Blues* provides an account of this habit among Sydney beach-going teenagers during the 1970s, though the tendency has also been noted on the US West Coast and elsewhere in that country. But it was not new in the 1970s in Australia.

The folk plural YOUSE, a characteristic of Irish speech, is still so frequently heard around the country that it is included in *The Macquarie Dictionary*. Other examples of pronunciation include the pronunciation of words like milk and film as 'miluk' and 'filum' and the still very common rendering of the final 'g' in anything and many other words, as 'anythin_k_', as well as the use of 'f' where the standard pronunciation is 'th', as in 'any_fi_ng'. A 'p' and a 'k' may be added to something, producing 'sum_p_thin_k_'. 'Would of' and 'should of' are still heard as substitutes for 'would have', as in 'I would _of_ gone if you'd _have_ let me' and 'we should _of_ given her the letter'. The construction 'mustn't have', as in 'They mustn't have been at the game' seems to be an Australianism. 'I seen' instead of 'I saw' and 'I come' instead of 'I came' are also not uncommon, nor is the expostulatory intensifier WOULD I, WHAT! used to indicate intense enthusiasm or agreement. Stupid may be pronounced as 'shtoopid' in some areas and 'arks' for ask has also been reported.

As well as these interesting aspects of pronunciation and usage, there is a good deal of variation in regional vocabularies where the same objects may have quite different names from State to State. For example, a DRINKING FOUNTAIN in Perth and southern Queensland is what is known as a BUBBLER in New South Wales. A cocktail frankfurt is a CHEERIO in both the Northern Territory and in Queensland, but is a LITTLE BOY in Melbourne. DEVON in Sydney is GERMAN SAUSAGE or STRASBURG SAUSAGE (STRAZ) in Melbourne, FRITZ in Adelaide, WINDSOR SAUSAGE in Queensland and POLONY in Perth. Likewise a KABANOS in Perth is known as CABANOSSI in Sydney. SPOUTING in Melbourne is known as GUTTERING just about everywhere else in the country. The VERGE in Western Australia is referred to as the NATURE STRIP in some eastern States or even the FOOTPATH in Queensland, a usage which causes great confusion with the denizens of those States where a FOOTPATH is just that. (PAVEMENT is also used in New South Wales in much the same way that FOOTPATH is used in Victoria and elsewhere.) A CONCRETER in Sydney is a person who lays concrete slabs for buildings; the same person in Perth is often called a GRANO-MAN, from the local, much older, term granulated concrete and he is more than likely to lay down a CONCRETE PAD. You put your waste in the RUBBISH BIN in Perth, but in Brisbane and Sydney it goes into the GARBAGE BIN and in Melbourne and Adelaide into the DUST BIN. The person who used to be known as a MARINE DEALER in Western Australia and South Australia is a BOTTLE-O in New South Wales and elsewhere. In Brisbane the piece of furniture in the bedroom that holds clothes, make-up, and just about everything else is called a DUCHESSE, rather than a dressing table, the name by which it is known elsewhere in the country. The conveyance for pushing babies around is a STROLLER in New South Wales, but is likely to be called a PUSHER in South Australia where hairclips or

HAIRPINS are what are known as BOBBY PINS in New South Wales and Victoria.

Probably the most confusing one of all involves the numerous terms for the 'shorts' worn when swimming, known variously as BATHERS (Western Australia), SWIMMERS (New South Wales), COSSIES or COSTUMES (New South Wales and Victoria), TOGS (Queensland) and SPEEDOS, or TRUNKS in different parts of the country. (Regionalisms are also discussed in relation to children's speech in chapter 6.) A 1970s Sydneyism for the briefer male swimming shorts (as opposed to board shorts) is SCUNGIES, deftly described by Kathie Lette and Gabrielle Carey in their Lingo-filled classic of beach culture, *Puberty Blues* (1979): 'The ultimate disgrace for a surfie was to be seen in his SCUNGIES. They were too much like underpants. The boys didn't want us checking out the size of their dicks.'

Each State has developed its own little lingo for physical and cultural features of the environment, especially for winds. In New South Wales the strong gusts bearing rain that occasionally break the heat and humidity of summer days are known as SOUTHERLY BUSTERS. The BRICKFIELDER also originated in Sydney, taking its name from the hot dusty wind that early Sydneysiders associated with blowing the heat and dust of the brickworks on Brickfield Hill into the city. The term was commonplace in Sydney by the early 19th century and was being used in Melbourne by at least the middle of the century, reaching Central Australia by the early 20th century. Before that it had blown into Western Australia, probably via the influx of T'OTHERSIDERS during the gold rushes of the 1890s. The west also specialises in coastal 'doctors' that sometimes come in off the sea to relieve the mid-afternoon heat. The most famous of these is the FREMANTLE DOCTOR, but there is also an ALBANY (pronounced 'AL-bany') DOCTOR, an ESPERANCE DOCTOR, a GERALDTON DOCTOR, a EUCLA DOCTOR and probably as many more as there are coastal settlements. There are also said to be a PERTH DOCTOR, a SOUTHERLY DOCTOR and a NULLARBOR DOCTOR. In South Australia they have WHIRLIES (usually known as WILLY-WILLIES elsewhere) and in most places dust storms are referred to as SHOWERS, usually prefixed with a local place names, as in COBAR SHOWER (NSW), though in Queensland they are just known as a BEDOURIE.

One wind whose name is not restricted to a State but mainly to the north of Western Australia and the Northern Territory is a COCKEYE or COCKEYED BOB, generally said to be a small but powerful whirlwind that arises unpredictably. The term is first recorded in print during the early 1890s, by which time it was well established in the regions of its usage. The origins of this term are, as with much Lingo, obscure. One explanation is that it is an anglicisation of the Aboriginal term KIKKOBAR (or *kack-ay*) which may or may not have anything to do with wind. Another appeared in the *Bulletin* in 1926. According to this version 'Old north-westerners relate that it originated on a pearling lugger whose captain and owner was named "Bob". His sight was not the best, and his Aboriginal diver, seeing a miniature cyclone approaching, used to warn his skipper by singing out "Cockeye, Bob"!'

Western Australia is the most isolated and independent of the Australian States and Territories. This may account to some extent for the great diversity of Lingo that has evolved there, a diversity reflected in a recently published dictionary of West Australianisms that notes more than 400 distinctive usages and terms unique to THE WESTERN THIRD. Excellent as it is, this dictionary did not get all the groperisms. Here are a few that give an idea of what variety may develop from State to State and from region to region.

BEACH SHACK — pretty much the same as 'a weekender'

'Bine' — an English migrant (from 'Woodbine', the brand name of cheap cigarettes favoured by British migrants)

BIRRIDA COUNTRY — claypan

BOONDY — a rock or projectile made of sand. Also COONDY and ROONDY)

BREAKAWAYS — a Kimberley term for gullies formed by erosion.

Chuditch — (Nyungar) native cat

CONGALONG — camel bell

CROSSWALK — pedestrian crossing (from the USA)

DING — derogatory term for a southern European migrant, frequently Italian.

'factions' — school teams; comparable to houses

FREO — shortened form of Fremantle (the proper West Australian pronunciation being 'FR'mantle rather than FREEmantle)

gidgee — (Nyungar)) spear

GOBBLEGUTS — windy harbour term for a local fish, also heard more widely

HONKY NUTS — large gum nuts

JARRAH JERKER — timber-getter. (The 'Jarrah Jerker's Jog' is a race unique to Western Australia)

JEWFISH, JEWIE (often spelt dhufish and noted as early as 1851) — the *Glaucosoma hebraicum*, found only along the West Australian coast. (JEWIE is used on the east coast too, though it refers there to a different fish)

jilgie or *gilgi* (Nyungar) — local freshwater crustacean, hence the saying TO DO A JILGIE meaning to back out of a commitment

KAL — shortened form of Kalgoorlie

KALAMAZOO — Western Australian fettlers' term for a three-wheeled hand-operated flat car

kneelo — an outdoor bar

Leper Line — the 20th parallel of latitude, a once legal boundary that Aborigines were forbidden to cross in an attempt to stem the spread of leprosy. It presumably did not apply to non-Aboriginal lepers

MARGARETS — south-west West Australian term for large surfing waves experienced near Margaret River

marron (Nyungar) — freshwater crustacean, since at least the 1880s

munjongs, sometimes *munjons* (Yindjibarndi and surrounding languages) — raw newcomers. Also applied to an Aborigine who has had little contact with non-Aboriginal culture

NOR'-WESTERS — Kimberley dwellers

PEDONG — a desert Aborigine

QUOKKA SOCCER — kicking the delightful quokkas native to Rottnest Island

SCHEME WATER — water piped from a government irrigation program

T'OTHERSIDER — anyone from the eastern States of Australia. Now mostly obsolete, but its essential meanings live on in THE EAST, the place from where all evil comes, easterly winds, taxes, drugs, serious crime, and in the term for those who come from such places, EASTERN STATERS

WALKABOUT DISEASE — fatal disease of horses that eat rattlepod (Kimberley)

wongi (Aboriginal) — an Aborigine from the Kalgoorlie area.

Local names for native and other flowers, trees and shrubs are also a fertile field of Lingo. The now widespread term for the edible pear-shaped fruit known as a CHOKO, probably originated in Queensland as a derivation of the Brazilian Indian term *chuchu*. In Western Australia there are terms derived from Aboriginal languages such as BY BY for cycad seed and MORRELL for eucalypt. Other folk terms for flora include BLACKBOY, EGG AND BACON PLANT, STAR OF BETHLEHEM (blue tinsel lily), TRIGGER PLANTS, SUN DEWS, WESTERN PRICKLY MOSES, MAIDA VALE BELLS, GUILDFORD GRASS, WOOLLYBUSH, SWAN RIVER MYRTLES and many, many more, varying from region to region. Then there is the unforgettable SNOTTYGOBBLE, usually applied to a West Australian genus of *Protaceae* and its fruit. Unfortunately, West Australians cannot claim this one as their own. It is a British dialect term for a yew. BROOME TIME, THE LAYUP SEASON and the SHINJU are, however, all genuine Western Australianisms, referring respectively to Broome's relaxed attitude to time, the lay-off in the pearling business during the cyclone season and the multicultural Broome festival, the *Shinju matsuri* (Japanese for pearl festival).

Fish are another generator of regional and local terms, with wild and innumerable variations, not only from State to State, but from region to region. SERGEANT BAKER, WOBBEGONG, NANNYGAI, MOWIE and TRAG (abbreviation of teraglin) are all used in New South Wales, though not necessarily elsewhere. Other New South Welshisms include PITT STREET FARMER, one who owns a rural property, but hires another to operate it; BROWN BOMBER, a parking inspector (even though the colour of parking police uniforms have long changed this term is still in use with the newer term, GREY GHOSTS); THE BAY, as well called the LBJ — the gaol at Long Bay; BONDI YUNCTION is a local name for Bondi Junction and a reference to the large number of Jewish people in that area. In the 1970s Bondi was usually said to be over-run by KIWIS, a subject on which there are a number of quite unprintable jokes; today it is a popular stopover for BACKPACKERS. In New South Wales REGO is an abbreviation for registration, the annual payment to license a car, though the term is not used in Western Australia, for instance, where the same bureaucratic necessity is a 'licence'. Sydney's red-light district, King's Cross, is THE CROSS; THE DOM is the Sydney Domain; The Gap is a cliff at Watsons Bay favoured for TOPPING YOURSELF, 'top' being an 18th-century underworld term, as in 'topsman', the hangman. TO GO OVER (or OFF) THE GAP means to commit suicide; THE LOO is Woolloomooloo; THE ROYAL is the Royal Easter Show, held each year and often known as THE SHOW. A SYDNEY ROCK is a Sydney rock oyster.

Victorianisms include LITTLE LON for Little Lonsdale Street; BALLARAT LANTERN for a candle held in the neck of a bottle; NATURE STRIP for a strip of grass between the PAVEMENT or the house and the road and a COLLINS STREET FARMER, the local equivalent of Sydney's PITT STREET FARMER. A TOORAK RICKSHAW is a taxi, known as a DALKEITH RICKSHAW in Perth. Queenslanders refer to BECHE or sea slug (trepang); to policemen as CANARIES; to Cape York Peninsula as THE CAPE; to residents of Cooktown as PEANUT-GROWERS and to swimming trunks as TOGS. South Australians call the *Adelaide Advertiser* THE 'TIZER and use the rhyming slang JOE BLITZ as the local version of the JIMMY BRITTS. The CROW-EATERS also seem keen on confections and soft drinks with names like HOCK AND LEMON, LONG JOHN (ice-cream, cream, nuts and a cherry on top) and (in Whyalla), SLIME — soda and lime. LAY YOUR GOOG is a South Australianism for getting angry. In the tropics, which means the

Northern Territory and the TOP HALF or TOP END of Queensland and Western Australia, they use the terms THE WET for the monsoon season and THE DRY for the rest of the year. The train that ran between Darwin and Birdum for many years was known as LEAPING LENA. In TASSIE they have some quaintly appealing words like a YAFFLER for someone who talks too much and too loudly (probably from late 18th-century convict cant 'yaffle', to eat), while a NOINTER is a TASWEGIANISM for a precocious child or youth destined for a bad end.

These and other differences of little lingo reflect to some extent the opinions each State or region holds about most of the others. Research into the stereotypical views that each State held of each other was carried out in the late 1960s by social psychologist J.W. Berry at the University of Sydney. Although Berry's findings were based on surveys of rather limited groups (first-year psychology students) and are now quite old, the results he published probably reflect accurately what most Australians did think about other States — and most of them probably think much the same today. Queensland was believed by most to be casual, friendly, outdoor, apathetic and carefree. New South Wales was sporting, competitive, suburban, materialistic, and cosmopolitan. Victoria was seen as suburban, respectable, conservative, materialistic, and conforming. Tasmanians were said to be apathetic, conservative, friendly, hospitable, and unsophisticated. South Australians were conservative, apathetic, hospitable, sporting, traditional while West Australians were seen as friendly, sporting, casual, apathetic and easygoing.

The extent to which apathetic, casual and easygoing turn up in these descriptions relates to the often-alleged indolence of Australians. Beloved of efficiency analysts and free-trade advocates, the idea that Australians do not work hard enough has been around since the earliest days of settlement when the convicts were thought idle because they often had to be flogged to labour. Indeed, in the criminological thinking of the 18th century and much of the 19th century, idleness was thought to be the cause of criminality. Very few suspected that it might be related to poverty and the general economic structure of the period. The use of terms like SHE'LL BE RIGHT, mate, SHE'LL BE APPLES, TAKE IT EASY, and DON'T BUST A GUT, are often presented as evidence of an economically undesirable casualness. Even Aboriginal Australians have been accused of this shocking reluctance to work for someone else. Instead, it is said, they would rather go WALKABOUT. How this supposed idleness relates to the backbreaking labour that did, and still does, go into pioneering and farming the land and in turning out molten metal and other products in the factories of the nation is something never explained by the accusers. Interestingly, the further one moves from the metropolitan nexus of Sydney, Melbourne and Canberra the more pronounced are these excessively casual attitudes. Could this have something to do with regionalism?

Regional rivalries, well aired through the various football codes, cricket and other sporting activities, have also contributed their share to the Lingo, great and small. Probably the best-known rivalry is that between brash, commercial Sydney and sober, intellectual Melbourne, an antagonism that has, at various times, had Melburnians refer to Sydneysiders as 'Our 'arbers' from their pride in the Sydney Harbour. In revenge, 'Sydneyites' call the Melburnian's pride and joy, the River Yarra, THE RIVER THAT'S UPSIDE DOWN and OLD MUDDY, a derogation that one CORNSTALK put to good use in the put-down AS USELESS AS THE YARRA — TOO THICK TO SWIM IN AND TOO THIN TO PLOUGH. A *BULLETIN*ISM of the 1860s referred to the non-Aboriginal residents of Tasmania as TASMANIACS, a usage rarely heard these days, though according to a 1982 edition of the *Bulletin*, the word still had currency in Sydney, at least. Queenslanders usually refer to anyone unfortunate enough to be living south of the border as MEXICANS, a reference to the supposed economic superiority of their State and an instance of the feared Americanisation. This term is also used in New South Wales along with WETBACKS, referring to Victorians. Western Australians, known with a hint of admiration as SANDGROPERS, call persons from anywhere other than THE TERRITO-RY, EASTERN STATERS, a modern continuation of the traditional T'OTHERSIDERS that developed during the Western Australian gold rushes of the 1890s, though the term also has earlier currency as a description of the eastern colonies. The TOP HALF or TOP END, refer-ring to that part of Australia roughly north of the Tropic of Capricorn, is widely believed by most other Australians to be 'the last frontier', full of beer-swilling COWBOYS, an image that TOP-ENDERS usually take great delight in encouraging.

Regional distinctiveness also surfaces, not surprisingly, in the vari-ety of names for the glasses from which the AMBER FLUID is con-sumed. To some extent the traditional names for different glass capacities are fading away, but a good few are still current. In New South Wales there are, from the smallest to the largest, a PONY (5 fluid ounces and now obsolete, though also used in Victoria and Western Australia), a SEVEN (7 fluid ounces, also used in Queensland), MIDDY, a 10 fluid ounce glass (though the same order will only get you 8 fluid ounces in Perth) and SCHOONER (15 fluid ounces). A long glass of beer was known from the mid-19th to the late 19th century as a BISHOP BARKER, after a very tall Sydneyside cleric. The practice of serving beer to a woman in a distinctively curving, narrow glass gave rise to the term A LADY'S WAIST in Sydney and in some other parts of New South Wales, though this term does not seem to be more widespread, despite the still-encountered practice of serving a beer for a woman in a tall, narrow glass, rather than in the rounder glass that signifies BLOKE. South Australians have a BUTCHER (since at least the 1880s when it held a pint, but subsequently hovering mostly about the 5 fluid ounces to 6 fluid ounces capacity and now standardised at 170 millilitre). In Western Australia the Perth term for a 6 fluid ounce glass was a BOBBY while a GLASS of beer currently gets you a medium-sized drink. The term POT has been used in Victoria, Queensland and Western Australia at different times to mean a medium-sized drink of beer and it is still possible to order a PINT in Western Australia and in some other places. A JUG is nowadays a popular order for a group of drinkers all around the country, keeping everyone's THIRST at bay, for at least a little while.

3

LAGS, LARRIKINS AND LAIRS

...I think that 95 per cent of the confidence tricksters in this
country either come from or have lived a long time in Australia.

DETECTIVE'S EVIDENCE AT TOWER POLICE COURT, LONDON, 1938,
QUOTED IN SIDNEY BAKER, THE AUSTRALIAN LANGUAGE

LAGS

One of the most interesting of our many little lingoes was that spoken by the convicts transported to Australia — LAGS as they called
themselves. This criminal argot, or FLASH LANGUAGE, used for clandestine communication within the convict subculture, gave quite
a few terms to the broader vernacular. A number of these are still
in use, including SWAG, SNOWDROPPER and BLOKE. An essential
Lingoism, even if not unique to Australia, BLOKE has an intriguing
past. It apparently derived from Shelta, the ancient Irish tinker language that originated as a secret form of Irish Gaelic back slang.
There may also be a connection between the convictism LAG and the
same Shelta word which meant to lose or to pawn, both meanings
having suspiciously underworld resonances. (Shelta, by the way, is
probably the origin of the Australianism SKERRICK, as in THERE'S NOT
A SKERRICK OF TRUTH IN THAT, from the Shelta *skurik*, originally
meaning a farthing or an almost worthless coin.)

The earliest account of the FLASH speech is that of Watkin Tench
in his *A Complete Account of the Settlement at Port Jackson in New
South Wales*, published in 1793. Tench was a captain in the Marines
who saw convict society at first hand and from its earliest days on
these shores. He had very definite views on the FLASH or KIDDY (after

KID, the FLASH term for deceive or mislead, still with us in JUST KID-DING and similar uses) language spoken by the transportees. Tench tells us that it was sometimes necessary to have an interpreter in court to translate the evidence of witnesses and accused. He thought that abolition of this speech would go a long way towards the moral and legal rehabilitation of the criminal classes:

> ...my observations on these people have constantly instructed me, that indulgence in this infuriating cant, is more deeply associated with depravity, and continuance in vice, than is generally supposed...

The observant and articulate captain also made the explicit connection between language and behaviour that has since been at the root — if not always so explicitly — of many descriptions of Australian English: 'I recollect hardly one instance of a return to honest pursuits, and habits of industry, where this miserable perversion of our noblest and peculiar faculty was not previously conquered.'

Tench was the earliest of a long line of complainants about the undesirability of Australian Lingo. In many ways he was our first WOWSER, even though that term for excessive puritanism did not arrive until the late 19th century. Accounts from this period agree on the range, crudity and ubiquity of swearing among convicts, a good proportion of whom were Cockneys, a London folk group noted — and usually lamented — for their linguistic skills. At least one Cockney favourite is still shared with Australian Lingo — CHRONIC for anything considered especially dire. Also noted for their linguistic abilities are the Irish, a large group among both transportees and free emigrants. Contemporary observers, and listeners, routinely used phrases like 'profane swearing' and the 'blasphemy of his [the GUMSUCKER's] language'. (GUMSUCKERS is also a term for Victorians.) Complaining of the depravity of female convict servants, no less a person than Charles Darwin, passing through on the *Beagle* in 1835, expressed his concern for the effect of their 'vilest expressions' on the children in their charge.

Various collections of convict slang exist, the earliest being that of James Hardy Vaux who compiled his *Vocabulary of the Flash Language* in or shortly before 1812 (published 1819). Vaux's work shows that the convict lingo was basically the cant language of the 18th-century British underworld. Cant was the name by which the speech of the criminal and economic underclass of Britain had been known since at least the early 17th century. It consisted of technical terms for the equipment, methods and targets of criminals as well as the colloquial speech of the urban working classes. Usually no

COLCHESTER

distinction was made between the criminal and the underprivileged, the whole being lumped together in such terms as THE MOB, the people and even less pleasant descriptions. A number of cant dictionaries were compiled by scholars and educated rakes but it was the formation of official police forces in the 18th century that sparked a more serious, practical interest in cant. The police, often recruited from different social groups than those they were to pursue, found the language of the underworld incomprehensible. The necessity to understand this code led to intense collection and study of underworld slang and its codification into police publications and individual notebooks. In the State Archives of New South Wales, for instance, is a book kept by an anonymous Sydney policemen from 1841–45 titled *Registry of Flash Men*, a list of criminals known to the compiler and an indispensable tool of the detective's trade, then as now. As a result of this activity, we have a pretty good idea of the language of the 18th-century British underclasses. It was this language that, along with its speakers, was transported to Botany Bay and other places of penance from 1788 and, along with smatterings of proper English and military jargon, was the earliest form of Australian speech spoken by 'the people'.

Cant included such terms as the already mentioned LAG, though this referred not only to a convict but also to the sentence received and the act of transportation. To be LAGGED meant being caught and convicted. A LAGGING was a sentence. An OLD LAG was one who had served out his or her transportation and who might be either free or perhaps serving another. Even at this early period the Lingo was displaying its hallmark characteristics of flexibility and efficiency. Ned Kelly was still using the term as part of everyday speech in the late 1870s when he referred to being LAGGED INNOCENT in his Jerilderie Letter, meaning being unjustly imprisoned. Noted convict poet Francis MacNamara, known as Frank the Poet, reportedly uttered a poetic farewell on his leaving a lengthy stint at the notorious penal station of Port Arthur during the 1840s which goes, in one of its several variants:

> *Land of lags and kangaroo*
> *Of 'possum and the scarce emu.*
> *The farmer's pride but the prisoner's hell*
> *Land of buggers, fare-thee-well.*

The word was still serving time in underworld slang at least as late as the 1970s, when TO LAG was to inform to the police or to prison authorities.

Other terms from the FLASH LANGUAGE noted in the colony by Vaux included:

BASH — to beat
BLOW THE GAFF — reveal a secret
BOUNCE — bully
CHATS — lice
CHEESE IT! — stop it
DOLLOP — a large quantity of anything
FENCE — receiver of stolen goods
FRISK — to search
GRAY — coin with two heads or tails
GRUB — food
KID — to deceive
MIZZLE — to run away
NUTS ON — infatuated with
OFFICE — hint, signal (to 'give the office')
PUT UP AFFAIR — preconceived plan
RAMP — trick, offence
RING IN — to defraud
SCHOOL — a number of persons met together to gamble
SHAKE — to steal
SHARP — gambler, swindler
SNITCH — to betray
STINK — an uproar
TURN (IT) UP — to cease, stop
UP THE SPOUT — in pawn

Quite a number of these very early convict terms are still with us in the Greater Australian Lingo. TURN IT UP, to CAUSE OR CREATE A STINK, to KID, to BE NUTS ON someone or something, to BASH a person. A PUT UP AFFAIR has become a PUT UP JOB, but we still refer to two-up gamblers as a SCHOOL, to betrayal by telling tales as SNITCHING, a DOLLOP is still a large lump of something and TO FRISK someone is to search them (also used in the US underworld and police slang). CHATS, while now obsolete, was a common item of World War I Australian soldiers' slang, body lice being a continual and irritating aspect of trench life — WE'VE CHATS IN GALORE, complained one itchy Anzac in understandably non-grammatical verse.

In the mid-1990s M.A. Chalmers conducted research into the survival of Vaux's FLASH LANGUAGE in present-day Australian speech. Taking 200 of the 400-odd words mentioned by Vaux, Chalmers found that 120 of them are still being spoken, even though their meanings and their status might have altered. Of the FLASH terms in Vaux, in addition to those just mentioned, Chalmers notes the following survivals: AWAKE, as in TO BE AWAKE or A WAKE-UP to someone or something; a BEAK is still a magistrate or judge; A BEAN is a guinea or money in general, retaining this meaning in the phrase WITHOUT A BEAN; while BOLT still means to run away, a FLASH term that originally meant to escape into the bush and, ultimately, to range the bush as a bushranger. CONK in the sense of nose survives. The term DANNA was FLASH for excrement and has given us, through the British dialect term 'dunnaken/kin', a privy or toilet, that superlatively Australian icon and the word that describes it, the DUNNY. DUNNY has also allowed us the evocative combinations DUNNY MAN, DUNNY CART and DUNNY DOOR.

Other cant words are still in regular Lingo usage. Well established in the underworld speech of late 18th-century England were words like BLUBBER, to cry, BOOSE for drinking alcohol and BOOSY for having too much of it. Some surprisingly modern-sounding cant terms were also in use then, such as SCREW for copulation and WELL HUNG to describe an impressive set of male genitalia.

On the western side of the Australian continent there is also evidence of convict little lingo. A policeman in the Swan River colony made a collection of the terms used by the convicts in his charge and wrote them down on the back of the Occurrence Book of York lockup. His list recorded the language in use by the convicts of the late 1850s and early 1860s, about half-a-century after Vaux's compilation. Quite a few of the words and terms have not changed at all. Some of them, like BLOAK (BLOKE) are still part of the Australian vernacular. Others, like DEENER for a shilling, are only relatively recently obsolete due to the changeover from sterling to decimal currency in 1966.

The Swan River list also included terms like ON THE CROSS, meaning to steal or carry out some illegal activity, its opposite being ON THE SQUARE, still used in its original sense of being beyond suspicion. ON THE CROSS and variants was a term widely used throughout the Australian colonies to describe crimes, especially those relating to stock stealing and highway robbery. A thief was a CROSS COVE. Recorded as cant speech as early as 1608, COVE is even today heard occasionally in the bush and from older speakers as a term for man, a synonym of BLOKE and often used in the same way, even down to its application to THE BOSS. It was also used extensively in LARRIKIN street slang, a fact exploited by C.J. Dennis in such combinations as GORSPIL (gospel) COVE, meaning a clergyman. SNOWDROPPING was stealing linen from a hedge or wherever it had been left to dry, a term that is still with us to describe a man who steals women's underwear from clothes lines — a SNOWDROPPER. TO HOCUSS (sic) meant to drug someone, usually in a brothel, a practice that was widely suffered by itinerant bush-workers, as expressed in the bush song 'Across the Western Plains' or 'All for Me Grog': 'Then damn that shanty grog, that hocussed shanty grog;/The beer that's loaded with tobacco. . .', a reference to the practice of dosing the already near-lethal alcohol sold in SLY GROG shanties with tobacco in order to stupefy the client so that whatever was left of his CHEQUE — his payment for a season's hard work — could be spirited away. Clothes were referred to as TOG-GERY which has a faint echo in the modern Lingo term of TOGS for trousers and in the collocation SWIMMING TOGS. A SWAG was (and still is in underworld slang) stolen property though the term has of course been extended to the bundle carried by a wandering worker, a swagman or SWAGGIE. To be BOOKED was to be caught or taken, a term that remains in Lingo and with faintly criminal associations, especially applied to traffic offences.

The anonymous policeman-lexicographer in the Swan River colony also provides some illuminating examples of reasonably lengthy exchanges between speakers of this argot:

> I pulled down a fan and a roll of snow. I starred the glaze and snammed 16 redge yacks. My joiner stalled. I took them to a swag chovey bloak and got 6 finnips and a cooter for the yacks. A cross cove who had his regulars lowr, a fly grabbed him. I am afraid he will blow it. He has been lagged for beaker hunting. Was a mushroom faker, has been on the steel for snamming a wedge sneezer so I must hoop it. Tell swag chovey bloke to christen the yacks quick.

This translates as:

> I stole from a shop door a waistcoat and a web of Irish linen. I broke the corner of a window and got 16 gold watches. My fancy girl stood close by and screened me from observation. I took them to a person who buys stolen property who gave me 6 five pound notes and a sovereign for the watches. A fellow thief who shared the money with me is taken by a policeman. I am afraid he will turn informer. He has been transported for stealing poultry. He used to travel about the country mending umbrellas and has been in prison for stealing a silver snuff-box. As I must run away, tell the person who bought the watches to get the names altered as soon as possible.

A further specimen was also provided in the form of a letter:

> Dear Dick, I have seen this swag chovey bloak who christened the yacks quick. I gave him a double finnip. I am now on the shallow. I have got

the yacks so do not come to fight cocum. I am at the old padding ken next door to the padding crib. I am gadding the hoof but quick, be a duffer now on the square. I want a stalsman buttoner to nail prads. I last week worked the bulls. I have lost my joiner. Mum now.

In English:

Dear Richard, I have seen the person who bought the watches, he altered the name immediately. I gave him a ten pound note for doing it. I am now going half naked to avoid suspicion. I have got the watches back again, so do not turn informer. Be wary and sly. I am stopping at the old lodging house next to a boys lodging house. I am going about without shoes but shall turn hawker. I am at present honest, but want a partner. Will you join me to steal horses. Last week I got through many bad 5 shilling pieces. I have left my girl. Be sure you say nothing.

Whether this fascinating glimpse of colonial criminality is authentic is impossible to know. But it looks real when compared with the con-victisms of the period and sounds right when read aloud. It gives us some idea of how the FLASH LANGUAGE sounded when spoken, rather than given as a list of words and definitions. These snatches of long-gone convict conversation also reveal the existence of terms similar to those still in use, such as BLOW IT, sounding fancifully genteel in these days of go-for-the-jugular expostulations. As well there are terms that passed into the general vocabulary of 19th-century and early 20th-century bush vernacular, like GADDING (usually PADDING) THE HOOF for going about barefoot or poorly dressed and PRAD for a horse. One of the interesting points of comparison here is that the cant version requires considerably fewer words to convey its meaning than does the official English translation, another example of the general economy and efficiency of Lingo.

The convict FLASH LANGUAGE continues to influence contemporary colloquial speech in many ways. NEW CHUM, originally meaning a new convict and recorded by Vaux, later came to mean any new-comer to Australia, a sense in which it may still be heard. Other convict terms that are either still with us or have only relatively recently dropped include: FENCE, FLASH, JEMMY, KID, LARK, LEARY (leading to LAIR), MUG, OUT AND OUT, PINCH, PLANT, QUEER, RACKET, SCRAGGED, SCREW (a prison warder), SEEDY, SERVE, SNITCH, SPOUT, STASH, STRETCH, SWAG, TURN UP, and YARN. Interestingly, PAL, then spelt 'pall' and meaning a criminal accomplice (originally from Romany), remains with us as friend, though like MATE and SPORT it can be used in a menacing, warning manner, as in WATCH IT, PAL.

LARRIKINS

Not unrelated to the argot of the convict and of the underworld was the lingo of the LARRIKIN, a word of unknown origin, though usually thought to come from the Irish term 'larracking (or larking) about', or making a noisy nuisance of oneself in public. The term first appears in print in the 1860s, though those 19th-century and early 20th-century street persons it described had been making parts of Sydney and Melbourne notorious for some time before, already being referred to in 1825 as 'larky boys'. The LARRIKIN provided one of our most popular literary figures, most famously in C.J. Dennis's *The Songs of A Sentimental Bloke* and, a little later in the character of 'the Bloke's' mate, Ginger Mick. While these became the most widely known and loved representations of LARRIKINISM, they were preceded by considerable literary interest in this topic, including a much more realistic portrayal of LARRIKIN life in Sydney at the turn of the 20th century in Louis Stone's novel, *Jonah* (1911), still a very readable compendium of LARRIKIN street talk. Other writers had flirted with the LARRIKIN's colourful lifestyle and distinctive speech, including Lawson, most notably in 'The Captain of the Push' and, perhaps most linguistically accurate of all the poetic representations of the LARRIKIN, Louis Esson's little-known, but evocative, 'Jugger's Out Ter-d'y'. In this poem, the hero 'Jugger' has just been released from gaol: 'Jugger got er sixer/Toppin' orf a John, Stoushed 'im wi' er bottle/Back o' Little Lon.' All Jugger's old mates and girlfriends are looking forward to a grand celebration — 'Won't we blow the froth orf!' and the return of some decent MIX-UPS, there not having been a proper fight since Jugger went away. Now, 'All the tarts iz waitin'/Linin' Little Lon.,/In their flashest clobber,/Battlin' ter git on.' The speaker of the poem's greatest anticipation is the effect that Jugger's release will have on the police: 'Won't it nark the rozzers!/Jugger's out ter-d'y.'

As the extracts from Esson's verse show, LARRIKIN lingo often collided with that of the criminal and included terms from the convict past, such as MAGSMAN (a swindler or CON MAN in more recent slang, also surviving perhaps in the current use of MAGGING for talking) as well as one or two that are still with us in the Great Australian Lingo, even if only spoken now by a dwindling number of older Australians. These include ALSO RAN (an unimpressive performer), HARD CASE (a tough person), BLOKE (continued from the earlier convict usage), DROP YOUR BUNDLE (to give up, admit defeat) and GET THE BIRD — to be treated derisively.

The LARRIKINS organised themselves in gangs called PUSHES, also termed the TALENT. Vanity was a typical LARRIKIN feature, exhibited in a distinctive style of dress that included bell-bottom trousers, waist-length jacket, high-heeled boots, colourful scarf, pipe, and hat. Their women also dressed colourfully, though being careful never to outshine the male of the species, not noted for his chivalrous behaviour towards his female companions. LARRIKINS had some unpleasant pastimes, as can be guessed at by their use of such terms as JUMPING THEIR LIVERS OUT, a practice celebrated in a piece of 1893 LARRIKIN verse titled 'Kicking Their Livers Out', one stanza of which reveals a good amount of LARRIKIN slang and also something of the relationship between the LARRIKINS and the forces of law and order:

> *If a Sydney trap arrest you, though you're simply doing nix,*
> *Don't attempt the least resistance, or he'll get you in a fix,*
> *He will grab you by the collar and the bosom of your breeks,*
> *And upset you in the manner of the ancient wrestling Greeks;*
> *He will use both boots and knuckles, he will bark your bleeding shins,*
> *While you've simply got to bear it with the meekest of your grins;*
> *For he'll charge you with offences of the most atrocious kind,*
> *And he'll swear you tore his tunic though you're paralysed and blind,*
> *And the beak will give him credit, and he'll send you up the spout*
> *If the 'garjun' of the brothel even jumped your liver out...*

LARRIKIN PUSHES were often named after their area of origin, such as The Rocks Push in Sydney's sailor town, the Gore Hill Tigers, the Blues Point Mob, or the St Peter's Push after what was in those days a fringe suburb of that city. Others had a connection with certain occupations. Makers and carters of bricks were the main membership of the Black Reds, while the Liver Push or simply the Livers mostly worked in the Glebe Abattoirs. In Melbourne, the only other city to exhibit serious 'pushism', the street gangs were similarly known by local place names, including the Bowerie Street Push, the Montague Dingoes and the Fitzroy Murderers, while the Melbourne gang referred to in Esson's poem were The Flying Angels.

In common with other denizens of the streets, LARRIKINS also used back slang. Back slang is created by pronouncing words and phrases backwards. The British slang term YOB, now heard in Australian Lingo, is back slang on 'boy'. LARRIKIN back slang formations included OCCABOT for tobacco and DAB for bad. Sometimes these formations were not always strictly logical, the necessities of pronunciation seeming to interfere with the spelling. Thus the police became ESCLOPS, DELO NAMMOW is an old woman and a bad sort became a DOB TROS. This form of communication could be used as a secret language — at least until the listener caught on or was already aware of this linguistic trick. Secret languages of one type or another have long been characteristic of underworld and peripheral social groups like the LARRIKINS, and also among children as discussed in chapter 6.

RORT is an interesting word with specific Australian connotations. Known in Britain from around the mid-19th century, it originally had a sexual dimension, meaning to enjoy oneself boisterously and sexually, rather like the modern term RANDY. The sexual overtones seem to have gradually faded in Australia. By the early 20th century (when the word was first recorded here), it simply meant to have a good old time and was used by LARRIKINS in this sense, as in an old LARRIKIN song that includes the lines:

My name it is McCarty and I'm a rorty party
I'm rough and tough as an old man kangaroo.
Some people say I'm crazy
I don't work because I'm lazy
And I hang around with the boozy crowd
At the pub at Woolloomooloo.

A poem published in the LARRIKIN newspaper *The Dead Bird* in the early 1890s began with an arresting line describing the doings at 'Fanny Flukem's Ball' in such impeccable LARRIKIN lingo that it seems worth quoting in full, especially as it also highlights the use of the lurid nickname, an outstanding feature of Australian vernacular usage:

Now, listen, rorty bummers,
And line up where I stand,
I'll tell you of a ryebuck spree—
Gor', blue me, it was grand.

Twas in Conky Bob's old stable,
Who had lent it to the boys
On condition that they'd not get juiced
Or kick up any noise.

There was Paddy down from Gipps Street,
And Micky from the Rocks,
And Ginger from the Glebe way,
With blue metal in his socks.

A couple of blokes from Tempe,
With two molls from Waterloo,
Who tried to brush in on the nod,
But found it wouldn't do.

For Little Ginger kept the door,
And swore 'Lor', strike him fat,'
If they didn't part their deeners up
he'd lay 'em cold and flat.

Fat Mag came down from Crown Street,
With little flat-foot Poll,
And Sally Jerks, the ice-cream bart,
And Bluey Murphy's doll.

They had lancers, waltz and polka,
Fitzroys and Alberts, too.
And Fat Mag performed the barn dance
With a bloke from Woolloomooloo.

When Sal Jerks got the needle,
And, with many jeers and scoffs,
Says, 'Blue me, I know people
Who fancy they are toffs.

I'm a cut above such jigs as that;
For, spare me days, I am,
But it narks a bloomin' girl to see
Such trollops put on jam.'

Then Fat Mag sailed in and mixed it,
And said, 'You ice-cream trash,
I didn't come in on the nod,
But parted up my smash.

'My old man's not in Sturro,
My brother ain't done time.
You are only bones and leather,
While I am fat and prime.'

Then Micky from the Rocks jumped up
And said 'blame 'er, you know,
If any bloke in the bleeding crowd
Would like to have a go.

'I'm quiet, I am, till I'm narked;
My talent are the same,

But when we deal it out you'll find
We are no mugs at the game.'

'Line up, boarders,' cried out Ginger.
'Let 'em have it,' says Fat Mag;
Our trouble's for such cadgers,
If we have to do a drag.'

Then Paddy down from Gipps Street
Socked Mickey from the Rocks,
While Ginger made things lively
With the metal in his socks.

The Tempe blokes just stopped one each
And then they guyed a whack.
'It isn't on our programme
And, Gor' bli'me we are jack.'

The cops then came upon the scene
And lumbered one and all.
A quid and costs was the result
Of Fanny Flukem's ball.

Today, though, a RORT is the unprincipled manipulation of the system — 'politicians rort system' or similar often appears as a newspaper headline — for personal gain, a quite different meaning. How RORT, RORTY and RORTING changed in this way is unclear and it seems that both the festive and the morally dubious senses of the term existed about the time of World War I.

This was the period in which the great popular versifier C.J. Dennis wrote his LARRIKIN classics *The Songs of a Sentimental Bloke* (1915) and *The Moods of Ginger Mick* (1916). One of the most notable and lauded features of Dennis's work is his use of LARRIKIN-ese in the dialogue of his characters. Here 'the Bloke' describes his love, Doreen:

A squarer tom, I swear, I never seen,
In all me natchril, than this 'ere Doreen.
It weren't no guyver neither; fer I knoo
That any other bloke 'ad Buckley's 'oo
Tried fer to pick 'er up. Yes, she was square.
She jist sailed by an' lef' me standin' there
Like any mug. Thinks I, 'I'm out 'er luck,'
An' done a duck.

From what is known of LARRIKIN speech it seems that Dennis, to say the least, gilded the lily for literary effect. He uses terms like BUCK-LEY'S and 'in all me natchril' (natural) that were (and, in these cases, still are) part of the larger vernacular of the time along with an arsenal of LARRIKINese — SQUARE TOM, an upstanding girl or woman and NO GUYVER, not make-believe, true. It seems extremely unlikely that LARRIKINS ever spoke the way Dennis has them speaking, even without the poetry. Suggestive evidence for this is the lengthy glossary that was usually published in the back of *The Songs of a Sentimental Bloke* and *The Moods of Ginger Mick*. The vocabulary that Dennis uses is suspiciously free of those commonplace LARRIKIN terms for prostitutes, brothels, gaols and various forms of crime. Dennis had the advantage of coming at the end of a considerable period of literary interest in the LARRIKIN, which had seen poetry from Lawson, Esson and a host of others. The author of *The Songs of a Sentimental Bloke* and *The Moods of Ginger Mick* was able to build on this tradition to present a lovable, sanitised LARRIKIN in the form of 'the Bloke' and, later, a slightly harder case, the rabbit-selling Ginger Mick who nevertheless ends up dying for his country at Gallipoli — that is, DOING THE RIGHT THING, something that many real LARRIKINS avoided. Still, for generations Australians thought of 'the Bloke' and Ginger Mick as typical AUSSIE street heroes. Many still do. In 1997 a novelistic treatment of Dennis's characters and their speech, titled *Cobbers*, was produced by a major publisher, together with a reasonably lengthy glossary.

We are never far from the murky depths of the convict underworld and of the later colonial criminal subgroups when discussing the way LARRIKINS talked. Much of the LARRIKINS' little lingo was also the argot of the underworld. Words like ACADEMY (prison), BAGGED (imprisoned), ANOINTED (flogged), BLUEBOTTLE (policemen), among many others reflected the LARRIKIN's uneasy existence along the fuzzy line between working class life and criminality. Frequently it was difficult, if not impossible, to distinguish between the lawful and the lawless, a difficulty that saw many LARRIKINS LUMBERED by the TRAPS or ROZZERS, brought in BARNACLES (handcuffs) before the BEAK (magistrate) and taking a little AIR AND EXERCISE inside. A longer gaol term of three months with hard labour was called a DOSE or a DRAG.

Other LARRIKINISMS related closely to their preferred entertainments. Prize-fighting was a religion to LARRIKINS, who would travel miles in their best CLOBBER to watch a bout, accompanied by their female DONAHS. This word is variously said to be derived from Spanish, Portuguese, Italian or the earliest European pidgin, Polari, known in later versions as 'parlary', a restricted language spoken by actors, costermongers, showmen and other such low types in the 18th and 19th centuries. DONAHS were also known as CLINERS, from the German *kleine*, little or small). A fixed fight was known as a BARNEY and a crooked fighter was reviled as a BRUISER. Obviously, there was no shortage of either. Football came a close second to boxing in the LARRIKIN sporting pantheon, with the now-common BARRACK being a LARRIKIN invention, though then more usually BARRACKIN. Gambling on horses also took a lot of the LARRIKINS' time and money. A dishonest bookmaker was called a BESTER while a horse certain to win was a DEAD BIRD, terms that also belonged to the parlance of the wider fraternity of the turf.

LARRIKINese included many terms relating to 'the oldest profession'. A CAB and DRUM were terms for a brothel — CAB MOLLS, or just MOLLS were those who worked in them. Interestingly, MOLL, used to describe low women in 18th-century cant or underworld slang, was also revived in the USA during the depression of the 1930s to refer to a gangster's mistress. Today, the word has sunk even lower. Pronounced MOLE it has been in use since at least the 1950s to mean a girl or woman who bestows her favours frequently and without much discernment; almost synonymous with BIKE (a woman who allows anyone to RIDE her, as in THE TOWN BIKE). Other LARRIKIN terms illuminate those things that were important in their knockabout lifestyle: MOOCHING for idling; STOUSH (in print from the 1890s, though derived from the English term for a commotion, 'stashie', and no doubt in use for some years before), STOUSH-UP and to be STOUSHED are all terms for fighting, while A BUNCH OF FIVES was a fist, as it still is in Lingo. PUTTING THE BOOT IN is still pursued today and was a well-attested larrikin pastime, colourfully commemorated in 'The Bastard from the Bush', Lawson's own parody of his much more respectable 'The Captain of the Push'. In 'The Bastard', the Captain asks the stranger: 'Would you stoush a blanky Chinky?' And the stranger replies, 'My colonial oath I would!'

The many other terms for fighting give an idea of the importance of this activity in LARRIKIN life. BUMP, COMB DOWN, DISH, DONG, JOB, SPIKE, SORT OUT, STONKER, RIP INTO, DO, GO THE KNUCKLE ON, WEIGH INTO, WIPE and QUILT were among 40 or so terms identified by Sidney Baker in *The Australian Language* as part of the LARRIKIN lexicon of STOUSH. Some of these, notably SORT OUT, RIP INTO, DO, and WIPE, are still in our mouths. Baker also traces a number of phrases to the LARRIKINS, including GAME AS NED KELLY, GAME AS A PISS-ANT, FOND OF THE KNUCKLE and FIGHTS LIKE A THRESHING MACHINE. Anyone who failed to measure up to LARRIKIN notions of pugilistic excellence COULDN'T FIGHT HIS WAY OUT OF A PAPER BAG or was A GUTLESS WONDER, both phrases continuing a healthy existence today.

Although not a specifically LARRIKIN term, the general Lingoism for a fight is a BLUE. Someone can PUT ON A BLUE, BUNG ON A BLUE or even STACK ON A BLUE. In any case the result is the same. The origins of BLUE for fight seem obscure, as they are for its usage as a term for swag or bundle. Another meaning of BLUE (also a common nickname for a red-headed male), however, is to make a mistake. This is said to derive from the woolsheds of the 1890s where the newly introduced shearing machine blades needed frequent sharpening. If the job was badly done by the person responsible the metal blades would TURN BLUE, slowing down the shearer's output of shorn sheep and making him unhappy enough to stack on a BLUE. Lexicographer Sidney Baker claims to have heard this interesting dual etymology from a shearer, a species of bush-worker renowned for their ability to spin a yarn.

A fight, by the way, is often described simply in Lingo as being on (PUT IT ON; BUNG ONE ON; IT'S ON FOR YOUNG AND OLD), a term celebrated in the late Don Henderson's classic song 'It's On', the chorus of which went something like this:

And it's on
All reason and logic have gone.
Winning the fight won't prove that you're right,
It's sad and true,
But it's on.

Closely related to LARRIKINISM is a vintage Lingoism. Although of British origin, BLUDGER was first recorded here in the early 1880s meaning, as it had for some time before reaching print, a male who lived off the immoral earnings of one or more women. (HOON, a word of unknown origin, also had this meaning.) From this specialised underworld usage, BLUDGER came to mean in the larger Lingo anyone (though usually a male) who was lazy and shiftless or attempting to avoid responsibility. While its more specific meanings have gradually declined into a generalised insult, the term had a return to its sharper meanings during and since the 1970s with the arrival of the DOLE BLUDGER, a man or woman who, in popular perception at least, prefers to collect the DOLE (a term used for all social security benefits), rather than to work. 'Dole' is an old English term for charity that reached its current Australian usage during the depression of the 1930s. In 1990s rhyming slang it has become the ROCK AND ROLL, a usage also known in Britain.

Another of our most cherished Lingoisms and the national myth it stands for also has murky origins. According to the *Bulletin*'s Red Page of 17 December 1898, a prostitute was known as a BATTLER. Since then though, BATTLER has covered itself with glory becoming something of a compliment to those who struggle on against adversity and overwhelming odds, as in Kylie Tennant's award-winning 1941 novel about life on the road during the depression of the 1930s, *The Battlers*. In the remarkably short time of less than 30 years BATTLER moved from the bottom of the Lingo to the top. At election time, politicians of all persuasions still claim to represent THE AUSSIE BATTLER in the hope that this will win them extra votes. The 1996 Federal election campaign rhetoric made absurdly excessive use of this term.

Has the heyday of the LARRIKIN passed, another casualty of the sea-changes in Australian society since the 1980s? In the *Weekend Australian Magazine* of 11–12 February 1996, there appeared a feature article on the painfully self-conscious AUSSIE actor, Bryan Brown. The JOURNOS puffed Bryan as 'the last larrikin', though it seems unlikely that he will be the last to make use of this enduring image.

THE UNDERWORLD

Crime was not restricted to the doings of some LARRIKINS and criminals in the cities. Highway robbery, attacks on stations, banks and even towns the size of Bathurst were the stock-in-trade of bushrangers (thought to be an Americanism) almost from the first days of settlement. As pastoralism developed, so did the stealing of stock. The popularity of this form of robbery can be judged from the various terms used to describe it — PODDY-DODGING, DUFFING, GULLY-RAKING. Other terms associated with rural crime included SWEATING as in SWEATING A HORSE, to do it ON THE CROSS, as already mentioned (CROSS-BRANDING was a related term meaning the illegal alteration of a cattle brand) and simply LIFTING, a word that is still in use for stealing.

The surviving writings or dictations of Ned Kelly, himself an expert and self-confessed PODDY-DODGER, are excellent repositories of the lingo spoken by both bushrangers and more respectable country folk during the last half of the 19th century. Apart from demonstrating his unequalled ability to curse and malign, Ned Kelly's letters contain phrases like 'the ground was that rotten it would bog a duck'; 'my fist came in collision with McCormack's nose and caused him to lose his equilibrium and fall postate [sic]'; 'he was as helpless as a big guano (goanna) after leaving a dead bullock'; 'I could have spread those curs like dung in a paddock'; 'they will be heels up in the murroo'; 'their hounds were barking at the wrong stump'; 'hard working innocent men who would not know the difference [between] a revolver and a saucepan'; 'deceit and cowardice is too plain to be seen in the puny cabbage hearted looking face'; 'the biggest mud crushers in Melbourne'; 'big and ugly enough to lift Mount Macedon out of a crab hole' (here Ned is describing the police), and 'he knows as much about commanding Police as Captain Standish does about mustering mosquitoes and boiling them down for their fat'.

These gems are from the Jerilderie Letter of 1879. They reveal Ned Kelly as an outstanding wielder of the Lingo, especially when describing policemen, using patterns of speech and phrase formations that are still very much part of modern popular parlance. It does not come as a surprise to find that Ned and his bushranging companions were also LARRIKINS, members of the Beechworth Mob whose distinguishing feature was wearing the chinstraps of their hats beneath their nose, an affectation later adopted by sections of the AIF in World War II.

The Kellys and other members of the Beechworth Mob were also LAIRS, although the term in favour then was FLASH, another convictism. LAIR in the sense of a male who dresses and acts in a FLASH way turns up in print during the 1890s. Since then (and no doubt before) it has developed a number of deviant forms, notably to LAIRISE, or to LAIR ABOUT meaning to act irresponsibly and ostentatiously and the closely related forms TWO-BOB LAIR, a useless and/or worthless person and MUG LAIR, used to describe a male acting in a stupid and vulgar manner, often under the influence of GROG, one of our earliest Lingoisms recorded in 1832 and in the mouths of the people for much longer. GROG, originally rum, often mixed with water but soon extended to any alcoholic drink, has given us a number of combinations, such as SLY GROG, the illegal alcohol sold in SLY GROG huts and sly grog tents during the 19th century and even later. Then there is GROGGING ON, GROG ARTIST, ON THE GROG and a GROG UP.

All these terms, along with dozens more, for the consumption of alcoholic beverages give a clear indication of the general popularity of drinking in Australian society. Such an enthusiastic demotic practice could hardly fail to excite a backlash from those who did not imbibe and who did not want anyone else to enjoy the demon drink. These killjoys were dubbed WOWSERS by the irreverent and muckraking *Truth* newspaper of Sydney near the end of the 19th century. Probably derived from the British dialect term 'wow', meaning bark or howl, like many Lingoisms wowser has a folk etymology that claims it is an acronym of 'We Only Want Social Evils

Righted/Rectified/Removed', a FURPHY put about by *Truth*'s prodi-
giously alcoholic founder and editor, John Norton. Norton also gave
differing accounts of his invention of the word, at least one of which
deserves quotation for the flavour and vigour of his ability to use
the Lingo with wicked effect, especially in political disputation, a
tradition that still enjoys a virile existence in the BEARPIT of Federal
parliament:

> I invented the word myself. I was the first man to use the word. I first
> gave it public utterance in the City Council, when I applied it to
> Alderman Waterhouse, whom I referred to…as the white, woolly,
> weary, watery, word-wasting wowser from Waverley.

Whatever its origins, Norton's use of WOWSER made it an immediate
success and the word is still hurled occasionally today.

The success of WOWSER probably put paid to the popularity
of another, possibly New Zealand term for excessive puritanism, a
SNUFFLEBUSTER. First put in print in 1890, this one has a whiff of journalistic invention about it, supported by the fact that most of its cita-
tions in *Australian Words and Their Origins* are from periodicals. One
of these, though, from the Sydney *Worker* of February 1895, is worth
quoting as an example of the skilled use of Lingo in political invective.
An apparently anonymous author wrote: 'Painted by him I am a narrow, bigoted, snuffle-busting son of a gun whose grog blossomed
"conk" [one of our earliest convictisms] gives the lie to his watery
protestations.' This is very much in the style of Norton, and echoes
some of Ned Kelly's maledictions quoted above and elsewhere.

Sidney Baker's *The Australian Language* includes a chapter on
the underworld and its lingo, based largely on his extensive network
of informants, mostly of the 1920s and 1930s. Baker presents a
breathtaking variety of historical and contemporary argot of convicts,
WIZZERS, TRAPS, WALLOPERS, HARDHEADS, CON ARTISTS, prostitutes
(those who HAWK THE FORK), RAZOR-SLASHERS, STANDOVER MEN,
GLIM-FAKERS, ILLYWHACKERS and assorted thieves, assassins and
informers, to mention only some of the little lingo terms of our
home-grown rogues' gallery.

One of the points that comes very clearly through Baker's discussion of these terms is that while a good many are Australianisms,
there are plenty derived from British and US criminal slanguages.
From Britain comes 'lurk', hanging around with criminal intent. By
the 1880s this was being used in Australia as DEAD LURK, meaning to
rob a house while the occupants were at church. The term crops up
again as 2nd AIF slang during World War II in the form LURK MEN,

meaning those who sought to avoid work and/or military service. Since then the word has been used in the wider Lingo as a description of a criminal or, at least, a dubious scheme of some kind, as in A BETTING LURK and, more generally, to mean a SOFT COP, an easy and/or remunerative job or activity. BRASS, meaning money and dating from the 16th century is also still heard, as is PINCH, to arrest and to KNOCK OFF, in the sense of stealing, rather than finishing work. Other terms that remained fairly firmly in the little lingo of the CRIMS included DO A BUST, to escape from custody; DARBIES for handcuffs; FAN, to search, STIR for gaol and COPPER'S NARK, meaning a police informer. NARK, of course also appears more generally as a term for being annoyed, as in DON'T GET NARKED or DON'T NARK ME, as it has now for well over a century.

Contacts with the USA have given us SHILL, a CON-MAN's collaborator; STOOL-PIGEON, an informer; ICE for diamonds; STRONG-ARM, to physically intimidate; and probably HEAT, meaning pressure from the authorities and familiar through generations of US television crime shows. Other imports from this favoured source include BLOW, to depart; BOOB and CAN for gaol (the latter meaning toilet in current US vernacular); GAT, a hand gun; SPRING, to bail someone out of custody and SNOW for cocaine, among numerous others, including SPIELER which many fondly think of as uniquely Australian.

Those criminalisms that Baker does identify as peculiarly Australian are discomfitingly many. Terms for a MUG (originally English), also noticed briefly in the chapter on 'Sports and Rorts', include ALEC, DILL (long since promoted to the greater Lingo as a term for a fool); SIM; LOLLY and the accurate BUNNY. TALE, PITCH and RORT are used in criminal parlance to refer to the line of talk used by a showman or confidence trickster. TO BITE or LUG is to borrow money; a SHODDY DROPPER is a hawker; THE COME ON is the method used to entice a potential BUNNY; STANDOVER and SHAKEDOWN, to bully or to frighten with potential or real violence and COP, denoting a profitable operation of some kind, a term also used in the wider Lingo with a similar meaning in the combination A SWEET COP or TO COP IT SWEET — though one may also COP IT, of course, which means getting into trouble. Equally Australian are a number of terms for the person who keeps guard for those involved in criminal activities, including COCKATOO, NITKEEPER (one who KEEPS NIT), the crickety-sounding LONG-STOPPER and FIZZ-GIG, or FIZZER now used widely to mean a police informer. Related to these activities is the term for those who brought news of what the TRAPS or TROOPERS were doing to the bushrangers with whom they sympathised — BUSH TELEGRAPHS. BUSH TELEGRAPH and the even more evocative MULGA

WIRE are still in use to describe mostly, though not exclusively, rural rumour networks.

Also associated with the underworld, mostly by necessity, sometimes by choice, are those charged with the duty of keeping it under control. The little lingoes of Australian police forces would make a linguistic study, probably a number, of their own. As well as the word DOG to describe an informer, the Victorian police still use the convictism LAG as a term for one who informs especially, though not exclusively, against his or her fellow-officers. Often there is a brisk interchange between the terms used by police and their targets, the CRIMS, but each group also has its own extensive argots. The New South Wales Royal Commission into Police Corruption that ran during the mid-1990s to late 1990s produced a number of interesting examples of police usage and abusage with such terms as THE LAUGH, for taking bribes, THE RENT, meaning the division of the spoils between police officers and the venerable DARLO DROP, said rather colourfully to be the practice of throwing a prisoner towards the ceiling and allowing him or her to return to the floor unrestrained. In fact, the DARLO DROP is used to mean any kind of police brutality that takes place while the victim is in custody and has been so used in Sydney for a very long time.

Australians are known for their tendency to make heroes of underdogs and criminals. Certain bushrangers are celebrated, as are the characteristics rightly or wrongly associated with LARRIKINISM and even with convicts. Many of these qualities are also linked with the heroic Australian foot soldier, THE DIGGER.

4

FIGHTING WORDS

> ...if an average Australian averagely slang-acquainted were set
> down to-night in one of our tents in France and listened to the
> boys as they talk and joke and chaff he would not understand
> the greater part of their conversation. It is not the words them-
> selves so much as the manner in which they are used and the
> significance that attaches to them that would puzzle him. For
> the war has brought with it a great increase in our vocabulary,
> and the slang dictionary will have to be re-compiled to
> be up-to-date.
>
> LIEUTENANT C. G. PRESCOTT IN THE ANZAC MEMORIAL, 1917

Wars have been significant watersheds in both the Great Australian Lingo and in some little lingoes, especially those associated with the volunteer infantryman, THE DIGGER. The large-scale mobilisations of civilian troops characteristic of the major conflicts of the 20th century have been forcing grounds for the speedy adaptation and creation of the Australian vernacular.

World War I, the Great War, 'the War to End Wars' was an especially potent moment for Australian nationalism and for the closely related development of Lingo. Although the country had been officially federated into a Commonwealth of States and Territories in 1901, there was an emotional absence waiting to be filled with great and symbolic deeds of national glory. That, at least, was how most Australians saw things at the time. Lacking many traditions, apart from those derived from an Anglo-Celtic heritage and a shared language, Australians also had little in common apart from the harsh experience of pioneering a country that few understood and many hated. These things were already coagulating into the national mythology of the bush and the pioneering past when Britain went to war in August 1914. Andrew Fisher, prime minister at the time, declared famously that Australia would fight 'to the last man and the last shilling' on behalf of the British motherland and her great empire. Most Australians agreed with him and the young men left the farms, the counters, the factories, and wherever else they laboured to join up. The 1st AIF (Australian Imperial Force) was formed from this enthusiasm and, in conjunction with New Zealand troops, became known as the Australian New Zealand Army Corps under the command of the British army.

The acronymisation of the telegraphic code ANZAC into Anzac is well known. It is an example of a word that had a rapid rise from a specialised usage to the official designation for Australian–New Zealand troops. Within a year of its invention Anzac had been the subject of Federal legislation. On 20 October 1916, the *War Precautions Act* was proclaimed. Part of the Act forbade the use of ANZAC, or any words resembling ANZAC, as the name, or part-name, of any private residence, boat, vehicle, or charitable or other institution. The penalty for so doing was a fine of £100 or six months imprisonment. In response to requests from the Australian government, the British also (reluctantly) banned use of the term for trade or profit in December 1916. Before this, though, a competition to name a new residential subdivision on the south coast of England was won with the suggestion of 'Anzac-on-Sea'. Disappointingly, no more was heard of this reverse linguistic colonisation.

Most of the other words and phrases the Australian and New Zealand troops created from the moment they gathered together in the great convoy that sailed from King George Sound in Albany, Western Australia, late in 1914, stayed firmly in the realms of Lingo. Some of them are still there. One especially powerful term was a relatively late invention of the Great War.

DIGGER

The word most Australians associate with the actions of Australian troops at Gallipoli in April to December 1915, did not come into general use until at least early 1917. The Australian and New Zealand soldiers at Gallipoli were sometimes referred to as Anzacs and often still are. More usually they are described with the word that all Australian foot soldiers are known by — DIGGERS, but as an Anzac writing to the *Bulletin*'s famous Red Page of 8 June 1922 claimed: '...there were no Diggers at Gallipoli where we dug most — the word had not come then!' The correspondent was right. How then, and when, did the word come about?

The sometimes handwritten newspapers and other publications printed under difficult conditions by Australian and New Zealand troops at Gallipoli, as well as their letters and diaries confirm that no-one was called a DIGGER at Gallipoli. Soldiers are referred to as privates, Australians, men or troops. Nor does the word appear in the 1917 *Anzac Memorial*, published on Anzac Day by the forerunners of the Returned & Services League of Australia (RSL). In an extensive glossary of Australian soldier slang, titled 'Anzac Vocabulary', we read about POSSIE (position), the weather and the food being CHRONIC, a CUSHY JOB (an easy job), and a variety of other terms mangled out of Arabic and French — but not about DIGGER.

So DIGGER was not commonly in use to describe Australian foot soldiers in January 1917. But in the 12 February 1917 issue of *The Rising Sun*, this humorous anecdote appears :

> Do the Sappers Wish They Did?
> Returning to Camp on Christmas Eve from the trenches, a voice was heard inquiring:
> 'Hey, Digger, do yer know the duck walks down to the Engineer's Camp?' Came the answer out of the dark. 'Trés bon, trés bon; I'll tell old Tom, our cook, about that.' Result, mystified look on face of inquirer.

Here the word is used in its familiar meaning and fits well with lexicographer Eric Partridge's personal observation that Australians used the term in their conversation, to describe others and that others called them DIGGER. But he implies that the term was not used widely to describe Australian soldiers.

When did this important item of Australian folk speech and national image arise? The earliest reference given for the use of DIGGER in its wartime, rather than its goldfields sense, is in the diary of C.A. Hemsley, 12 August 1916, where an Australian soldier used the term in jest to an officer addressing a parade — 'The officer in charge of the parade was addressing the men, and at some kindly expressed sentiment one wag interjected with "Hear, hear, old digger" .'

According to the official war correspondent, Charles Bean, writing in the *Official History*:

> It was at this stage [June–August, 1917] that Australian soldiers — in particular the infantry — came to be known as 'diggers', together with the New Zealanders, who are said to have inherited it from the gum-diggers in their country. It carried so rich an implication of the Anzac infantryman's own view of his functions and character, that it spread like fire through the AIF, and by the end of the year was the general term of address for Australian and New Zealand soldiers.

Bean, a fine journalist whose ear was always close to the ground, probably picked up that DIGGER was being applied generally by the Australians to themselves, and by others, fairly quickly. It seems that the term came into general use as the preferred description of the Australian soldier probably a little before Bean's estimate, in the first months of 1917. Bean was certainly unaware of it in November 1916 when he penned a reasonably extensive discussion of the term Anzac and the importance of what Australian (and New Zealand) soldiers called themselves for the London-produced *Anzac Bulletin* of 6 December. DIGGER does not appear in this discussion, an inconceivable omission if the word had by then achieved its defining status.

When it did catch on, though, DIGGER spread like a bushfire. By mid-1918 the word had been promoted to the masthead of the weekly newspaper *The Digger,* 'published with authority' of the Australian bases in France. This very official organ even included a verse in its September 1918 edition that summed up one central element of DIGGER philosophy and activity:

THE DIGGER'S TOAST
The Frenchman likes his sparkling wine,
The German likes his beer,
The Tommie likes his half and half
Because it brings good cheer.
The Scotsman likes his whisky,
And Paddy likes his pot,
But the Digger has no national drink,
So he drinks the blanky lot.

No sooner was the word out, it seems, than disputes arose about the origin and ownership of the term. DIGGER, even more than POMMY, is probably the most contested single word in the Lingo. The famous newspaper *Aussie* began publication at the front in January 1918 and from issue number 2 in February that year carried impassioned correspondence on the origins and ownership of DIGGER. Claims for a New Zealand origin were put forward; that it was first used on the Salient; and that it came from the military necessity of digging-in. A poem titled 'The Dinkum Oil About "Digger"' appeared in number 4 and correspondence wound on through subsequent issues into 1919. (The terms DINKUM OIL or THE GOOD OIL, by the way, are said by linguists to be a transfer of the use of oil to ensure the efficient running of a machine to the need to have good information in order to fight effectively. It seems more likely that the term is related to the earlier use of OIL for alcohol — and still current as THROAT-OIL or

NECK-OIL. At a time when alcohol was often adulterated, GOOD OIL meant the genuine, full-strength brew. This very easily transferred to a description of hard information.)

The Digger in France also carried extensive correspondence about its namesake, including further claims for a New Zealand origin, and the columns of the postwar publications, such as *Aussie*, the *Bulletin*, *Smith's Weekly* ('the Diggers' Bible') and the numerous returned soldiers' newspapers and journals frequently addressed the issue in the postwar years.

But it was in the appropriately named 'Digger's Diary' column of the *Western Mail* for 9 January 1930 that ex-serviceman Cyril Longmore put forward a particularly convincing claim for a West Australian genesis of DIGGER. According to Longmore, members of the 3rd Division's 11th Brigade, a West Australian unit, were in training on England's Salisbury Plain in September and October 1916. An officer, seeing the troops practising trenching techniques referred to them as DIGGERS. The 11th Brigade jokingly took up the term, using it to describe themselves. When they shipped out to fight in France late in 1916, they took the term with them and it spread rapidly throughout the AIF from early 1917. Longmore's version fits very comfortably with the newly established dates for the origins of DIGGER, though this is unlikely to stem controversy about the term which crops up from time to time in newspapers, magazines and PUBS around the country.

DIGGER is the focusing concept, the keyword, for the wartime and postwar culture of the Australian civilian infantryman. Inventiveness, anti-authoritarianism, sardonic humour and casual gallantry are the essentials of this Australian military myth that developed rapidly from dawn on 25 April 1915, to be transmitted down the subsequent generations. The DIGGER soldiered on through the Somme, through the Western Desert and the New Guinea jungles of World War II through to Korea, then on into the more recent conflicts of Vietnam and the Gulf War where, even though no infantry fought, the image of the DIGGER was invoked by press and politicians. DIGGERS were also involved in peace-keeping operations in Somalia and Namibia. The staying power of the image probably means that it will remain with us through the 21st century as well. Fundamental though the disaster in the Dardanelles was to this image, there were no DIGGERS at Gallipoli.

DIGGERESE — WORLD WAR I

Despite the late arrival of DIGGER into the folk speech of the DIGGERS themselves and, very quickly thereafter, into the national lexicon, the men of the 1st AIF and the nurses who tended them were not slow in coining new words. Out of their experiences in Egypt, on Gallipoli, in France and occasionally on leave or in hospital back in Britain, or BLIGHTY (a Blighty was also used for a wound serious enough to be hospitalised in Britain, though not serious enough to cause permanent disability) the necessities of war sprouted many strange new terms that grew into the DIGGERS' lingo.

Almost as soon as the AIF was formed and it became known that soldiers were to be paid six shillings a day they were dubbed SIX BOB-A-DAY TOURISTS. In comparison with most other allied soldiers, Australians were very well paid. Just as quickly came the term CHOCOLATE SOLDIERS, referring to soldiers believed to be reluctant to fight. Although CHOCOLATE CREAM SOLDIERS had been in use since the late 19th century in British parlance, Australians adopted it as their own, rapidly abbreviating it to CHOCS.

Training in Egypt brought the Australian soldiers face to face with a people and a culture which were wholly alien to most of them. Their immediate response to the Egyptians, conditioned by decades of British imperialism and its accompanying mentality of colonialism, was to refer to them as GYPPOS and WOGS. The 1st AIF's typical experience of Egypt, apart from the monotony and discomfort of training and camp life, was of the drinking places and brothels of Cairo, relieved now and then by some sightseeing to the pyramids and other historic sites. It was the former pursuits, though, that contributed most early terms to the slang lexicon of the AIF.

SAIEEDA came to mean goodbye, goodnight, good day. IMSHI was the soldiers' version of the Arabic for go, as was YALLAH. When these terms were used together, they magnified each other, according to a contemporary writer, and were to be understood as meaning GO TO BLAZES. BAKSHEESH meant money, a term that is still heard occasionally, now meaning usually a bribe or KICKBACK. A variant of this, also still sometimes heard, is BUCKSHEE, to get something for nothing, from the Egyptian term for alms. MAFEESH meant to finish, the end. Women, in DIGGERese, were BINTS (from Arabic), a term used by World War II diggers and even occasionally today, and TABBIES, a term taken from pre-war street slang, though 'tabby' has a longer history in British and US slang as a term for an elderly spinster.

One especially notorious incident that has passed into the mythology of the DIGGER also seems to have given us a still current Lingoism. On Good Friday 1915, Australian, New Zealand and some soldiers of other nationalities rioted in the red light district of Cairo, known as the Wazzir. The riots seem to have been based on the belief that the Egyptian prostitutes were knowingly infecting the men with venereal disease and that, to make matters worse, they were being overcharged for their pleasures. (The high incidence of venereal disease in Australian soldiers returned home, unfit for duty from Egypt, provides some evidence to substantiate this perception, though there is also a likelihood that many were infected by Australian prostitutes before they left these shores.) The riots were bloody and brutally suppressed by the Military Police in the usual way. A number of people were killed and many injured. To go TO THE TOP OF THE WAZZA (Wazzir/Wazza) is still used to mean taking something to excess.

The soldiers were not shy, either, in borrowing a number of terms from the French language. One example was FINEE, heard frequently in the evocative phrase *après la guerre finit* (after the war is over). The French *il n'y a plus* became NAIPOO, sometimes NAPOO, meaning nothing doing or no way, probably borrowed from the British TOMMIES. This term also provided the name of a popular gambling card game, NAP, commemorated in a ditty of the time:

> 'I'll go one', said England;
> 'I'll go two', said France.
> 'I'll go three', said Germany and put them in a trance.
> 'I'll go four', said Russia, 'and wipe them off the map'.
> But they all dropped dead when Australia said
> 'We'll go nap.'

From French the soldiers mangled *trés bon* into TRAY BON for very good which commonsensically in English at least led to NO BON for no good. But the Australian soldiers' use of *bon* was not derived exclusively from wartime contact with the French. BON had been in Lingo usage for more than a decade before World War I began in such combinations as IT'S A BON, AIN'T IT? to mean something good and in numerous variants including BONSTERINA, BON TON (said to have been pronounced 'bong tong') and BONTOSHER. Many of these seem related to another archetypal Lingoism, the term BONZER for something good, though this seems to have reached us from the Spanish via the Americanism for a large, rich mine or other source of wealth, a bonanza. Also from the soldiers' ear rendition of French came PLONK for cheap wine, slurred from *vin blanc* (white wine), *Compris* became COMPREE, understand, more usually NO COMPREE and *manger* became MONGY, to eat, or the meal itself.

As in everyday life, the soldiers had plenty of euphemisms for death and for the devices that brought it. These included to GO WEST (also claimed as an Americanism of World War I, though definitely used before the entry of the USA into that conflict), TO STOP ONE, as in a bullet; to GET IT IN THE NECK; to GO OUT TO IT; to TAKE THE COUNT (both from boxing), the Americanism to PASS IN YOUR CHEQUES (checks) and the laconic SMUDGED, meaning that someone had been blown to bits. A DAISY-CUTTER was a term used widely in the British forces to refer to an anti-personnel bomb, but it seems to have originated with the Anzacs. Many of these terms are still used.

On Gallipoli the Anzacs soon made the acquaintance of body lice, or CHATS, a term also common in US folk speech. The enemy became JOHNNY TURK or JACKO (also used in Australia for Aborigines, though once applied to the kookaburra, from one of its Lingo names THE LAUGHING JACKASS. The call of this bird was also known as THE SETTLERS' CLOCK during the 19th century.) The firing position became a POSSIE and home for most was a DUGOUT. They made JAM TIN BOMBS and PERISCOPE RIFLES and told FURPHIES, or rumours, a word originating in Egypt and derived from the name of the manufacturer of the water and sanitary wagons used by the AIF in Egypt, Furphy and Sons. The soldiers used to stand around these wagons (the water carriers, not the others presumably) which bore their manufacturer's name boldly forged into the end of the tank, and discuss the war, swap news and generally try to find out what was going on as they were told almost nothing by the military command. The rumours, speculations and desperate guesses that circulated in these conversations were soon given the general name of FURPHY.

The popularity of rhyming — and other — slang (discussed in more detail elsewhere) at this time can be heard in this probably apocryphal exchange between an American and an Australian soldier, late in World War I:

> The Yank: 'Say Guy, how far to battle?'
> Aussie: 'Well sonny, I guess it's about five kilos. Just 'pencil and chalk' straight along this 'frog and toad' till you come to the 'romp and ramp' on the 'johnny horner'. Then dive across that 'bog orange' field till you run into a barrage. That lobs you right there. D'ye compree?'

Many other ANZACAL terms also have a recognisably Australian character, such as the term unpleasantly familiar to soldiers on Gallipoli and to those who nursed them on hospital ships and in Egypt — the GALLIPOLI GALLOP for dysentery. To BLUDGE, while not originating with the soldiers, certainly attained the momentum that still propels it in current Lingo. A 'bludger' was 19th-century British slang for a man who lived off the earnings of a prostitute. It was also used in Australia with this sense. The soldiers' contribution seems to be the disengagement of the term from most, if not all, of its underworld associations and the use of it in the two modern senses of doing nothing, lazing about and to borrow, as in TO BLUDGE A FAG. This latter was the main sense in which the word was being used in the AIF by 1916, along with cognate terms such as NIPPED, HUMMED, and CADGED, the last a continuation of much earlier convict argot.

A colourful in-group language of its own, ANZACAL, as one soldier described it when writing home from Gallipoli, was an amalgam of bush slang, LARRIKIN slang, army acronyms and Australianised foreign phrases, mainly Arabic and French. From the existing Australian Lingo of the time the troops preserved and extended such terms as CHIV, said to be derived from the rhyming slang for face — CHEVY CHASE, in use from at least the late 19th century; COBBER, BONZER, PRAD (horse), BABBLER (from BABBLING BROOK, rhyming slang for cook used by shearers and other outback workers) as well as the term for a popular LARRIKIN practice of STOUSHING or fighting. C.J. Dennis's romanticised depiction of the war through Ginger Mick's eyes as just one big STOUSH was right on the mark as far as AIF slang was concerned. Reinforcements, for instance, were sometimes referred to as REINSTOUSHMENTS, in France, often chopped down to just REOS. Ginger Mick also saw the AIF as one big PUSH or LARRIKIN gang, a view that appealed strongly to the Anzacs who bought the book in tens of thousands.

The soldiers' ALPHABET, a verse-form that uses the alphabet as a framework for comic and satirical comment on the experience of war, was a favourite form of printed soldier entertainment. Many of these poems are based on soldiers' lingo as in the following example composed by L.F.S.H. of the 8th Light Horse Regiment on Anzac, December 1915.

ANOTHER ALPHABET
A is for Anzac, removed evermore,
B is for Beachy who busts on the shore.
C is for Colic, which follows directly,
D is the Dose taken paregorectly.
E is for Exercise climbing the hills,
F for Fatigues that come faster than bills.
G is the German who made the Turk fight,
May H____ be his portion or serve him well right.
I is for Indian, excellent fellow,
J is for the jaundice which makes us so yellow.
K is for Kobber, Australian for friend,
L is the Last Post, which comes right at the end.
M is the Mule who's game as a sparrow,

N is the Nuisance with saps much too narrow.
O is the Oaths, some of which are fair snorters.
P is the pain they produce at headquarters.
Q is the Quiver which runs down your back,
When R a big Rooster comes plunk from Chanak.
S is the Soft Jobs you get back at the base,
T is the Turk and a pretty tough case.
V is for Vickers, that man-killing pest.
W's the Whisky we sigh for in vain,
X is for Xcitement, "The mail's in again."
Y is for Yes, if we're asked to go home,
Z is for Zero — I'm chilled to the bone.

As well, not a few Anzacal terms went over the top into the linguistic battlefield of the Great Australian Lingo. A surprising number are still in use today, including: A GOOD POSSIE, to COME A GUTSER (to make a bad mistake or suffer serious misfortune or injury; though GUTS referred to hard information or news and became COMIC CUTS in rhyming slang) and the Cockney CHRONIC that, by 1916, had come to mean anything which was really bad which was a lot, including food, water, officers, the war, the lice, the mud, the heat, the cold…, one of the salient characteristics of the Australian soldier being his propensity to complain or to WHINGE. From Canadian soldier slang the Australian soldiers adopted BEAT IT, meaning to go quickly, a common wartime manoeuvre and one not unknown in peacetime where the term still has the identical usage. ONKUS means disagreeable or unpleasant and was used in civilian life between the wars, revived by the 2nd AIF (see below), only to stagger on well into the 1960s, though it is rarely heard today. The still-current term TO COME AT something originated in World War I. Now, as then, it means to take on something, to join in, to agree. The still-sometimes used term for British people, CHOOMS, also arose in World War I, deriving from the way that many TOMMIES north of Watford pronounced CHUM, closely equivalent to the Australian use of MATE.

Probably, the Australian soldiers developed another term that is still with us from their close contact with the CHOOMS during the war years. RAFFERTY'S RULES, meaning no rules at all, seems to be an Australianisation of a British dialect term for confusion or mess, RAFF or RAFFETY. Wherever it came from, the first-known printed reference to it occurs in the newsletter of a homeward bound Australian troopship in late 1918, the *Port Hacking Cough*, a good indication of its DIGGER origins.

Charles Bean, later to edit and partly author the *Official History of Australia in the War of 1914–18* was, as already noted, a close observer and recorder of the doings of the Australian soldiers from the start of the war right through to the bitter end. In his history Bean published what he heard a group of soldiers saying while they rested out of the line in May 1918. It provides a rare, presumably verbatim, example of some of the DIGGERS' language which, by the standards of World War II, was mild and by the standards of today is almost kindergarten talk:

> The language in the yard [of the building in which the troops were billeted] is such that you'ld [sic] think there was going to be a knifing every two minutes. 'Ah____ you, you lazy bastard.' 'Go to b_____, to hell wid yer.' 'Would yer, yer bastard!' — and you look out of the window and find that it is all spoken with a grin. The most ferocious oaths are flung between the passing men...

It would be CHRONIC to leave World War I without quoting an anonymous poem that appeared in a soldiers' newspaper handwritten on Gallipoli about seven weeks after the 25 April landing. This anonymous piece, titled 'The Trooper's Lament' gives an earful of what the Lingoists among the Australian troops were saying in 1915. Like C.J. Dennis's better-known 'The Australaise', this verse is also inspired by W.T. Goodge's 'The Great Australian Adjective' but has the added advantage of providing a brief narrative of the Light Horse experience of war to that point:

> *I come from good old Wamp-Wamp and me monicker's Gus*
> *Headers*
> *An' I joined the 4th Light_____ 'Orse out at Broad_____ meadows.*
> *I brings along me own old prad, and shove the claim in 'ot.*
> *But th'_____ vet 'e crools me pitch, an 'arf was all I got.*
> *I gathers in the _____ cash and gets off on the spree,*
> *And the CO ups and passes me a week's C_____B.*
>
> *GORSTRUTH!!*
>
> *Then off we goes to Egypt, and in th'_____ sand,*
> *I does a fortnight's doublin' with a rifle in me 'and.*
> *And then we took our _____prads an' stuffed 'em well with tibbin*
> *(Which sorter calms them down a lot and stops their_____jibbin').*
> *An' round about the Pyramids, the desert an' the Sphinx*
> *We does a five months' stunt among the flies an'_____stinks.*
> *But when we all gets pretty 'ot and fit to take the track,*
> *They hikes me off me 'orse an' makes me 'ump a _____pack.*

CRISE!!

Next thing I finds meself a-dodgin' shrapnel in the' trenches
Where a bloke can 'ardly turn around for periscopes and stenches.
'Owever, it's all in the game a soldier's got to play,
An' I'd rather be out 'ere than_____Egypt any day.
But let me feel just once again me old prad shy an' reef
An' you can 'ave me biscuit an' me tin of bully beef.

MY_____OATH!!

DIGGERESE — WORLD WAR II

The lingo of the DIGGER was formed in the experiences of Egypt, Gallipoli and the Western Front during the World War I and was carried on into later conflicts by subsequent generations of volunteer infantry. As well as this younger generation there were still enough men who had served in World War I fit enough to serve again. World War II AIF slang for these brave, or possibly foolhardy, men was RETREADS. When the next generation of DIGGERS returned to Egypt during World War II (1939–45), they also borrowed some of the same words and phrases from the local language like MUNGAREE or MUNGA for food or the eating of it, HARD MUNGA meaning iron rations and SOFT MUNGA being everyday food.

A portion of 2nd AIF slang was continued from World War I. Terms like SHEILA and BINT which had been applied to women and girls during the earlier conflict remained in use, as did BACKSHEESH, SHOOFTI for look (from Arabic) was a British borrowing that DIGGERS in the Middle East soon picked up, as in HAVE A SHOOFTI AT THAT, or in THE SHOOFTI ROOM, the viewing area of an Arab brothel. The originally derisive term for volunteer civilians used in World War I, CHOCOLATE SOLDIERS was common in the forms CHOCS or CHOCKOS. WOG, used of Arabs and subsequently of any non-European race, including Japanese, was resurrected from its World War I Egyptian usage. The variations on this term (given by Baker) make for a lengthy history, all of it unedifying. Enough to say that its widespread use in World War II provided the seedbed for its later civilian application to migrants in the late 1950s. GUTS, meaning news or hard information, survived from World War I, often in the acronymic GG or GOOD GUTS, sometimes GOOD GRIFF (from GRIFFIN, a LARRIKINISM for the truth), also a hangover from the past. FURPHY kept circulating, as did BLUDGER, among others. An unattributed verse from the New Guinea campaign provides a glimpse of the discomforts of war in that theatre, a smattering of World War II lingo and also shows how the term DINKUM continued to give good service, as it had in World War I:

> *The man-eating mozzies of Moresby,*
> *Their beaks are so big and so sharp,*
> *That a nibble or two and you're just about through,*
> *You may even be playing the harp.*
> *We don't give a rap for the buggering Jap*
> *We'll fight him like dinkum Aussies.*
> *But lord up above, if your children you love,*
> *Why in HELL did you ever make mossies?*

Some terms were altered slightly to suit new circumstances, titles and slang. The World War I BASE WALLOPER, a soldier who hangs around HQ in preference to going anywhere near the action, was called a BASE BLUDGER or a FOUNTAIN PEN FUSILIER. A SHINY ARSE was newly minted for World War II and indicated someone who worked at base behind a desk. CUT LUNCH COMMANDOS was another usually unfairly disparaging term applied to soldiers serving on Australian, rather than overseas, duties. Those who worked on propaganda, mainly through the Department of Information, were known as BLUE PENCIL WARRIORS. Staff of that organisation made the Chief Censor of the day, Edmund Bonney, the subject of a paranoid parody of 'My Bonnie Lies Over the Ocean':

> *My Bonney lies over the ocean,*
> *My Bonney lies over the sea,*
> *And sometimes I get the notion,*
> *Bonney also lies to me.*

In World Wars I and II, the Australian soldiers' attitudes towards those who were thought to have a SOFT SPOT were far from complimentary. A famous DIGGER song that did service in both wars makes this point very clearly and also shows how ANZACAL became more direct and 'bad' in the 1939–45 conflict. The earlier version of the song, peppered with DIGGERISMS of the day, depicts the soldier returning to London from the fighting in France and reporting to AIF Headquarters in the Horseferry Road:

> *...A buckshee Corporal said 'Pardon me, please,*
> *But there's dust on your tunic and dirt on your knees.*
> *You look so disgraceful that people will laugh',*
> *Said the cold-footed bastard that works on the Staff.*
> *The Aussie just gave him a murderous glance,*

And said, 'I've just come from the trenches in France,
Where shrapnel is falling and comforts are few,
And Aussies are fighting for cowards like you.
I wonder, old shirker, if your mother e'er knew,
That her son is a waster and afraid of the strafe,
But holds a soft snap on the Horseferry Staff?'

The World War II versions, usually called 'Dinky-di', from the nationalistic chorus that the song acquired somewhere between 1918 and the 1940s, sometimes switch the whereabouts of the fighting from France to Tobruk. Some representative verses show the use of World War I slang in the more directly critical context of the 1939–45 conflict:

He came up to London and straightaway strode
To army headquarters in the Horseferry Road
To see all the bludgers who dodge all the strafe
By getting soft jobs on the Headquarters Staff.

(Chorus) Dinky-di, dinky-di,
I'm an old digger and I won't tell a lie.

The digger then shot him a murderous glance;
And said 'I'm just back from the shambles in France,
Where the whizzbangs are flying and the comforts are few,
And brave men are dying for bastards like you.

'We're shelled on the left and we're shelled on the right.
We're bombed all the day and we're bombed all the night.
If something don't happen and that pretty soon,
There'll be no bastard left in the bloody platoon...

As the last of the two examples above shows, World War II DIGGERS, also like their predecessors, made good use of their lingo in verse. From one of the anonymous classics of the World War II usually known as 'Adolf Hitler's Isle of Doom', a reference to the ill-fated Crete campaign, comes these lines:

The water it was onkus and the tucker it was crook
I got fed up and slung me hook.

ONKUS, a word of unknown origin was, as we know, in use during World War I, though it does not seem to be a soldiers' word. It means, of course, something unpleasant or of inferior quality. CROOK is much the same and has a number of meanings, including to berate someone as in TO GO CROOK, to be of inferior quality and, as in this poem, or to be ill. (One of Sydney's major cemeteries is Rookwood and the local lingoism is CROOK AS ROOKWOOD.) To be FED UP is to have had enough and to SLING YOUR HOOK is a Lingoism meaning to leave, usually in annoyance.

In fact there are, not surprisingly, many World War II DIGGERisms relating to discontent. Probably the most famous is WOULDN'T IT ROOT YA?! ejected as an expression of disgust with pretty well any aspect of the war. It came in various euphemistic versions, including WOULDN'T IT ROTATE YER?! WOULDN'T IT RIP YER?! and WOULDN'T IT ROCK YER?! even politely as WOULDN'T IT ROT YOUR SOCKS?' though the discerning Lingoist would generally prefer the ROOT version. Often this exclamation became simply WOULDN'T IT?! in which form it is still heard today. Other well-used World War II complaints still in wide use today included WHINGE, BALLS-UP, FAIR CRACK OF THE WHIP, UP THE SHIT, also used in shortened form of UPTER, ON THE NOSE, to be JACK OF SOMETHING, possibly everything, and A LOT OF (HOT) COCK used to describe anything felt to be nonsense. The long-standing Australianisms revolving around BUCKLEY'S CHANCE were (and still are) in use, including such terminal combinations as WE'VE GOT TWO CHANCES — MINE AND BUCKLEY'S. Also still heard occasionally is NOT WORTH A CUNTFUL OF COLD WATER and its even cruder variants, like AS MUCH USE AS A CUNTFUL OF COLD PISS. CACTUS was 1940s RAAF slang for something that would not function. It experienced a revival in the 1980s, though seems to have dropped from most contemporary usage since, yet the exclamation that something is TOTALLY CACTUS is still met with on occasion. To COLLECT something or to be COLLECTED by something is another World War II-ism still in use, as in THE CAR COLLECTED THE BUS. Others still heard include GROUSE, meaning something exceptionally good as in WASN'T THAT A GROUSE FEED, a perversion of the use of the same term to mean complaining, and BINGLE, now meaning a slight car accident and used in 1939–45 to mean a skirmish, a brawl or a drinking party.

One negative lingoism of the World War II that is worth a little more attention is BODGER meaning something or someone thought to be of inferior quality or someone who makes a mess of things. The term derives, it seems from a British dialect word related to 'botch', a mainstream term for doing a job badly. Its interest here is that the word was the basis of the postwar name for the first Australian teenagers, the BODGIES, discussed elsewhere, another example of the tendency of Australians to use apparently self-deprecating terms to describe themselves. TWO-BOB LAIR and MUG LAIR seem also to have reached their current state of development during World War II.

There were, of course, plenty of newly coined expressions of unhappiness, most of which have now, happily in some cases, been lost. These included to GIVE THE GAME TO THE BLACKS, meaning that the speaker was unhappy with the army and/or the war, AFTERBIRTH for food, BAIT LAYER for an army cook, probably from pre-war bush usage, Q BASTARD for quartermaster, SNAKE PIT for sergeant's mess', and the like. Perhaps one of the most bitter of these terms was WHITE NIP or WHITE JAP, a term used in Japanese prisoner-of-war (POW) camps to describe any prisoner thought to be collaborating with, or in some way being favoured by, the Japanese captors. It was applied to certain officers in Changi and on the Burma Railway.

Australian prisoners of the Japanese swiftly developed their own little lingo. The Japanese themselves were variously referred to as LITTLE YELLOW MEN, JAPS, JEEPS, NIPS (from soldiers of Nippon), or simply LITTLE YELLOW BASTARDS. Not surprisingly, POWisms were sometimes full of nationalistic angst: the British officers' quarters, for example, were known to the Australians as the IMPERIAL WAR MUSEUM. The bamboo urinals were known by the euphonious term PISSAPHONES. Men thought to be too accommodating towards the Japanese were called JAPPY (a compression of JAP HAPPY); a secret radio was a BIRDIE and the so-called stew (white radish, water and maybe pepper) served up as food was known as DANUBE, a rhyming slang formation on BLUE DANUBE. Other rhyming slang terms included STEAMTUG for a bug and TO-AND-FROM for POM. Even in captivity the little lingo reflected the Australian need to stereotype others: the British were also referred to as KIPPERS while the Dutch were CHEESE-EATERS.

As in World War I, the 1939–45 conflict proved a fertile ground for the cultivation of lingo. To do any kind of justice to this colourful linguistic event would require a book-length study of its own. Here are some of the more arresting World War II inventions: WHEELBARROW, a conscript (because he had to be pushed); SPINE-BASHING, resting, sleeping or loafing; SKITTERBUG, a Bren-gun carrier; ANKLE-BANGER and HOCK-FLOGGER, both meaning an overcoat; DOOVER a general term for just about anything, still quite widely used; SNARLER from the abbreviation SNLR, Services No Longer Required, applied to men sent back from the Middle East, often on THREE P BOATS, meaning boats that contained pox, prisoners and provosts — 'Enough said', perhaps.

DIGGERESE—KOREA AND VIETNAM

Australian participation in the Korean War (1950–53) involved a continuation or adaptation of World War II terms. These included BAGGIE for a subaltern, derived from the earlier BAGGIE-ARSED; the almost surreal COCK OBOE for commanding officer and related to the World War II COCK ORANGE and MUNGAR a new version of the ANZACAL for food (probably influenced by Italian rather than French or Arabic). SKIPPER or SKIP mostly used to mean a platoon commander, was an extension of its previous use by subalterns to address a captain and also by World War I Anzacs who had an aversion to using the term 'sir' of officers, a long-standing Australian tradition of anti-authoritarianism that was highlighted when civilians enlisted to fight.

In Vietnam the Korean War term HUTCHIE, a dugout or bunker (from the Japanese for house, *uchi*) was revived, as was CHARLIE, referring in the Korean conflict to the enemy. The North Vietnamese communists were also referred to as GOOKS while Vietnamese in general were known as NOGGIES, an interesting continuation of a Korean War lingoism for Asians, probably derived from the British euphemism for NIGGER, NIG-NOG.

Other Vietnam DIGGER terms included BUSH-BASH, derived from the outback driving practice of taking short cuts by four-wheel drive through bush scrub and applied in Vietnam to a jungle patrol. The term FRAG meant the killing by his own men of an officer believed to be foolhardy in exposing his charges to danger. This term, like many others such as GRUNT for an infantryman, was shared with US soldiers as was, it is rumoured, the practice itself. There were, of course, plenty of terms related to off-duty socialising. Many related to venereal infection, such as SAIGON (or VIETNAMESE) ROSE, for a particular strain of venereal disease; a MAMMASAN was the boss of the bar or brothel and SAIGON TEA was a whiskey and coke. Also shared with the Americans was the term for the last day of a tour of duty, a WAKE-UP, usually rendered by the Australians and New Zealanders as a WAKEY.

The development of DIGGER lingo since Gallipoli has been marked by an increasing tendency towards worse language. The swearing in the 1939–45 war was far more colourful than that of World War I, it seems (though this could be a result of the print proprieties of the period) while there were few punches pulled in the lingo and lore of the Vietnam conflict. A Vietnam DIGGER parody of 'Jingle Bells' gives a relatively sedate hint of the soldier slang of that particular war. 'Christmas in Vietnam' presents a jaundiced view of Christmas festivities from the point of view of the troops serving in that country. The chorus, in which VC stands for Viet Cong, goes:

Jingle Bells, mortar shells, vc in the grass
We'll get no merry Christmas cheer until this year has passed.
Jingle Bells, mortar shells, vc in the grass,
Take your Merry Christmas cheer and shove it up your arse.

Another Vietnam ditty, this one said to be known by every Australian soldier, was called 'Cheap Charlie'. To the tune of 'This Old Man' or 'Nick, Nack, Paddywhack', this one is also full of Vietnam DIGGER-speak. *Uc-dai- loi* means Australian, while CHEAP CHARLIE means stingy.

Uc-dai-loi, Cheap Charlie,
He no buy me Saigon Tea.
Saigon Tea costs many, many P [for Piasta — money]
Uc-dai-loi he Cheap Charlie

Uc-dai-loi, Cheap Charlie,
He no give me MPC (Military Pay Certificate)
MPC costs many, many P
Uc-dai-loi he Cheap Charlie

Uc-dai-loi, Cheap Charlie,
He no go to bed with me
For it cost him many, many p,
Uc-dai-loi he Cheap Charlie

Uc-dai-loi, Cheap Charlie,
Make me give him one for free.
Mamma-san go crook on me,
Uc-dai-loi he Cheap Charlie

Uc-dai-loi, Cheap Charlie,
He give baby-san to me;
Baby-san cost many, many P,
Uc-dai-loi he Cheap Charlie

Uc-dai-loi, Cheap Charlie,
He go home across the sea;
He leave baby-san with me,
Uc-dai-loi he Cheap Charlie.

Back in Australia terms like NASHO for national serviceman had been around since national service was introduced in the 1950s. It was joined by a more chilling term, CONSCRIPT, when the government reintroduced conscription in November 1964, officially as national service. Those who reached their twentieth birthday had that date entered in a lottery. If the date was drawn that male was required to become a conscript or national serviceman, soon reviving the older NASHO. The national service lottery was widely resented and fiercely resisted as part of the growing antagonism to the Vietnam War, particularly as those required to go, should their number come up, had not reached the then-legal voting age. Those who were conscripted in New South Wales were often sent to Puckapunyal army camp for training. A contemporary parody of 'Bye, Bye Blackbird' expresses the prevailing mood:

> *Pack up all your bags and kit*
> *Puckapunyal's up to shit*
> *Bye bye Pucka.*
> *Stew for breakfast, stew for tea,*
> *No more bloody stew for me,*
> *Bye bye Pucka.*
> *No more climbing over bloody mountains,*
> *We'll soon be drinking Fosters out of fountains.*
> *No more blanco* (canvas whitening), *no more brass,*
> *You can stick them up your arse.*
> *Pucka, bye bye.*

Relatively little Vietnam War DIGGER slang transferred into the wider Australian vernacular. A couple of examples that did last were ZAP and WASTE, both terms meaning to kill, and both American. Another, R AND R for Rest and Recreation, the official term for leave away from Vietnam, had a few years of use, but mostly faded away, along with the recuperating soldiers and the popular memory of the war. About all that remains now are terms associated with the devastating technology of that war, including NAPALM (also used in Korea) and AGENT ORANGE.

The DIGGER and Anzac legends have also added a number of distinctive words and terms to the vernacular. ANZAC DAY became such in 1916. It has been joined by THE MARCH, referring to the parade of RETURNED SERVICEMEN that forms the essential spectacle of the ONE DAY OF THE YEAR. EX-SERVICEMEN is something of an Australian peculiarity. Other countries call their war heroes veterans, a usage that is now becoming common in Australia, partly through its adoption by the Vietnam Veterans' Association (often called VETS) and the use of Department of Veterans Affairs by the Federal Government since the 1980s. And while many Australians will associate veteran with US usage, it is also the preferred term in Britain. The Australian use of ex-servicemen is perhaps related to the fact that, while an individual may leave the services after the war, returning to CIVVY STREET, he nevertheless always remains, in the popular mind, at least, a DIGGER. This term and its surrounding associations has been kept powerfully alive by ex-service organisations, notably the RSL from quite early in World War I. The term ex- servicewomen has also, rather belatedly, begun to feature in the official discourse of returned organisations.

Closely related is the usage RETURNED SOLDIER recorded first here, though known elsewhere. Miners who returned home from the Australian diggings were called RETURNED DIGGERS in the mid-19th century. It was used of troops returning to these shores from the South African War of 1899 to 1902 and was simply revived during World War I, being with us ever since. A term that is closely associated with the Anzac tradition is the DAWN SERVICE, the simple but powerful ceremony that begins the Anzac Day formalities and which, for many Australians, is really what THE DAY is all about. There is a considerable amount of folklore about the origins of the term and the practice. The most well developed of these is that what we now know as the DAWN SERVICE was begun in Albany, Western Australia. According to this story, a Reverend White held a 'Requiem for the War Dead' at 6 am in St John's Anglican Church, Albany, on 25 April 1929. This was to parallel the exact hour of the Gallipoli landing in 1915. In later years White continued this service and followed it with a pilgrimage up to the top of Mt Clarence, Albany. In the sea below, near the area in King George Sound from which the original Anzac convoy had departed in November 1914, wreaths were thrown into the sea from a small boat. Whether or not the Reverend White can claim credit for the first DAWN SERVICE, a dawn ceremony, initially without religious content, was instituted in Perth on Anzac Day 1929. Alas for regional pride, similar, apparently spontaneous, ceremonies were held in Sydney two years earlier.

5

WHATCHAMACALLIT AND OTHER MONICKERS

'Wot's in a name' she sez…An' then she sighs,
An' clasps 'er little 'ands, an' rolls 'er eyes.
'A rose', she sez, 'be any other name
Would smell the same.
Oh, w'erefore art you Romeo, young sir?
Chuck yer ole pot an' change yer moniker!'

C.J. DENNIS, 'THE PLAY',
FROM THE SONGS OF A SENTIMENTAL BLOKE, 1915

One of the most important functions of the vernacular is to name things — or to re-name them. There are not too many aspects and activities of everyday life that have not been, to some degree at least, well and truly Lingoised. In Australia, we name and re-name ourselves, our jobs, our cars, our buildings, our homes and our PUBS. We even like to use rhyme occasionally. An especially rich area of naming, encountered in a number of contexts throughout this book, is the personal — and the impersonal — nickname.

NICKNAMES

A basic characteristic of Lingo is the creation of informal names for almost anything and anyone. A glance through the police gazettes of New South Wales and Victoria for the 1820s reveals the extent to which individuals were habitually identified by their nicknames, rather than by their proper names, a habit that has stuck. There are even Lingo names for those things we cannot remember the names of —WHATSIT, DOOVERLACKEY (or just DOOVER), WHATCHAMACALLIT, THINGUMEBOB, THINGY, WHOSAMAJIG, WHATASAMAJIG, THINGUMAJIG,

WHATSIT, WHAT'S-HIS-FACE and WHOSEMAWHAT. As well as these various terms for that which has been forgotten or of which we do not wish to speak (TELL WHATSHISFACE TO PISS OFF, for instance), occupational speech is full of nicknames like THE JUDGE, so-called because he is often called to the bar; LIGHTNING for someone noted for slowness (another example of the frequent perversity of Lingo); THE GRIZZLY BEAR for someone who is frequently grumpy; THE DRONE for someone who just goes on and on…So popular is nicknaming in the great Australian Lingo that we even have one for God — HUGHIE, as in the plea for rain: SEND 'ER DOWN, HUGHIE. God's son also has a MONICKER — JC.

Taffy Davies made something of a study of nicknames in his *Australian Nicknames* (1977) and *More Australian Nicknames* (1978). These two compilations reveal the extent and inventiveness of our nicknaming skills, including such examples as: THE LAWYER who fancies a say in everything, KANGA who is always on the hop and WILLIAM THE SILENT, described as the bosom companion to WHISPERING SMITH.

Since 1968, folklorist Chris Woodland has been collecting nicknames from just one town, Mulwala, on the Murray. It seems that just about everyone in this area is known by their informal MONICKER (the origin of the term monicker, also used in the USA, is usually said to be the Irish tinker language, Shelta). So far, he has recorded more than 130 nicknames for locals, derived from their physical appearance, habits, some event, tradition (SPUD MURPHY) and a number named after sundry television characters (MAGOO from the 'Mr Magoo' cartoons, STEPPY — from the early English sitcom 'Steptoe and Son'). Sometimes, many people are unaware of the real name of the person. Woodland also noted that a good many of the nicknames were made up by women, even though the vast majority were applied to men.

Prominent people (especially sports stars, as discussed in 'Sports and Rorts') are frequently nicknamed. Politicians with unofficial titles include RED TED Theodore, Jack Lang, THE BIG FELLA, BLACK JACK McEwan (leader of the Federal parliamentary Country Party, 1958–71) and Paul Keating, when treasurer, was known as MR CHEATING; Neville Wran when premier of New South Wales was known as NIFTY NEV, or just NIFTY for short. Brian Burke, when Western Australia premier was often referred to as BRIAN BLOKE or more simply just as BURKIE. Western Australian politician Reg Withers was, and still is, known as THE TOECUTTER while his colleague Wilson Tuckey glories in the nickname IRONBAR. Gareth Evans when appointed attorney-general in 1983 received the nickname BIGGLES for authorising a spy flight over the Franklin River area of Tasmania. Some politicians have even attracted more than one nickname. That great political character and Queensland Premier Joe Bjelke Petersen was known by all sorts of nicknames, including BJELKE JOE (Joe's wife, FLO — Florence – of course is known by that name throughout the land, along with her pumpkin scones) and Robert Menzies was known as PIG-IRON BOB, a reference to his decision to ship iron ore to Japan shortly before World War II began, despite warnings that the ore would return as Japanese bullets and bombs. Menzies was also known as MING THE MERCILESS, often shortened to MING, in accordance with his reputed political ruthlessness. On the other side of the political divide, Robert Hawke before and during his prime ministership gloried in the nicknames THE MILD COLONIAL BOY, referring to a perception that he talked tough but acted less so, and THE SILVER BODGIE, derived from his greying hair and his reputation as a bit of a LARRIKIN with the SHEILAS (A NOTED PANTSMAN) and the GROG. In 1996, a man long-known as LITTLE JOHNNIE HOWARD and, sometimes, as HONEST JOHN, became prime minister.

Nicknaming is not restricted to those in politics. Some widely known nicknames of NON-POLLIES include THE ELECTRONIC DICK, Dick Smith's self-inflicted advertising persona, one that has stuck with him ever since. The adman, John Singleton, is known as SINGO and a famous female television journalist is, apparently, widely referred to as THE PERFUMED STEAMROLLER, to mention only one or two of many possibly defamatory examples.

In earlier times even a public hangman could earn a Lingo MONICKER. NOSEY BOB was the nickname of Robert Howard, official executioner of New South Wales from 1874–1904, who suffered a disfigurement in that region of his MUG. Another early nickname, redolent with associations, was the name of a denizen of Sydney's Rocks, PIG MARY, a large Irish woman so-called from her occupation of retrieving slaughterhouse offal from the Darling Harbour swamp and selling it in the streets as pig food. Early Rocks personalities with colourful nicknames also included OLD COMMODORE, the ferryman BILLY BLUE and one of his lesser rivals, FRENCH PETER. Street sellers — described in the late 1820s as crying their wares with strong Cockney accents — also attracted memorable rhyming and alliterative monickers like ABBY DABBY and RICKETY DICK.

A notable nickname from the past is that of William Francis King, an unusually strong man whose claim to fame was to run, walk and lift weights. Often he did all three at the same time, being celebrated for his ambulation from Sydney to Parramatta in three hours carrying a boy on his back. On other occasions he shouldered dogs, goats and, it is said, cats, rats and mice — three hundred of them and all at once. King's main means of livelihood was selling pies, a trade that, in conjunction with his feats of strength and endurance, earned him the nickname FLYING PIEMAN. He died in 1874, broken and destitute, but lives on in a children's play, and a folk dance and tune especially composed in his honour.

Nor is it only public personalities who attract nicknames, but also prominent institutions. Some, such as AUNTIE for the Australian Broadcasting Corporation (ABC) are known nationally. (The ABC Public Relations department was once known as the SECRET SERVICE in deference to its perceived inability or reluctance to publicise almost anything.) Early to mid-1990s ABC parlance also includes the fallout of political correctness with a person of Non-English-Speaking Background, officially acronymed to NESB, being known in Lingo as a NESBY.

Others, such as GRANNY for the *Sydney Morning Herald* (also applied to various other newspapers since the late 19th century) and the TIZER for the *Adelaide Advertiser* have a more localised currency. Qantas used to be described by many of its employees and the general public as QUAINT-ARSE or CHARLIE QUAINT-ARSE and, as a consequence of its late 1990s advertising slogan, the Commonwealth Bank is now referred to throughout the nation as WHICH BANK?

This application of folk names to official institutions is a longstanding Australian custom. A colourful example is the local name for an alleyway in Sydney's Rocks district. Built and named in the 1840s, this narrow thoroughfare became a torrent of water and effluent during rainstorms. Despite a number of other official re-namings the locals persisted in calling the alley SUEZ CANAL, a nickname now officially adopted by the tourism-conscious keepers of that heritage precinct.

Then there are names of places and the people who come from them. KIWIS come from MAORILAND, THE LAND OF THE LONG WHITE CLOUD or the SHAKY ISLES, otherwise known as New Zealand. MAORILANDERS are well known in Australia for being unnaturally attracted to sheep, a slur typical of mainlanders against those from outlying landmasses or islands such as Tasmania where the locals are all known to have too many toes as a result of long in-breeding. SANDGROPERS hail from Western Australia, or GROPERLAND; CORNSTALKS from New South Wales; BANANABENDERS or BANANALANDERS from BANANALAND or Queensland (capital BRISSIE or BRIS); WESTIES are residents of the Western Suburbs of Sydney, WAXIES are almost anyone who is not. Bushies are country folk while Darlinghurst, Fremantle and

Wollongong become DARLO, FREO and THE GONG. The exclusive Melbourne suburb of Toorak is known as TRAK to Melburnians, Perth's absurdly minuscule enclave of affluence, Peppermint Grove is PEPPY GROVE while Sydney's Double Bay (DOUBLE PAY) has been described in that scrawled form of Lingo, graffiti, as 'vogue on the outside; vague on the inside'.

Various colloquialisms are used by Australians to describe their homeland. These include OZ, OZZIE (not to be confused with AUSSIE, one who comes from Australia), DOWN-UNDER and even NED-LAND, after our national hero/villain (with those who came from the place called, naturally, NEDS). Given the problems that people have historically had in naming this part of the Earth since it was first thought to exist some thousands of years ago, this proliferation of terms is continuing a long tradition. Australia was known by such names as the Antipodes, Terra Australis (the south land), Terra Australis Incognita (the unknown southern land), New Holland and, even odder to our ears, 'the great south land of the Holy Spirit'. When Captain Cook took possession of the place in the name of King George III, he gave it yet another name — New South Wales. It is now just NEWSOUTH to most.

Vernacular names for occupations are plentiful. Usually involving contraction, a favoured technique of Lingo. It is almost as if we did not want to take the necessity for most of us to work too seriously. This casualness is reflected in the phrases THE LAND OF THE LONG WEEKEND sometimes used to describe Australia, or THE LUCKY COUNTRY from Donald Horne's book of that name in which lucky was used ironically, though it is now used quite without irony. A few further examples: HOSTIE — air hostess (also known as a TROLLEY DOLLY); JOURNO — journalist; MUSO — musician; WHARFIE — wharf labourer, stevedore; TRUCKIE — truck-driver; POLLIE — politician; CABBIE — taxidriver; BRICKIE — bricklayer; CHIPPIE — carpenter; CHALKIE — teacher. Closely related to the last is SCHOOLIES — nowadays usually applied to schoolchildren, though it may also be used to include teachers, a usage dating from at least the late 19th century.

Even vehicles have their own folk names: a utility becomes a UTE, a Volkswagen campervan is universally known as a KOMBI. Volkswagen sedans used to be widely known as VOLKSIES or BEETLES from their distinctive shape. Cars and other vehicles also feature in Lingo through sayings like SHE'S GOT MORE GUTS THAN A BEDFORD TRUCK and HE'S GOT A FACE LIKE THE BACK-END OF A BONDI TRAM. While there has been no operating Bondi tram for many decades now, the phrase is still heard in and out of Sydney with the mundane bus substituting for the much more colourful tram. A worn-out car is A BOMB, A WRECK or

A CRATE. Paradoxically, a vehicle that goes well and fast may be said to GO LIKE A BOMB. Context is all-important in Lingo.

Lovingly malicious names may also be given to public buildings like the Ministry of Education building in Perth, called from its metallic-style architecture, SILVER CITY. The Qantas twin towers in Sydney used to be known to Qantas staff as BULLSHIT TOWERS while the historical St Vincent's Hospital in the same city, known to cabbies and many Sydneysiders as VINNIES or ST VINNIES, also has a plush private section that revels in the title of the JESUS HILTON and, more prosaically, as the DARLO HILTON. The freeway cut beneath Melbourne's new, jumbo-sized casino is known to disgruntled locals as KENNETT'S KHYBER PASS, a revival of older rhyming slang of British origin. Headquarters of the Civil Aviation Authority in Canberra is unsettlingly nicknamed FORT FUMBLE. One of many oddities is the term used for the Sydney Harbour Bridge in South Australia and Victoria. In those States the structure is termed THE COAT-HANGER, something Sydneysiders hardly ever call it. To Sydneysiders it is simply THE BRIDGE. You will no doubt recall many such local names for buildings in your locality, some notable examples being attached to sporting complexes like the Queensland Cricket Association ground at Woolloongabba (an Aboriginal word), known as THE GABBA or the Western Australian Cricket Association ground in Perth, universally referred to as THE WAC(k)A — not to be confused with a WHACKER, for more on which, see below.

THE AFFECTIONATE (OR NOT SO) DIMINUTIVE

The affectionate or familiar diminutive is a term used by linguists to describe the practice of shortening words to end with 'ie', less frequently 'o'. The affectionate diminutive is widespread in this country. Although common here, however, it is not unique to Australia. Nor is its use always affectionate. Some less than complimentary examples include SECKO for a sex maniac or pervert, also SICKO for someone whose interests are off-centre, BLOWIE for a blow-fly and COMMO (or COMMIE) for communist, as in COMMO BASTARD, once a fairly serious insult though one that has, in later times, lost most of its sting. But generally our use of the diminished suffix is affectionate, rather than malevolent, as in the case of WHACKO, a shortening of WHACKER for someone thought to be dangerously unbalanced. A person described as WHACKO (not to be confused with the now largely obsolete exclamation whacko!) does not usually imply the same level of dangerous unpredictability as a WHACKER.

Other words affected by Australia's seemingly insatiable need to abbreviate in this way include PRESSIE, RELLIE, BICCIE, CHRISSIE,

FOOTY, COSSIE, MOZZIE, BLOCKIE (a person who lives and works on a small block of land), GROUPIE (participants in the largely ill-fated Western Australian Group Settlement scheme of the 1920s and 1930s); GLADDIE (gladioli) and the classic ARVO (afternoon) to name only some. ANOTHERIE for another has been in vogue for some decades but now seems to be on the slide, its main form of preservation being in the drinking song that has the refrain: SING US ANOTHERIE, DIRTY AS BUGGERY, SING US ANOTHERIE, DO. Particularly in Sydney, SERVO for service station seems to have crept into use in the early to mid-1990s.

One term whose diminutive has definitely been affectionate, if not downright essential, has been sanitary man, in use since at least the end of the 19th century. Widely lingoised as the SANNY or SANO MAN, this fast-disappearing trade is also known as the NIGHT MAN or simply the DUNNY MAN who comes to take the nightsoil away. In common with other everyday necessities, the DUNNY has left its mark in the Great Australian Lingo with terms like THUNDERBOX, THRONE, LOO, CRAPPER (after the inventor of the water closet, Thomas Crapper), BOG, DYKE and, of course, dunny itself, also used in a crude description of excessively frequent or enthusiastic copulation: BANGING LIKE A DUNNY DOOR IN A GALE (outdone only by the brilliantly alliterative BANGING LIKE A BUGGERED TAPPET). There is also the crass but widely used SHITHOUSE, a term which has generated many useful and colourful combinations — AS UGLY AS A SHITHOUSE RAT, BUILT LIKE A BRICK SHITHOUSE (that is, big and strong) and the simple description of something shoddy or inferior as SHITHOUSE. It is even possible, in Lingo at least, to describe one's general condition in this way: I'M FEELING SHITHOUSE TODAY.

Shrinking occupational names is especially notable in the area of delivery and takeaways. In earlier years home deliveries of commodities was an unremarkable aspect of everyday life, involving bread, milk, fruit, vegetables, patent medicines, and usually inferior clothing, the purveyors of which were once known as SHODDY DROPPERS. About the only partial survivor of these trades is the MILKO, the milkman, first recorded in print during the 1860s but in the mouths of Australians for many years before. In addition to the SANNY MAN mentioned above, there has been an ongoing need for refuse to be taken away from homes by the GARBO — garbage-man and the BOTTLE-O(H) who, in many though not all States, takes away the EMPTIES or DEAD SOLDIERS. That new term for takeaway, the Americanism TAKE-OUT is also catching on to describe is fast food or junk food of various types, such as pizza, CHINESE and KENTUCKY FRIED RAT.

In an article in *Australian Folklore* in 1993, the Director of The

University of Sydney's Language Centre, Brian A. Taylor, published a learned analysis of the codes by which Australians MUCK ABOUT with people's proper names. Taylor studied Sydney newspapers from 1982 to 1988 to discover the rules by which BOONIE, GREIGY, SIMMO, DAVO, RICHO and the rest (not forgetting the ultimate absurdity DUNNY for another unfortunate sporting CELEB) are inflicted on us. Four main methods are used to achieve these effects: an ending is added to the name, usually 'y', 'ie' or 'o'; a multi-syllabic name may be shortened to one syllable; this may happen and then be re-expanded with one of the usual endings; or a consonant at the end of the first syllable may be swapped for another, either in the shortened or re-expanded form. Taylor notes that these rules seem to apply reasonably well to a lot of the diminutive versions of place names — ALICE for Alice Springs, THE LOO for Woolloomooloo, and THE ISA and THE TOWERS for Mt Isa and Charters Towers respectively. The author of the paper also traces this habit back to Old High German and, tentatively, even further to the linguistic habits of the Gauls somewhere around the birth of Christ. A tough one to top.

Surnames are not the only formal names that get the short end of things in Lingo, forenames are also fair game. GAZZA for Gary, BAZZA for Barry, DAZZA for Darren, LOZZA for Laurie, KESSA for Kylie, but KEZZA for Kerry (a male) and TEZZA for Terry. Now obsolete as a usage of this sort but, having transferred its meaning, OCKER — short for Oscar, continues a lively existence in the vernacular as a shorthand for the 'ugly' Australian male, a subject treated in more detail in chapter 7.

BRAND NAMES

The commercial world has been a rich source of Lingo. One of the best-known brand names, Vegemite™, has given us the phrase 'HAPPY LITTLE VEGEMITES', widely used to describe satisfied people. The sticky brown substance known as Vegemite™ (blended brewery yeast extracts, celery and onion flavouring, together with a lot of salt) concocted by chemist

Dr C.P. Callister in 1923 is widely held to be quintessentially OZ, despite the fact that it has been owned and produced by the American Kraft company since 1926. The successful advertising campaigns for Vegemite™ (a registered trademark) run by the J. Walter Thompson Advertising Agency since 1931 have left their mark on the Lingo. Beginning in 1954 Vegemite™ was advertised on radio, using the slogan and jingle 'HAPPY LITTLE VEGEMITES'.

With the arrival of television in Australia in 1956 this campaign ran on THE BOX and was revived on the TELLY of the early 1960s through to 1967. In the late 1970s the advertiser decided to return to the 'Happy Little Vegemite' theme on the assumption that those parents who had been KIDS in the 1940s and 1950s would be nostalgic about these reminders of their youth and the persistent theme that Vegemite™ was good for you and so would buy it for their KIDS. It seems to be working still as Vegemite™ is as popular as ever. In KIDS' lingo, though, they have found a slightly irreverent but topical use for the ever-reviving 'HAPPY LITTLE VEGEMITES' jingle in the form of an unquotable folk parody.

Aeroplane Jelly Crystals is another brand name that has profited greatly from its TRUE BLUE image, its appeal to children and its ability to evoke nostalgia through the advertising anthem 'I Like Aeroplane Jelly'. Advertisers in the early 1990s revived what looks very much like the original film clip of the little girl in the swing singing the Aeroplane Jelly song, though the ball that used to rhythmically accompany the lyrics at the SAT'D'Y ARVO PITCHERS (or 'filums') has bounced into oblivion.

Commerce has given the language distinctive collective terms that are applied to all species of a product, regardless of its correct trade name. ESKY™, the portable ice chest introduced in the 1950s now does duty for any more or less rectangular container that is capable of being insulated and of holding of GROG. Some people use it to keep food cool, too. The VICTA, invented by Merv Richardson in his BACK SHED in 1952, is a generic term for all lawnmowers powered by an internal combustion engine, or something that purports to be one. Known for many years as TOECUTTERS, Victa mowers also contributed the well-known advertising slogan to the vernacular: IT TURNS GRASS INTO LAWN. PASS THE KLEENEX™ means hand me a tissue, so successful was the advertising of that particular brand of tissues. Speedo swimming costumes, produced since the 1920s (now owned by an overseas company), have long been closely associated with Australia and even dubbed THE GREAT AUSSIE COSSIE by an admiring journalist. In Lingo, SPEEDOS may refer to any make of swimwear. Chesty Bond was the hero of a newspaper comic strip by Ted Moloney that began in 1938. Since 1940 the character has been used to promote Bond's athletic singlets and other male apparel, hence the occasional use of the term CHESTY BOND to refer to an especially masculine type of Australian male or as a catch-all description of Australian men as CHESTY BONDS. The Cyclone fencing wire brand has given us, since early in the 20th century, CYCLONE FENCE and CYCLONE GATE and, more recently, Aerogard insect repellant has given us the term AEROGARD applied generically to such concoctions. MR WHIPPY is applied to any mobile ice-cream vendor, at least in New

South Wales, where the tinkling of the 'Greensleeves' tune through badly distorting speakers signals the coming of the Mr Whippy van.

The occasional complexity of the Lingo is well demonstrated in a widely used folk name for a barbecue-cleaning implement marketed as a BBQ-mate. These, and by extension any other such tool, are known as KENS, derived from the name of Barbie's friend, Ken. This is probably best conveyed through example: WHERE'S THE KEN, I'VE GOT TO CLEAN THE BARBIE. Got that!?

The Hills Hoist revolving clothes line, invented in an Adelaide shed in 1945, still dominates the backyards of suburbia and HILLS HOIST may describe a clothes line of any kind. More than five million hardy HILLS HOISTS have been sold and, legend has it, a solitary hoist was the only thing left standing in many Darwin backyards after Cyclone Tracy. Like the VICTA, the HILLS HOIST has its own load of legend and Lingo, early models being known as CHINWHACKERS or GUT-BUSTERS, depending on where the lever that then operated the beast came into painful contact with your body. The famous Akubra bush hat has been so popular that AKUBRA is used for any sort of wide-brimmed cowboy hat. The name of a popular breakfast cereal has come to be used as a mild insult. Someone who is a FRUIT LOOP is considered to be NOT ALL THERE, a term probably derived from the older insult a FRUITCAKE and the simile NUTTY AS A FRUIT CAKE.

A distinctive Australianism is TO HAVE A FEED, meaning to eat and it seems that food and related products have been especially influential in our folk speech. BIG BEN — a meat pie, from the name of the well-known Sydney comestible purveyed for many years by Tip Top, now Top Taste and long ago gobbled up by a multinational. This pie is immortalised in Lingo through the saying YOU COULDN'T WIN A PIE AT A BIG BEN PICNIC, a reference to pretty well total incompetence or terminal bad luck. A sort of homemade pie is a JAFFLE™, a sealed sandwich filled with sweet or savoury contents, that is toasted in a jaffle iron over a flame. A jaffle iron, a proprietary product, is a long-handled, metal contraption with one or more saucer- or square-shaped containers at the end into which the bread is placed for JAFFLING. Usually the sandwich is buttered on the outside before toasting to prevent burning. The containers holding the sandwich are then clipped tightly together, compressing the sandwich into a compact bulge. The bread acts as an excellent insulator, JAFFLE™, innards staying amazingly hot for a long time after they are cooked.

Other TUCKERISMS include the term CHEESE AND JATZ (from the name of a type of salted cracker biscuit marketed by Arnott's) which is sometimes used to indicate small party foods, also known these days as nibbles or, more POSHLY, as finger food. A GLASS-AND-A-HALF is a nickname that may be applied to someone who is unable to drink much alcohol without becoming inebriated. It derives from the advertising slogan for Cadbury's chocolate which contained 'a glass-and-a-half of that rich, full-cream milk'. Nor must we forget the popular use of the trade name Schweppes, long famous for carbonated waters, nowadays more familiar as lemonade (Schweppes Ginger Ale™ was a trade mark registered in 1906, by the way). In Lingo, SCHWEPPES is a euphemism for the exclamation SHIT.

Some of our other traditional TUCKERS have derived their official and Lingo names from their inventors or producers. Granny Smiths are green apples originally grown near Sydney by Maria Smith (1801–70). The lamington (LAMMIE, sometimes LAMMO) was probably named after Baron Lamington (Charles Wallace Baillie), Governor of Queensland from 1895 to 1901. Both the chocolate icing and coconut sponge cake and its name were well established by 1910. This easily cooked and relatively inoffensive cake, either produced in individual cubes or as a large slab which was cut into squares, has also established itself in Australian culture as the ideal fundraiser for schools, churches, community groups and anyone else who needs your charity. The LAMINGTON DRIVE is still as widespread in Australia as the CHOOK RAFFLE. Pavlova is a sickly sweet concoction of cream, meringue and fruit, said to have been invented in the 1920s as a tribute to ballerina Anna Pavlova (1885–1931), who toured Australia with the Russian Imperial Ballet. In Lingo, pavlova is usually rendered as PAV.

The brand names of other products have contributed in different ways: CLAYTON'S has assumed a wider meaning in Lingo. Derived from the early 1980s advertising slogan for a non-alcoholic beverage, Clayton's™ — 'The drink I have when I'm not having a drink' — the term has the implication that something essential is missing, or has been withheld from the experience or the item and so of a synthetic and unsatisfying substitute, as in IT'S BEEN A CLAYTON'S MATCH (an uninspiring FOOTY game); THIS IS CLAYTON'S LEGISLATION, and so on. Other such examples include EYES LIKE SHELL ROAD MAPS, a simile that graphically evokes eyeballs shot through with ragged red lines, just like the roads on a well-known brand of map. A CUP OF TEA, A BEX AND A GOOD LIE-DOWN and TAKE A POWDER both relate to proprietary brand medicinal powders that used to be consumed with dangerous frequency in post-World War II Australia and until well into the 1970s. People, especially though not exclusively working-class women, were prone to knocking back a BEX powder or a VINCENTS whenever they felt like a lift. When the harmful effects of this abuse on the kidneys became better known, consumption declined, but the Lingoisms derived from this era are still heard from time to time. DAKS™ may still be heard for trousers, after a 1950s and later brand name. To KIWI-UP was to smarten up your appearance. It derives from the trade name of Kiwi shoe polish and was widely used during the World War I and survived into World War II, though not far beyond. More recently the '57 varieties' of Heinz tinned products has given us the term HEINZ for a mongrel dog or BITSA.

Probably the most famous trade name to enter the Lingo was the term for a rumour — a FURPHY, already mentioned in chapter 2, and still in vigorous usage, especially in the rumour-prone world of high finance. Siroset was a brand name for a process of treating clothing material to encourage it to hold a crease, so-named after its invention in the Commonwealth Scientific and Industrial Research Organisation, the CSIRO. Another famous trade name is Laminex™. Patented in 1945, Laminex™ was a particular type of durable plastic laminated sheet widely used in kitchens and milk bars in the 1950s and 1960s. The word LAMINEX is now applied to just about any bright, durable surfacing laminate. LAMINEX is sometimes shortened to LAMMIE, not to be confused with the cake . . .

PLACE NAMES

The names of major Australian cities are generally standard English, usually derived from British places or eminent British people — Sydney, Hobart, Brisbane, Melbourne, and Newcastle. In the naming of lesser communities there is often more of an attempt to grapple with the names given to places by their original occupiers. Accordingly, many Australian place names are (often addled) attempts to adopt the local Aboriginal name. For example, Boomahomoonah (Victoria), said to be derived from an Aboriginal term, *boonah*, meaning a large kangaroo (though the word BOOMER for a kangaroo, as in the Rolf Harris Christmas song 'Six White Boomers', is said by our lexicographers to derive from a British dialect term for something large). Nimmitabel (New South Wales), supposedly yet another Aboriginal word for the place where the waters meet, has been known as Nimmitybelle, Nimithyball, Nimitubell and Nimoitebool, among other variants.

But even though many of our prominent cities bear official testimony to the MOVERS AND SHAKERS of their day, most have developed lingoisms. SYDNEYSIDE and SYDNEYSIDER are words with a long history. Less hoary, but more serious, especially during World War II, was the term BRISBANE LINE. This referred to a contentious plan to defend from the Japanese only that part of Australia south of a line drawn between Adelaide and Brisbane. While the existence of such a strategy has been denied by officials, the possibility still makes those who live to the north and west of such a line nervous. Brisbane, of course, is also known fondly as BRISSIE or BRIS while Rockhampton is just ROCKY. Hobart has its HOBART TRUMPETER (*Latris lineata*), a prized fish, so-called from at least the late 19th century while denizens of Adelaide (CITY OF CHURCHES since at least the 1870s) have been known, cumbersomely, as ADELAIDEANS since the 1830s and the crows they consumed when short of mutton (hence CROWEATERS) were known as ADELAIDE PHEASANTS. Melbourne is still referred to, or at least thought of by Melburnians (though hardly by anyone else), as MARVELLOUS and Perth has the rarely experienced cooling summer breeze, the PERTH DOCTOR. Perhaps the most mythic of all the capitals, Darwin, home of DARWINIANS or TOP-ENDERS, boasts a range of associated lingoisms, including DARWIN BLONDE, a part-European, part-Aboriginal girl or woman; DARWIN RIG, the local concession to the demands of formality, dark shoes, long trousers and a long-sleeved white shirt and tie — no jacket, and the impressive 2.25-litre beer bottle known as a DARWIN STUBBY.

Town names and place names may also have legends attached to them. The name of Jerilderie in New South Wales is derived from the local Aboriginal term for a reedy place. Local pioneer legend, however, has it that the name was derived from the habit of an early settler calling her husband 'Gerald, dearie'. According to Dyraaba legend, the naming of Joolinee, also in New South Wales, stems from the pursuit of a murderous giant by a young man. The giant got thirsty from the chase and stopped to drink from the stream where the young man heard him mutter *jooli, jooli,* meaning that the water was salty. This caused the area to be called Joolinee, meaning brackish water.

The unusually named Walkaway, about 30 CLICKS (kilometres) south-east of Geraldton in Western Australia has, not surprisingly, generated a number of legends about its origins. One is the usual suggestion that it is derived from the indigenous Nowkadja term for the area, in this case *wagga wah* (variously spelt), said to mean either a camp site or a break in the hills. Alternatively, it may be derived from the name of a local Aborigine at the time of the town's foundation in the mid-19th century. Another version is that because the Midland Railway ended a fair distance from the town itself, to go further you had to walk away, and the town was so-named. Yet another suggestion is that because the early settlers were not able to MAKE A GO of their properties, they had to walk away from them. And there are other variants of these tales, as well. Residents have become so tired of being asked how their town got its unusual name that their standard reply to all such queries is: 'If you saw the place, you would walk away too.'

While the adaptation of indigenous names is an inevitable and generally positive process it needs to be balanced with the equally common practice of simply extinguishing the indigenous name and replacing it with that of the new owner. So, near Perth, *Galup* became firstly Triangle Lake, then Mongers Lake, after being granted to an early Swan River settler of that name, and is now the more elevated Lake Monger. The Tasmanian place known as *Toorbunna* became, ridiculously, Ben Lomond, while the Victorian Rokewood replaced the indigenous *Conoreyalk*. This process was repeated many many times as the landscape was sequestered and progressively possessed through naming and re-naming.

But in Lingo, all is often not as it sounds. There are place names that have the look and lilt of indigenous languages, though closer inspection reveals the often odd truth. The town of Geekabee in Western Australia is derived from the initials and a few odd vowels of a man called George Kershaw Brown. Three Colac shire members named Barnard, Pink and Bath gave their partial contributions to the naming of Barpinba in Victoria. A glance through any collections of Australian place names will reveal many more such seemingly whimsical origins.

This process of slicing and then fusing two or more proper names together is also found in the names of businesses — Bevray Enterprises, from the joint operators Beverley and Raymond. It can also be used to create house names which sometimes move beyond the banalities of 'Dunro(a)min' and 'Thiseldo' to such inventive couplings as 'Dorwill' (Doris and William) and 'Ananart', from Anne and Arthur (Art) . A related practice is that of combining the forename initials of family members into a unique house name, as in 'Beema', concocted in the 1920s from the names of the children: Betty, Ethel, Elizabeth, May and the father, Alexander. Also included here must be the occasionally encountered reversals mounted on more than a few Australian homes —ESUOHRUO and EMOHRUO.

PUB NAMES

As noted in a number of contexts throughout this book, the essential accompaniment of just about all Australian activities is GROG at least it seems so from the frequency with which expressions about its consumption are heard. Some historical evidence also suggests an early ardour for liquid refreshment in New South Wales and elsewhere in the country. The rum trade profitably monopolised by the officers of the New South Wales Corps for many years resulted in the Rum Rebellion against Governor Bligh in 1808 (of *Bounty* notoriety;

he seems to have been prone to such incidents). A decade earlier and only eight years after the colony was established a licence was issued to a public house in Parramatta. It was called the Mason's Arms, a direct link and homage to the British traditions of drinking. A licence issued the following year introduced a colonial element into the naming of BOOZERS when a woman named Sarah Bird was granted a licence for the Three Jolly Settlers in Sydney, a nice combination of the traditional and the antipodean. But the British influence remained strong well into the 19th century and right around the country. A PUB called the Whale Fishery was licensed in Hobart in 1807 and possibly earlier. It was followed by others named Bird in the Hand, The Plough, Carpenter's Arms and, nostalgically, the City of London. In Western Australia The Stirling Arms in Fremantle received a licence on New Year's Day 1830, less than a year after the founding of the Swan River settlement, as did the patriotic George IV and, in Perth, the Happy Emigrant. Victoria followed the West Australian example of shrewd sycophancy and named its first licensed PUB the Governor Bourke (after the same) in 1836, followed the next year by an Angel Inn, and a Ship. South Australia was more inclined to the prosaic from the very first and named its PUBS in much the style that is now common. Guthrie's Hotel in Glenelg got a licence in 1837, as did the Victoria and the slightly more interesting Southern Cross. A similar tendency can be seen in Queensland where the Brisbane was licensed in 1842 and the Victoria in the next year which also saw the continuing English influence in The Woolpack and the Shepherd and Flock. Through this early period, and indeed for well into the 20th century, many places of refreshment were unlicensed, giving us the infamous SLY GROG shanties.

From the late 19th century it seems that PUB names tended more towards the local and downright descriptive in such titles as The Botany View or just someone or other's name — Johnson's, for example. The most common, Royal, is still with us almost everywhere, as are a few like Terminus and Railway Junction, inspired by the spread of railways towards the end of the 19th century. From early in the 20th century 'Commercial Hotels' became frequent. These and similar dull MONICKERS are the common run in Australian PUB names. The occasional oddity or striking name like the Australian Youth in the Inner-Western Sydney Suburb of Glebe leaps out, but names like the No Good Damper Inn on the Melbourne–Dandenong Road, the Doctor Syntax in Hobart and the Help Me Through the World that once graced Sydney's Rocks are a long way between drinks.

In Lingo, of course, many of these official names are shortened to localised versions — The Botany View becomes THE BOTANY, The Mason's Arms descends to THE MASON'S, The Paddington Inn inevitably becomes THE PADDO. The original and official name of the famous Young and Jackson's in Melbourne has long been forgotten, if it was ever known by drinkers. Young and Jackson bought the PUB in the 1870s and it has been known after them ever since. Since early in the 20th century the hotel's special claim to fame lay in its posses-sion of the once-daring nude painting of 'Chlöe' that hung above the bar. This famous work was painted in 1875 by the French artist Jules Lefebvre and came to Melbourne for the Great Exhibition of 1880. It was eventually bought by the-then co-owner of the establishment, Norman Young, in 1908, since when it has graced the saloon bar. OUR CHLÖE used to be the traditional response of MELBURNITES to the Sydneysiders gloating about OUR BRIDGE, OUR 'ARBER and OUR BRAD-MAN. The well-known simile for excess drinking — DRUNK AS CHLÖE is often thought to be derived from the famous painting in Young and Jackson's. But the term is recorded in print as early as 1823, more than half-a-century before the famous lady arrived in Melbourne, and seems to have belonged to the argot of sports and gambling.

Not only do hotels have their lingo names, so do the substances served within. Exotic names for mixed drinks have included STONE FENCE for ginger beer and brandy, a SMASH for ice and brandy, a HAND OF HOPE for the singularly unexciting lemon juice and water. A MADAM BISHOP was, it seems, a concoction of nutmeg, sugar and port and a LOLA MONTEZ consisted of water, lemon and ginger, mixed with rum. BLOW-ME-SKULL-OFF dates back to at least the 1850s and could refer to any number of poisonous concoctions. One recipe called for a mix of *cocculus indicus*, spirits of wine, opium, pepper and rum. Another included sugar, lime juice, ale, rum and brandy.

THE VERNACULAR BODY

Many Lingo terms refer to, involve, or name parts of the human body. We may be told TO KEEP YOUR HAIR ON; that we are OFF OUR HEAD; THICK in it or that we should HEAD OFF somewhere. We may EYE OFF, HAVE EYES ON, or be DONE IN THE EYE. Ears may be BENT, CHEWED, or we may be EARBASHED. We may be NOSEY, or ON THE NOSE, occasionally MOUTH OFF, or have A MOUTH LIKE THE BOTTOM OF A BIRDCAGE, or LIKE A GREEK WRESTLER'S JOCKSTRAP. Sometimes we have to TAKE IT ON THE CHIN.

If we STICK OUR NECK OUT, we run the risk of GETTING IT IN THE NECK. Something may cost us AN ARM AND A LEG. A brave person may have GUTS. Someone may TURN UP HER TOES (die), or HANG ON BY HIS FINGERNAILS. You can KEEP YOUR SKIN ON or alternatively JUMP

OUT OF YOUR SKIN, depending upon the circumstances, and ONE'S BLOOD CAN BE WORTH BOTTLING or, less happily, be ON THE WALLS.

Bodily and mental afflictions, real, imagined or fervently wished, also feature strongly in Lingo. One can be BLIND AS A BAT; DEAF AS A POST; SILLY AS A BRUSH or A CUT SNAKE; SILLY AS A WET WEEKEND; LAME AS A MULE; THICK AS TWO SHORT PLANKS; THICK AS PIG SHIT; QUEER AS A BEER; CAMP AS A ROW OF TENTS; CACK-HANDED (left-handed); UGLY AS A SHITHOUSE RAT or as A BAGFUL OF BUSTED BOILS; have A FACE LIKE A BUSTED SANDSHOE; be USELESS AS TITS ON A NUN; MAD AS A MEAT-AXE; THIN AS A RAKE, or as A BROOM, or a BEANPOLE, or even a DROVER'S DOG; be A GREAT LONG STREAK OF MISERY; a SHORTARSE, or A TUB OF LARD.

Then there are those terms for body parts and functions, many of which feature in other chapters. The extent and variety of the Lingo terms for genitals and other body areas hints at a determined, if perverse, use of euphemism to avoid the use of perfectly respectable words like testicles, penis, vagina, and posterior. Such terms, though, seem sterile and colourless to the Lingoist who prefers such delights as BALLS, KNACKERS, CRACKERS, ORBS, PRICK, DICK, OLD FELLA, TOSSEL, STALK, THROBBING GRISTLE, TROUSER SNAKE, BEARDED CLAM, BOX, DATE, FANNY, ARSE, BUM DOT, BACKSIDE (SPOT YOUR DOT being an affectionate invitation to take a seat), BLOT, to name only a very, very few of the available possibilities for the four delicate spots in question.

Bodily functions do not escape the Lingo. Defecation may be unappealingly described as GIVING BIRTH TO A COPPER (a policeman), or CHOKING A DARKIE. Urination may be a PISS, SLASH, SHAKE HANDS WITH THE UNEMPLOYED, GIVING THE WIFE'S BEST FRIEND A SHAKE, POINTING PERCY AT THE PORCELAIN, and so on. Flatulence — FARTING — is well represented, too. Various terms are used for the act itself, including OPENING THE SANDWICH BOX, CUTTING THE CHEESE, DROPPING ONE, DROPPING YOUR GUTS, LETTING OFF A BREEZER, among others even more vulgar. As well, there are traditional responses to this embarrassing, usually unpleasant, but totally unavoidable bodily function. These include such retorts as BREATHE IN DEEP AND GET RID OF IT and TURN ON THE FAN AND BEAT IT INTO SHIT which is probably quite enough on this subject except to say that one who is FARTING SPARKS is very angry indeed, possibly even more so than someone SPITTING CHIPS.

A DOG'S EYE AND DEAD HORSE

A pie and sauce, of course. A DOG'S EYE AND A DEAD HORSE is rhyming slang for this peculiarly Australian repast. The origins of rhyming slang are unknown, but it was spoken by Cockneys and criminals in London during the early to mid-19th century and is also found in the

secret language of Shelta where standard English words were sometimes rhymed, as in supper, known in Shelta as 'grupper'. The term
ELEPHANT'S TRUNK meaning drunk, for example, still part of
Australian rhyming slang, was recorded in England during the
1850s. As convict speech was derived initially from the cant language
of the British underworld, especially that large part of it in and
around London from whence many LEFT THEIR COUNTRY FOR THEIR
COUNTRY'S GOOD, it is no surprise to find rhyming slang featuring in
the Australian vernacular, especially as a form of naming.

Though it may well have been in use among restricted groups a
generation earlier, rhyming slang seems to have become more widely popular in the last years of the 19th century in this country, aided
to some extent by the popular theatre. Much of the rhyming slang in
use here is the same as that used in Britain, where it is still most closely associated with the speech of the London Cockneys, though it is
spoken much more widely in that country. PEN AND INK for stink;
TROUBLE AND STRIFE for wife; CHEESE AND KISSES for missus, are just
a few examples of rhyming slang terms common to Britain and
Australia. But as well as these borrowed terms, Australians have
developed a fair repertoire of their own rhyming slang that has a distinctively local flavour. Consistent with other aspects of the Lingo,
rhyming slang is liberally larded with offensive terms for 'others'.

It is sometimes said that rhyming slang is an obsolete form,
though a couple of comparatively new coinages suggest otherwise:
GERMAINE GREER beer and, especially piquant, KERRY PACKERED for
knackered. Another relatively recent coinage is REG GRUNDIES undies,
usually rendered more properly as REGINALDS. In fact, names of
prominent, and even not so prominent, people, and even department
stores, have always proved fertile sources of Australian rhyming slang,
such as BASS AND FLINDERS winders (windows); CAPTAIN COOK look,
as in TAKE A CAPTAIN COOK AT THAT, also used in Cockney rhyming
slang; CHARLIE WHEELER for SHEILA (a girl or woman), usually just
CHARLIE and originally from the name of artist Charles Wheeler
(1881–1977). Another rhyming slang term for SHEILA is POTATO
PEELER. Other examples of this process include: EDGAR BRITT for
SHIT, after the Australian jockey of the same name; FRANK THRING a
ring (finger), after well-known actor, the late Frank Thring; FRED
ASTAIRE lair; GORDON AND GOTCH (wrist)watch, after the name of a
well-known newsagents' distributor; HALLEY'S COMET vomit; HARVEY
DREW SPEW (vomit); HENRY BERRY sherry; JIMMY GRANT immigrant,
used in New Zealand since at least the 1840s and recorded in
Australia in the 1850s; JOE BLAKE snake and JOE BLAKES shakes,
usually those induced by excess consumption of alcohol and its

after-effects. JACK LANG means slang, though may also be applied specifically to rhyming slang, as in to TALK THE OLD JACK LANG; Jack Lang was a famous or infamous, depending upon your political views, Labor premier of New South Wales during the depression years of the 1930s. RED NED is cheap red wine and a TYRONE POWER is a shower. An UNCLE MERV means to PERV (as in ogle) and can be simply rendered as HAVE AN UNCLE. A WALLY GROUT is a SHOUT (as in buy a round of drinks) and ZANE GREY is pay, as in wages for work performed. Another recent invention is A BARRY CROCKER meaning A SHOCKER (something bad), after the well-known entertainer and star of the *Bazza McKenzie* films of the 1970s, often used in its shortened form of BARRY.

Fictional or mythical characters have also formed a basis for rhyming slang. MICKEY MOUSE is GROUSE (good), after the evergreen Disney character, though the lingoism MICKEY MOUSE is also used in non-rhyming slang form as a description of someone or something considered unreliable or faulty. A few other examples: MUTT AND JEFF is deaf, after the characters in a long-running Australian newspaper comic strip; DAD AND DAVE is shave, after Steele Rudd's famous characters; NELLY BLIGH is pie; NOAH'S ARK is shark; often simply NOAH or NOAH'S, after the biblical figure. This last is used both of the fish and of an individual believed to be a dishonest or untrustworthy dealer, especially in business matters. Since the late 19th century criminal argot has also used NOAH'S ARK to mean NARC, an informer. Others of this type include TOM THUMB for drum, as in IT'S THE TOM THUMB, meaning the truth, or useful information of some kind. A JOHN DORY is a story, usually with the connotation of fabrication or exaggeration.

Similarly, the names of places have contributed their share to the formation of our rhyming slang, often adding a local touch. A BAROSSA PEARL is a girl, from the name of a cheap white, sparkling wine that was a popular drink in the 1960s and early 1970s before we matured as a wine-drinking nation and pretended that we had transcended such embarrassments. Some other examples: BULLI PASS (sometimes simply BULLI or PASS) for arse (compare with the British 'Khyber Pass', or 'Khyber', which is also used here); COFF'S HARBOUR for barber; DAPTO DOG for WOG (usually just a DAPTO), from the famous New South Wales dog races, the Dapto Dogs; HAWKESBURY RIVERS shivers (usually HAWKESBURIES); KEMBLA GRANGE change (money); MALLEE ROOT for prostitute, a drollery on the slang term for sexual intercourse; MANLY–WARRINGAH'S for fingers (New South Wales version, a homage to a prominent local football club); ONKA-PARINGAS for fingers (South Australian version); RIVER MURRAYS (No) or NO WORRIES; SYDNEY HARBOUR for barber; TENNANT CREEK means a Greek (Northern Territory); WERRIS CREEK (Victoria and New South Wales) also a Greek, usually just WERRIS, NEW SOUTH for mouth, WARWICK FARM for arm (New South Wales) and WELLINGTON BOOT for ROOT (as in fornicate).

Then there are those things that form the basis for still more distinctively Australian rhymes, including: BABBLING BROOK for cook, often simply BABBLER; BAKED BEAN for QUEEN (male homosexual); BEECHAM'S PILL for dill, usually just BEECHAM'S; BILLY LIDS for KIDS; BUTCHER'S HOOK for CROOK, meaning unwell, sick; CATTLE DOG for catalogue; CHINA PLATE for mate, usually just CHINA, a Cockneyism; CHOCOLATE FROGS for WOGS (migrants from southern Europe); CHOCOLATE FROG for DOG, underworld slang for an informer and COCK SPARRA for Yarra (Melbourne). COMIC CUTS for GUTS means the truth, the guts of something and may be rendered just as COMICS. The word can also mean simply guts, as in intestines. A COUNTRY COUSIN is a dozen, usually bottles or cans of beer; DEAF AND DUMB is THE DRUM, as in GIVE US THE DRUM, meaning tell us the truth; an EGG AND SPOON is a HOON; FAIRY BOWER is a shower; FLAT CHAT means extremely busy; FORWARD PASSES are glasses (drinking); a GINGER BEER is A QUEER (male homosexual); a GOANNA is rhyming slang on rhyming slang for JOANNA, meaning piano; a HERE AND NOW is a CHOW (person of Asian appearance); a HOLLOW LOG is a WOG; HUNGARIAN CHAMPAGNE is soda water; an IN-BETWEEN is A QUEEN (male homosexual); JUICY FRUIT, after the brand name of a chewing gum, means ROOT (sexual intercourse); KANGAROO(S) are shoe(s), usually just KANGA(S); LAGER BEERS are ears; LOOP-THE-LOOP is soup; an OPTIC NERVE is a PERV (pervert, as in one who PERV[E]S at or ogles the opposite sex), often spoken as in COP AN OPTIC AT THAT, being an enthusiastic comment on the attractiveness of — usually — a woman. A male homosexual may be described as HE'S AS QUEER AS A BEER; the RED HOTS means the trots (harness racing) or THE TROTS, as in dysentery. RIDGY-DIDGE is an expression of approval, signifying that something is genuine. The related RIDGY-DITE means all right and is used to indicate that someone or something is genuine, to be trusted. ROTARY HOE means RIGHTIO (a term of agreement) and RUBBIDY-DUB, a PUB is often shortened to RUBBIDY, a usage recorded in the late 1890s, though certainly older. A SKY ROCKET is a pocket; a SLAPSIE MAXIE is a taxi; a SNAKE'S HISS is a PISS (to urinate); SOLDIER'S BOLD is cold, usually just SOLDIERS; STEAK AND KIDNEY is Sydney; a SUBMARINE is a QUEEN (homosexual); SUDDEN DEATH means breath, usually bad breath; a TEDDY BEAR is a LAIR; THIEF AND ROBBER is COBBER and TREY BITS means THE SHITS (TREY was the term for pre-decimalisation threepence; also used in card-playing for a three of any suite).

To VIOLET CRUMBLE is to TUMBLE, as in to understand something: OH, NOW I VIOLET CRUMBLE! derived from the name Violet Crumble bar, an Australian confectionery of chocolate-coated honeycomb.

While rhyming slang goes in and out of favour in the wider Lingo it does tend to be a constant in the little lingo of criminals. During the 1960s the following rhyming slang terms were reported as current in Sydney's Long Bay Gaol:

BOB HOPE — soap
BOB POWELL — towel
BO-PEEP — sleep
BRACES — horse or dog races
DAD AND DAVE— shave
FAIRY BOWER — shower
FRED ASTAIRE — LAIR
JOHN DORY — a criminal's story or alibi. More generally, any kind of an excuse.
ST LOUIS BLUES — shoes
TEDDY BEAR — lair
MICKEY MOUSE — grouse (meaning good, a total opposite to the larger Lingo use of MICKEY MOUSE — to mean something inferior or suspect in some way)
TOM THUMB — the drum (the truth, useful information)
YOGI BEAR — boob lair (boob meaning gaol)

Recent research indicates that rhyming slang still forms a portion of criminal argot with many of the above terms still in use.

Rhyming slang is not the only area in which rhyme is worked to good effect. A number of other common terms use this device, including: ARTHUR OR MARTHA (DIDN'T KNOW IF THEY WERE ARTHUR OR MARTHA) meaning confused; ARTY-FARTY for a person or thing considered to be frivolous, as in HE'S AN ARTY-FARTY WANKER; CHOCK-A-BLOCK — full up and related to the more respectable CHOCK-FULL. This Lingoism (also used in British and American slang) is usually shortened to CHOKKA, as in the probably apocryphal words of the airline clerk to the intending passenger SORRY, OCKER, THE FOKKA'S CHOKKA. As with many other terms this one also does dual service to describe the act of coitus, as in I WAS CHOCK-A-BLOCK UP HER. DEAD HEAD is a person of low intelligence; FROM GO TO WOE means from beginning to end; FUCK A DUCK! is an exclamation of surprise and/or anger; FUCK TRUCK as for SHAGGIN' WAGON (see below); HORSES FOR COURSES is an expression indicating that appropriate elements should be matched, such as putting the right person in the right job, making an appropriate choice of table wine, and so on; HOUSE MOUSE was a publican (obsolete); IN LIKE FLYNN means success, especially in relation to sexual conquest of a female by a male; KISS MY ARSE, FOR TOMORROW IT MAY PASS, a poetic expression of scorn; NO GO is a hopeless cause; NO SHOW, being without hope of success; ODDS AND SODS is bits and pieces, miscellaneous items or persons; OKEY DOKEY means the familiar form of OKAY, signifying equable agreement; OOROO is a term of farewell, derived from the earlier HOOROO; SHAGGIN' WAGON means a motor vehicle, usually a station wagon used for sexual intercourse and also known as a SIN BIN or FUCK TRUCK. SILLY-BILLY is mild term of abuse.

An apparently indigenous form of rhyming slang evolved here during the depression of the 1930s, according to Sidney Baker. This consisted of short rhymes on place names, usually with a sombre reference to unemployment and hardship, such as THINGS ARE CROOK IN TALLAROOK, GOT THE ARSE AT BULLI PASS and NO WORK IN BOURKE. During World War II there was a slight revival of this vogue with THINGS ARE CROOK IN OLD TOBRUK and, in New Guinea, THINGS ARE DRACK AT WEWAK (DRACK being soldier slang for bad, revived in 1990s youthspeak). Variations on this poetic form are still heard from time to time such as THE BEER IS WEAK IN JULIA CREEK, meaning poor beer, often abbreviated to JULIA CREEK or even JULIA and as a general expression of dissatisfaction. Other literary devices, such as spoonerism, are rare in Lingo; FLUTTERBY for butterfly seemingly the lone oddity.

6

LIFESTYLE LINGOES

The common speech of the Commonwealth of Australia
represents the most brutal maltreatment which has ever been
inflicted upon the mother-tongue of the
English-speaking nations.

WALTER CHURCHILL
(AMERICAN PHILOLOGICAL SOCIETY)
IN BEACH-LA-MER, THE JARGON OR
TRADE-SPEECH OF THE WESTERN PACIFIC, 1911

Australian vernacular, or 'common speech' as the American linguist quoted above puts it, makes careful social distinctions that the official language may not. For instance, a BIKER is a very different person leading a very different lifestyle to a BIKIE. The former is a person who rides a motorbike, probably has a job and solid family responsibilities. But in popular parlance and perception a BIKIE is a violent and menacing man, dressed in jeans and leather jacket, probably carrying concealed weapons and involved in drug-dealing. Whether the stereotype is accurate or not, the Lingo observes such gradations and nuances. A similar distinction is made in terms like surfer and SURFIE, the latter, like BIKIE denoting not simply a pastime or a means of transport but an entire lifestyle, with its own customs, costume, values and, of course, little lingo.

Lifestyle lingoes are terms and usages peculiar to lifestyle or leisure groups in Australian society. Although the Australian population is relatively small, the community has developed the full range of well-delineated groups that speak their own languages. As well as such social groups, there are speech communities to which individuals may belong by virtue of their sexual orientation, gender, or age. And there are those vocabularies that belong to groups created by particular historical experiences and ways of looking at the world. This chapter samples just a smattering of the many such little lingoes that exist, or have existed.

DOING IT TOUGH

During the depression of the 1930s many Australians were thrown out of work and out of their homes. Often they were forced to go ON THE ROAD in the same manner as the wandering bushmen of the not-so-distant past, carrying SWAGS and looking for work. Hard times and shared desperation made these people into a social group among whom there developed a lingo that was an amalgam of some older terms and a number of new ones. Many of these words became part of the folk songs and ditties of the period. Terms like 'dole', a much older English term for an act of charity, quickly came back into popular parlance. The Victorian bush singer and poet Simon McDonald wrote a poem at that time, chronicling the bitter experience of the era. Titled simply 'The Dole' the poem went, in part:

> *The Government gave us a handout*
> *That kept body and soul.*
> *Some people called it the 'susso',*
> *The out-of-work called it 'the dole'...*

There were many other depression ditties that introduced new or revived terms to the Lingo, terms that were a shorthand for deprivation, poverty and hopelessness: the DOLE, tolling like a funeral bell, the many receivers of which were known as DOLEYS, and SUSSO, short for the official Sustenance allowance, also known as THE SUSS and consisting only of the bare essentials needed to sustain life — sugar, tea, flour, a bit of meat. The SUSSO was immortalised in sharp parodies like this, to the tune of 'You're in the army now':

> *We're on the susso now*
> *We're not behind a plough*
> *We live in a tent*
> *We pay no rent*
> *We're on the susso now.*

HOOKING A RATTLER or HOPPING A RATTLER was to illegally catch a train, usually UP THE COUNTRY where it was hoped (usually unrealistically) to find work. Often these trips led to confrontations with the

police (WALLOPERS) or DEMONS (detectives) as outlined in a song
from the time that includes a good deal of depression lingo, including
BAGMAN, an old variant of swagman that became especially widespread during this period.

> *A strapping young bagman lay dying,*
> *His nosebag [swag] supporting his head;*
> *All around him his mates were a-crying*
> *As he rose on his elbow and said:*
>
> *Wrap me up in my old police blanket*
> *And bury me deep down below,*
> *Where the demons and the wallopers can't worry me,*
> *In the shade where the old rattler blows.*
>
> *He'd jumped every freight in Australia,*
> *Botted handouts by the score.*
> *He'd learned all the rorts as a whaler,*
> *But alas he will battle no more.*
>
> *Those coppers that wait at Rockhampton ,*
> *Those demons that wait at Yarell;*
> *The bastards can wait there forever,*
> *I'm catching a fast freight to hell.*
>
> *(Final chorus) Wrap him up in his old police blanket*
> *And bury him deep down below,*
> *Where the squatters and coppers can't touch him,*
> *For he's going where all bagmen go.*

BAGMAN was also used in such terms as BAGMAN'S GAZETTE, meaning
the rumour mill or BUSH TELEGRAPH system that operated effectively
along THE TRACK and also in the form of the BAGMAN'S UNION, a
mythical set of rules for proper conduct of those TRAVELLERS who
were ON THE ROAD during the HUNGRY THIRTIES, itself a continuation
of the equally fictitious SWAGMAN'S UNION. There was also a complaint known as BAGMAN'S LEG that came about from the loss of the
leg beneath the wheels of a train when trying to HOOK A RATTLER
(freight train) or TAKE HER ON THE FLY, as in Jack Wright's song of
the period, 'Battler's Ballad':

> *You are just a lonely battler and you're waiting for a rattler,*
> *And you wish to heaven you were never born*
> *For you ran to dodge the coppers and you came an awful cropper*
> *And the skin on both your hands is cut and torn . . .*

Then you hear the bumpers crashing, see the green light flashing
You feel that great big engine rushing by
With your swag held at the ready, you're nerves are not so steady
For you know you've got to take her on the fly...

The term BOTTED, meaning borrowed or cadged and used in 'The Dying Bagman', has been in use in Australia since at least the 1880s with a number of related meanings. Used as a term for an agricultural parasite pest, a BOT-FLY, a BOT was also used to refer to an illegal or crooked scheme of some kind, appearing in Boldrewood's *Robbery Under Arms* (1888) with this meaning. The suggestions of parasitism and unsavouriness continued into World War I when the term attained its now near-obsolete meaning, replaced by HIT UP, as in HE HIT ME UP FOR A SMOKE.

RELIEF WORK entered the Australian vocabulary and GETTING RELIEF referred to work provided by the government, mainly on public works projects, such as land-clearing, road-building, and the notorious construction of the Sandy Hollow Railway line in New South Wales. One of the workers on this project, Duke Tritton, wrote a poem about his experience in which he referred to the workers and their treatment: 'We were no better than convicts, though we didn't wear the chains.' Other ditties of the day were even more direct:

The songs that we sang
Were about old Jack Lang [then Premier of New South Wales]
On the steps of the dole-office door.
He closed up the banks,
It was one of his pranks
And he sent us to the dole-office door.

We molested the police
'Till they gave us 'relief'
On the steps of the dole-office door...

Evictions became common, known in Sydney at least as GETTING THE BUNG. The bailiff, accompanied by police, or JOHNS, arrived in force. Sometimes they had to fight their way into the house through an angry crowd of neighbours and sympathisers in order to eject the rent- or mortgage-defaulting tenant. DOSS HOUSES became common, as did SOUP KITCHENS where you could get a plate of LOOP-THE-LOOP (rhyming slang for soup) if you were lucky. HAPPY VALLEYS sprang up. These were shantytowns of cardboard, tin, and anything else that the unemployed could scavenge to build a shelter for their families. To the tune of 'When Your Hair has Turned to Silver' they sang this song:

When your hair has turned to silver
I will still be on the 'dole'
And we'll live in Happy Valley
Where the 'reds' [Communists] *have got control*
You can draw the weekly ration
And the child endowment too,
And when I get the old age pension
I will leave the rest to you.

While Australians have long prided themselves on their ability to MAKE DO with very little, often in very difficult physical circumstances of climate and geography, the experience of the depression years gave the term DOING IT TOUGH even greater resonance.

TAKING IT EASY

After World War II and until the 1980s Australians generally enjoyed an affluent lifestyle. This allowed many to indulge those hedonistic, leisure-loving urges so often held against us by outsiders and some insiders. Condemnation of Australian casualness expressed in phrases like SHE'LL BE JAKE, SHE'S APPLES and NO WORRIES, is nothing new. It is a subset of WOWSERISM and has had something of a revival in the economic rationalist 1980s and 1990s. Little of the bean-counting of monetarists, efficiency experts and quality auditors seeking excellence has had much effect on popular attitudes, nor on the Lingo that carries such attitudes. We still take our leisure pretty seriously, going on HOLS frequently, enjoying the 'weekender' or beach shack as much as possible, PARTYING and RAGING (an Australianism now adopted by the British via the television SOAPS 'Neighbours' and 'Home and Away') seemingly AT THE DROP OF A HAT and still indulging in the communal consumption of fairly significant amounts of GROG. The PRAWN NIGHT is still with us, a latter-day continuation of the earlier smoke night/smoke concert/smoker (first in print in New Zealand in the 1880s), as are such hallowed activities as Bingo and QUIZ NIGHT. Our interest and participation in sporting activities is well known and includes not just the FOOTY and cricket, but lawn bowls, gymnastics, surfing, netball, and every other active pastime imaginable. As well, Australians are great consumers of culture in their leisure time (even though we use the disparaging terms CULTURE VULTURE and ARTY-FARTY in Lingo). This includes such popular forms as rock music, dancing, restaurants and cinema but also the higher brow stuff known sometimes as THE YARTS — ballet, opera, classical music, theatre, libraries, galleries, museums, and so on. In short, the Australian attitude to work has been that it is a necessary evil to be accomplished as quickly and as efficiently as possible, so that we have both the financial means and the time to pursue leisure interests.

It may be that this attitude lies behind our reputation as great adopters of new technologies, especially those that are either labour-saving or are related to leisure in some way. The PITCHERS or the FILUMS were enthusiastically embraced by us all as soon as the local industry got off the ground in the early 20th century. Radio, THE WIRELESS, caught on quickly from the 1930s, only to eventually be superseded by television from the mid-1950s, known variously as THE TELLY, THE BOX, the THE BOX IN THE CORNER and THE ONE-EYED MONSTER. We have also taken up the VIDEO (video cassette recorder) with alacrity, as well as the home computer or personal computer (PC), the facsimile transmission machine (FAX) and, most recently, the Internet, usually just THE NET, though increasingly called THE WEB (see also chapter 9). Other gadgets from kitchen whizzes and microwave ovens to vacuum cleaners (THE HOOVER) to washing machines, dishwashers, toasters, and the FRIDGE, are now so much a part of everyday life that we take them all completely for granted.

This much-condemned Australian interest in taking it easy may stem from the persistence of our pioneering myths of hardship and the equally powerful popular image of deprivation associated with the depression. Folk memories of that event have been passed down the generations, instilling a fear of recession and its social and eco-nomic consequences that makes us very keen to own our own home, a kind of hedge against another economic disaster. As banks well know, Australians will make almost any sacrifice to keep up the mort-gage payments on the family home. Other Lingoisms related to Australia's love affair with consumerism and comfort include THE NEVER-NEVER, referring to hire purchase schemes, on the LAY-BY, the Australian term for paying a small deposit on an item, allowing it to be held until the full price is paid at a later, often distant, date. Sometimes LAY-BYS can be paid off in regular or irregular instalments. The LAY-BY system, in operation since at least the 1920s, faded away in the good times of the 1980s but has made a solid return in the more austere 1990s. REPO is the repossession of cars, homes, or other goods on which regular payment has been abandoned (a REPO MAN is one who does this unpopular job for a living), THE PLASTIC or PLAS-TIC MONEY means credit cards while SUPER is superannuation (though in the bush it may also mean the manager or overseer of a property or the fertiliser, superphosphate). Tax avoidance and BOTTOM-OF-THE-HARBOUR SCHEMES, THE VOLVO SET and THE WHITE SHOE BRIGADE are further testament to our double-edged enthusiasm and disdain for taking it easy.

BILLY LIDS

BILLY LIDS, sometimes TIN LIDS, is rhyming slang for KIDS. Adults have some other Lingo terms for children, including LITTLIES; ANKLE-BITERS; RUG RATS; BREAD-SNAPPERS, and CHIPS OFF THE OLD BLOCK. But KIDS have their own lingo as well. It includes names for toys and games, such as marbles, of which the following is only a sampling: DUBS, STONKS, AGATES; EMMAS; REELS; CATS EYES; SATELLITES; GALAXY (dark blue and flecked with white), POO (unpleasantly brown), PLAN-ET, CHINA ALLEY; NIGHT; TOM BOWLER (or TOMBOLA, usually an extra large marble), COKE; BLOODSUCKER; PRATE; BIRD'S CAGE; BLOOD NOSE; BIRDSHIT; DR SPOCK; BLUSH; BLUE SNAKE; BLUE BELL; BLUE JET; KINGS; SPACEYS; TINTS; BLUE MOON; GALAXIAN; COCKY CAGE; CLEARY; BALL BEARING; NORMAL, and PEE WEE. Some of the names of marbles on this list are quite old, DUBS, STONKS and CATS EYES probably dat-ing back to the19th century. Many are of relatively recent origin, as can be deduced from the names themselves, like DR SPOCK and SPACEY. Marbles also boasts terms like MULLY GRUBS, KNUCKLEDOWN, FUDGING, and THE CHINESE FLICK, among other esoterica.

Children's games and associated equipment have generated lots of little lingo terms around the country. The term KIDS use to indi-cate that the speaker gives up or is in a safe place and cannot be attacked, tagged, or otherwise made 'it' varies from State to State. In Perth it is BAIL-EASE, in Sydney B-A-R BAR, in Melbourne BARLEY, in Adelaide BARLEYS and in Brisbane just BAR. In Tasmania, the KIDS do not seem to use this term. Skipping rope games may be called SKIPPY or SKIPPINGS. While Adelaide, Brisbane and Sydney refer to them as common old RUBBER BANDS, they are LACKY BANDS in Western Australia and LACKER BANDS in Melbourne. This variation also applies to the playground game involving skipping a circle of rubber or elas-tic into convoluted shapes and designs. Sometimes the game is known as LACCIES, and sometimes as ELASTICS. The children's cricket game in which you run whenever you hit the ball is called TIP AND RUN in Perth, HIT-AND-RUN or TIP-AND-RUN in New South Wales, but is TIPSY RUN in Brisbane and TIPPETY-RUN in Victoria. In parts of South Australia it is called TIPPY GO.

KIDDY lingo also displays a good deal of the regional variation already noted in grown-up practice. For instance, a HILL TROLLEY in Perth is a BILLYCART just about everywhere else, though both these usages seem to be declining in favour of GO-CART. In South Australia the same type of vehicle was known as a BITZER. The metal or plastic thing you slither down on is a SLIPPERY DIP in South Australia and a SLIDE (sometimes a SLIPPERY SLIDE) in New South Wales. Staid Victorians are content with SLIDE, as it is also usually called in Western Australia, though SLIPPERY DIP is not unknown there either and is the favoured term in Brisbane. The practice of giving your friend a lift on your BIKE is mostly called DINKING or GETTING A DINK in Victoria, Tasmania and southern New South Wales. Further north, into Queensland and in Sydney it is usually called a DOUBLE. In South Australia the terms are either GETTING A DINKY or GETTING A DONKEY. Western Australia has settled for GETTING A DINKY. In parts of South Australia, at least, the word for carrying a friend behind on one's bicycle is TO PUG. Perhaps the most widely known regional variation is the term for the bag in which a child carries schoolbooks. This is usually simply a schoolbag, though in Queensland and in northern New South Wales the term PORT is used, as it is for more general types of luggage-carrying bags.

The armoury of childhood violence includes a diversity of regionalisms. In Brisbane, Melbourne and Adelaide small boys try their hardest to kill small animals and birds, not to mention each other, with a shanghai. The same device is a GING in Western Australia and a slingshot in New South Wales. (South Australian KIDS, by the way, call young sparrows SPOGGIES.) BOONDIES, YONNIES or GOOLIES are mud clumps or rocks that are thrown at tin lids (GOOLIES is also a term for testicles, though not in KIDDY culture). At least they are if you come from, respectively, Western Australia, Victoria (where the same projectile may also be called a BRINNY, noted earliest by Baker in the early 1940s) or Brisbane. Elsewhere the ANKLE-BITERS seem content to simply hurl ROCKS at each other. You can get yourself a BLOOD NOSE in South Australia, Tasmania and most of Victoria. Elsewhere you are more likely to get, or to be given, NOSE-BLEED, BLOODY NOSE or BLEEDING NOSE, but all are equally unpleasant.

Food occupies a good deal of childhood attention. Words for different foodstuffs especially appealing to children are numerous. An ICEBLOCK in Brisbane and Sydney is an ICY POLE in Melbourne, Adelaide, and Western Australia. The morning school break at which food is consumed is often known as RECESS in Adelaide and Sydney, though in the case of New South Wales this is probably relatively recent usage. In the 1950s the term was PLAYLUNCH, which also referred to the food lovingly packed by mum for her child's consumption at that time. In Perth younger schoolchildren use the term PLAYTIME while older ones prefer the more grown-up and US-sounding RECESS. (The food eaten at this time used to be called MORNING PIECE). In Brisbane the KIDS say the charming LITTLE LUNCH, but it is a no-nonsense PLAYTIME in Melbourne. LUNCHTIME, the midday food break is pretty well all over the country except in Queensland where the term is BIG LUNCH, logically counterpointing the LITTLE

LUNCH of younger years. PEANUT PASTE in Adelaide, Brisbane and Perth is PEANUT BUTTER in Melbourne and Sydney. Ice-cream comes in BUCKETS in Perth, Brisbane and Sydney, but in a DIXIE in Victoria and a DANDY in South Australia. TUCKER (originally British), near-obsolete in adult lingo, lingers on in TUCKSHOP at a few places, though this term for the school food shop seems to be almost universally superseded by the prosaic CANTEEN.

Like other well-defined social groups, especially those at the lower or outer edges of mainstream society, children have secret lingoes of various kinds. One of these is usually known as pig Latin, involving a reversal of the syllables of words, so that the first sound is placed at the end of the word, as in 'Can you come?' which turns into the amusing 'Ancay ouyay umcay?' gibberish to the uninitiated teacher or parent. This kind of linguistic play has been observed in children of many cultures and, according to Baker, was once known in Queensland as LOTUS LANGUAGE.

One of the most fertile areas of KIDspeak is the not so gentle art of parody. Parody is a constant in the expressive culture of all social groups, of course, though with KIDS it is often right up to the minute and refreshingly free of the inhibitions that trouble their parents. In fact, one of the functions of children's parody is to subvert, verbally at least, the stuffy, confusing world of grown-ups. The introduction of television in Australia from the mid-1950s provided many new opportunities for parody, as indicated in the following random sampling from a vast range of possibilities.

In the 1970s the 'Addams Family' television show theme song became, in KIDDY culture:

The Addams Family started
When Uncle Festa farted,
They thought it very funny
When he blew up the dunny
And landed in the sewer -
A drain of raw manure.
the Addams family,
Blurt, blurt.
or
The Addams Family started
When Uncle Festa farted,
The children were disgusted,
They stuck their dicks in custard,
The Addams Family.
Drop dead.

Advertisements for Sorbent toilet tissue could hardly have escaped the parodic urge. The original became:

What's the softest fibre
You can use to wipe your khyber?
New, new, new newspaper.
If it's aggravating,
You can read it while you're waiting,
New, new, new newspaper.
If you've got the runnies,
You can always read the funnies,
New, new, new, newspaper.

There was no doubt at all about the virtues of Carlton Bitter — at least among Melbourne children:

Carlton Bitter, Carlton Bitter,
Carlton bitter, can or draught.
It's the health food of a nation,
Stick the ice-cream up your arse.

Just in case this retrospective gives the impression that modern Aussie KIDS do not do this sort of thing anymore, here is a 1990s children's parody to the tune of the ABC's long-running children's show, *Playschool*, which began broadcasting in 1966:

There are people in there
With hand grenades
And lots of AIDS
Open wide, come inside
It's gay school...

GAY, by the way, has been reported in use among 1997 pre-adolescent schoolchildren as a mid-range derogation similar TO DORK.

YOUTHSPEAK

The world of childhood and adolescence is continually adapting new terms from the world of adult lingo and from children's media of all kinds. In the late 1980s KIDS around Australia (and around the planet) were talking TURTLE-TALK, derived from the enormously popular films of the Teenage Mutant Ninja Turtles. COWABUNGA (already known to an earlier generation of Australian surfers as a term of exultation used as the surfboard slides down a large wave), HUMUNGUS,

TOTALLY AWESOME were a few of the more popular utterances that have now abated. At the time of writing, BILLY LIDS seem to have reverted to their tried-and-true linguistic adaptations and inventions. Some terms in use among primary schoolers in Western Australia during the early 1990s included DORK, DWEEB (a SPASTICATED DWEEB is a REAL DORK, at least it was in the early 1990s)— all insults — and GROSS for almost anyone or anything perceived as undesirable. In the late 1990s the word GOOBER (spelling and derivation unknown, possibly related TO GOB, an earlier youthism for spit?) was in use to mean spit or dribble. One who dribbled was said to be GOOBERING.

The following general terms of insult were in common use among an earlier generation of 16-year-old Sydney schoolgirls in the late 1970s: TROG, DAPTO, MANG, POONCE (continuing an earlier usage) and NERD, the last being still in use with this age group and also in the larger Lingo. NERD has even become an almost formal description for one who is excessively involved with computers and computing. Persons of Greek descent were called CHOKOS, A CAT was a male homosexual, as it had been in prison little lingo and more widely for a considerable time. In an interesting case of back slang occasioned perhaps by the onset of political correctness, GOW meant WOG.

Almost 20 years later, on the other side of the continent in Perth, Western Australia, 13- and 14-year-old schoolgirls numbered WICKED and ALL RIGHT... as terms of approval in their repertoire of little lingo. Anything that was not liked would be GROSS. An attractive boy might be referred to as CUTE, A ROOT or, reflecting the gender-bending creeping into Lingo, A BABE. Boys not considered in such a favourable light were MUMMIES' BOYS. Disapproving terms for females included BUTCH, SLUT, TRAMP, MOLE, and COW, all used in the wider Lingo. Terms for (male) masturbation used were FLOG THE LOG and SPANK THE MONKEY. Generalised insults included DICK-WIPE/KNOB/HEAD/WIT, DOODLE-HEAD/BRAIN and a TRY-HARD, someone thought to be putting too much effort into being liked or accepted, but also used in a generally derogatory manner. Insults also included PIZZA-HEAD and the poetic PIMPLE ON THE PENIS OF LIFE. Someone who did not fit the norms of the group in any way, such as being over-fond of academic studies, was called A SQUID and, in a continuation or revival of 1950s youthspeak, was SQUARE. GROOVY, COOL, FUNKY and RIGHT ON seem to have made a comeback in 1990s youthspeak, presumably inspired by the revival of 1960s fashions and music. Interestingly, PSYCHEDELIC is used to mean something colourful. Parents may be requested not to CHUCK A SPAZ when remonstrating with some less than satisfactory aspect of their adolescent offspring's behaviour.

Other terms of current — that is, mid-1990s to late-1990s vintage— include: SCUNTED, meaning to be caught out doing something and MUNTED, meaning deformed, ugly, unpleasant; BIMBO, a silly girl; DANIELS, people who are rowdy; MOSH PIT, the heaving mass of adolescent humanity directly in front of the stage at rock concerts, hence the verb TO MOSH; while GIGSTERS or PUNTERS are those who attend such events. UNCO, a shortening of uncoordinated, is used to describe anyone or thing that is thought to be less than competent or pleasing to regard. A NIGEL or a SCOTT is an awkwardly alone male at social gatherings. HOMIES, an Americanism, refers to those who wear expensive brand-name clothing, such as Nike and Adidas. Wollongong little lingo for such people is PUNCY-PUNCES, an allegedly onomatopoeic reference to their preference for a style of popular music that uses a rather restricted range of sedate rhythms, similar to the TECHNO fad of a few years before. A 1960s youthism, GROUSE, seems to have been revived in Melbourne and possibly elsewhere in the eastern States. The northern English and Scottish rendering of SHIT, the almost Shakespearean 'shite', seems to have come into fashion here through the film, *Trainspotting*. As a general observation, it seems that the f-word has taken the place of BLOODY in youthspeak, a process of amelioration familiar to linguists, in which previously taboo terms become more acceptable with succeeding generations.

The speed with which youthspeak changes can be breathtaking and also crucial to one's relationships and general social standing. Discussing current terms with a 13-year-old in late 1997 I uttered what I thought was an excellent example of my up-to-date COOLness — MEGA, an intensifier usually used to mean very big or capacious and in vogue earlier in that year. I was greeted with a wrinkling of the nose and the retort: 'Use that word and you go straight down the social scale.' At the same time members of this age group were also using JOY as a general expostulation of delight, as in YOU'VE JUST WON THE LOTTERY. JOY! This is mentioned here only for the sake of the linguistic record, as JOY will no doubt have gone the way of MEGA long before this book is printed.

In keeping with the Lingo tendency for words to take on sometimes totally opposite meanings, youthful persons are currently using words like HELL, to mean something exceedingly good. So THAT WAS A HELL PARTY means that the experience was intensely enjoyable and not, as we might logically be tempted to think, incredibly bad. Just why this reversal has come about is unclear, though it presumably is part of the same process that uses words like WICKED to mean something approved of, rather than something decried, as in its mainstream meaning. The term is also used to intensify, as in HELL GOOD or HELL SCARY.

With the arrival of the Internet and the tendency for youth to be among the medium's most enthusiastic and adept communicators, youthspeak is becoming even more rapidly internationalised. In English, at least, the dominant language of THE NET, we can see this process in action where teenagers swap their local lingoisms with NET SURFERS from around the world. Youthspeak for something good can range through ZESTY, MAD, SICK and BAD while terms for something bad or undesirable include FESTY, SEEDY, SAD and CRUSTY. Terms like HOES, derived from the US — and so international — rap music slang (it is a variant of WHORES) are used in Aussie youthspeak, in GANGSTA RAP lingo, in US youthspeak and in the globalised netspeak. If these trends continue, it will mean the end of books such as these which attempt to explore the intricacies of national vernaculars. We are already hearing, and seeing, the global colloquial speech of the 21st century — the INTERLINGO (see chapter 10). An interesting aspect of language and the Internet is the fact that communication is written, rather than spoken. How this will affect the development of INTERLINGO, if at all, will provide research topics for future linguists and lexicographers.

SHEILASPEAK AND FAMILYSPEAK

Some years ago the late Nancy Keesing wrote a book titled *Lily on the Dustbin* 1982) in which she drew attention to the particular qualities of Australian women's speech and speech in the family which she labelled, respectively sheilaspeak and familyspeak. One of the strengths of Keesing's work is that it was based largely on a survey of what women actually said, rather than depending on literary and journalistic sources, as is the case with many dictionaries of colloquial speech. Keesing's informants provided terms such as LIPPY for lipstick (first noted in print 1955, but certainly quite a bit older), A LICK AND A PROMISE for a hasty grooming; MY STOVE IS AS SLOW AS A WET WASHDAY and the title of the book itself, A LILY ON A DUSTBIN, a useful item of sheilaspeak that could refer to a variety of situations, including being stood up by a friend (similar to being LEFT LIKE A SHAG ON A ROCK) or a sardonic reference to the glamorous aspirations of many women tied to the drudgery of parenting and housework. A SPOT was a term used by and to women for an alcoholic drink, apparently originating as a euphemism in the 1930s. Women do not get drunk, or any of the many other lingoisms describing that term, instead they get TIDDLY, or MERRY, or even more politely, A LITTLE FLUSHED.

Other items of sheilaspeak that might be mentioned include those related to conversation (something women are generally more adept at than men in Australia, where the STRONG, SILENT image still holds great power), such as HAVING A CHINWAG and HAVING A NATTER.

Men generally seem to prefer more four-square terms like JAWING and HAVING A YARN for their conversational exchanges). The contraction of darling, DARL, is used exclusively by women, though may be applied by them to either sex. Terms for women's clothing, accoutrements and activities include CARDIE (cardigan); NIGHTIE; STEP-INS; FLATTIES (low-heeled shoes); to PUT ONE'S FACE ON; to POWDER ONE'S NOSE, and to SPEND A PENNY. ON THE RAGS; THE CURSE; MY FRIEND, and THAT TIME OF THE MONTH, are all lingoisms for menstruation which may sometimes be referred to by male names, as in 'I'VE GOT CHARLIE/FRED, ETC. TODAY', an eloquent expression of some women's view of the male. The adult male member of the household, should there be one, may be called HUBBY among other things, such as HE ONLY THINKS OF HIS BELLY AND WHAT HANGS ON THE END OF IT. Women are also said to prefer the term HAVE KITTENS when describing a crisis or panic of some kind, rather than, say, DOING THEIR BLOCK or SPITTING THE DUMMY or CHUCKING A MENTAL or A WOBBLY (despite the modern sound of this one it goes back to at least the early 20th century), all of which, despite the dummy reference, are masculine idioms. According to some observers women may also use modified and sanitised versions of Lingo in their speech — PIG'S BUM instead of PIG'S ARSE, for example. While this may be true in some circles, there are many women who wield the Lingo as well, if not better, than men. A late-1990s women's description for well-toned and well-defined stomach muscles— male — is A SIX-PACK.

Non-Lingo words may be used in ways that are special to their users. In the 1990s it has become common for women to describe males that they find especially attractive as 'beautiful', a usage that would occur to very few Australian men, even in these liberated times. While not exclusively female usages, some terms used to describe a promiscuous woman are more likely to be used by women than men, such as ROOT RAT, TART, HUSSY and SLEAZE.

Folklorist Gwenda Davey has published a number of collections of family sayings, including *Snug as a Bug* and *Duck Under the Table* in which she presents sayings collected by her and her students over many years. Davey included parental retorts to silly questions from children, such as A WIG-WAM FOR A GOOSE'S BRIDLE, a traditional response to the question 'What are you making?' Other such retorts, some of which are also reported by Nancy Keesing, collected from a number of English and other language sources included:

What's for dinner? Shit on toast.
What's for dinner? Bread and butter and duck under the table.
An alternative answer was 'My liver and kidneys.'

What's for tea? Pig's bum and gooligum. Or Wombat on toast.
How old are you? As old as my little finger and a little bit older
than my teeth, or 'Old enough to know best.'
What's that? 'Flypaper for a stickybeak.'
What'll I do now? Fart in a bottle and paint it blue.
Where are we going? Up the bum of a big black chook.

Other familyisms include FULL AS A GOOG (egg), FULL UP TO PUSSY'S BOW and FULL UP TO THE DOLLY'S WAX (first noted in the 1940s, but in use for at least a generation or two previously), all terms for being replete with food — rather than alcohol, for which there is a different set of fullisms, noted elsewhere. AS FULL AS THE FAMILY PO (chamber pot) is also applied to filling the tummy with food. Remonstrations to miserable children or spouses include YOUR LIP WOULD TRIP A DUCK and YOU'VE GOT THE COLLYWOBBLES, also used to mean literally having a stomach-ache. Terms used in the wider Lingo may also be used in this family context , including FACE-ACHE and MISERYGUTS. Terms related to the domestic sphere, especially child-rearing, while not exclusively feminine, are often used more by women than by men. Examples of this kind are being CLUCKY, meaning wishing to be with child; JAMIES for pyjamas and NIGH-NIGHS for going to bed and, hopefully, to sleep, a state encouraged with this ditty:

Good night, sleep tight,
Mind the fleas (or bedbugs) don't bite.
If they do,
Squeeze them tight.

BODGIES, WIDGIES AND YOUTH GROUPS

The earliest Australian TEENAGERS were the BODGIES and WIDGIES (sometimes WEEGIES), often shortened to just BODGE and WIDGE. Inspired by US fashions, films and music, the BODGIES and WIDGIES had their own little lingo. Although BODGIES and WIDGIES were a post-World War II phenomenon, observers at the time were not slow to link them explicitly and their rowdy activities with those of the LARRIKINS. In 1956 J.E. Webb wrote in his *So Much for Sydney*, 'The children of the new slums are natural recruits for the strange legion of 1955–56 larrikins and larrikinessess called "BODGIES" and "WID-GIES"...'

BODGIE is usually said to derive from the British dialect terms 'bodge' and 'bodger', meaning, respectively, to work in a careless way and one who does such work. It also has a subsidiary meaning of worthlessness, inferiority. During World War II, the term BODGER was in use among AIF personnel to describe something of poor quality or a fake. Just how the term was taken up by the BODGIES themselves or was applied to them is not clear, although some authorities claim the word has a US origin. But by 1950 the term was in general use in Sydney at least, where it appeared in the *Sunday Telegraph* of 7 May of that year in a description of the BODGEY dress — '. . . belted velvet cord jacket, bright blue sports shirt without a tie, brown trousers narrowed at the ankle, shaggy Cornel Wilde haircut'. The hairstyle referred to here was usually known as a CORNEL WILDER and was one of a number of US cuts affected by BODGIES, including the short all over CREW CUT, the almost bald GI CUT and the longer DUCKTAIL TAIL. The rock-and-roll variant of these styles was usually called a DUCK'S ARSE.

The BODGIES' girlfriends were known as WIDGIES, a term whose origin is unclear, but which has been variously explained as related to RIDGY-DIDGE, WIGEON, a young girl and a journalistic corruption of WEAKIE (that is, a poseur). YOU PAYS YOUR MONEY AND YOU TAKES YOUR CHOICE, as they sometimes say in Lingo. Whatever the origins of WIDGIE, those women identified as such took a subservient role to the male. The WIDGIES' dress varied according to place and time, but pegged gabardine skirts, often with a wide leather belt, jeans, flat-heeled shoes for dancing and short hair and, sometimes in the earlier days, bobbysocks were all possible elements of the wardrobe. Later the flared skirt, tight sweater and thrust bra became recognised as the standard WIDGIE costume. The WIDGIE was easily outshone by the flamboyance of her male companion, much as the CLINERS of the LARRIKINS had generally been upstaged by their men.

In his study of the BODGIES and WIDGIES, *The Young Ones*, Jon Stratton traces the origins of this youth group to the influx of US popular culture during and after World War II. In particular the BODGIES and WIDGIES were obsessed with clothes and with dancing. The clothes were as described above, though the US ZOOT SUIT or DRAPE JACKET was also popular. Dancing was heavily influenced by US styles drawn from the jazz dances of the 1930s and which developed into the jitterbug and the jive. Needless to say, these 'immoral' dances were greeted with the usual parental horror, though the sexual connotations of the youthful contortions involved are quaintly innocent in comparison to the gyrations of many subsequent dance trends. The difficulty that Australian (and New Zealand) society had in dealing with this postwar manifestation of youth was neatly, if chillingly summed up in the title of a study published in 1958 by A.E. Maning, *The Bodgie: A Study in Psychological Abnormality*.

The little lingo of the BODGIES and WIDGIES included words that, in variant form, would crop up in the speech of their younger brothers and sisters when they in their turn reached adolescence in the 1960s. A BODGIEism for something that looked or was considered extremely good was a concertina word formed from ABSOLUTELY FABULOUS, ABFAB, in use from the early to mid-1950s. In the 1960s this reappeared in youthspeak as simply FAB, most notably applied to The Beatles pop group that was incessantly described as THE FAB FOUR. In the 1990s the term has had yet another revival in the name of a popular English television comedy series, 'Absolutely Fabulous'.

The BODGIES transformed by the mysterious processes of youthful progression into the ROCKERS of the late 1950s and early 1960s. ROCKERS were influenced by the motorcycle and car-orientated antics of Marlon Brando and James Dean in films like *Wild Ones* and *Rebel Without a Cause*. They wore black leather jackets, black oily jeans and greasy — preferably black — hair. The ROCKERS were opposed to the blond SURFIES that also arose as a recognisable youth group at about the same period, along with the British-influenced Mods who wore fashionable clothes and rode motor scooters. Gang warfare between Mods and Rockers was legendary, though the Mods seem to have been more in tune with the ethos of the early 1960s, often identifying strongly with British bands like The Beatles and The Who.

The 1960s was very much the decade of youth groups. The hippies quickly became the dominant group, developing a coherent and cogent social and political philosophy that is still with us in some aspects of the New Age. The hippies were the first global youth movement and were opposed in many countries by other youth groups. In Australia, at least in Sydney, their deadly enemies were the SHARPIES. SHARPIES appeared about 1966. The males wore high-waisted jeans, often with braces, T-shirts with collars, sandshoes without socks, very short haircuts (sometimes longer at the back), and perpetually menacing expressions. They were forerunners of the later BOVVER BOYS, sharing much of the same neo-fascist philosophy of violence and petty criminality. Their little lingo does not seem to have been recorded, but it certainly depended heavily on vulgarity and invective drawn from the larger armouries of the Australian Lingo. SHARPIE girls looked a bit like an aggravated version of the DOLLY BIRDS of the time, though they usually pierced their ears and cultivated a similar fearsome visage to that of their boyfriends. Tattoos were favoured by both sexes. The term SHARPIE was also used to refer to anyone who dressed in an often ostentatiously fashionable style and it is occasionally still heard in this way.

JUNKIES, HEADS AND DOPERS

In the mid-1960s to late 1960s the youth drug subculture introduced a range of new little lingoisms to our vernacular. Many of these terms were derived from overseas usage, especially from the USA. Obtaining drugs was called SCORING or MAKING A BUY, usually achieved through a MEET with a PUSHER, a DEALER, or THE MAN. A DEAL was a greater or a larger amount of purchased drugs while a STASH was a person's individual supply. A HIT was an intravenous injection of a narcotic, variously HORSE or H (heroin), MORPH (morphine), PETH (pethidine), or a cocktail of these and other drugs. The equipment used for these injections was a syringe, needle and tourniquet, the latter a luxury often avoided by the substitution of a belt. These items were referred to as a KIT, GUN (the syringe) and THE WORKS and sometimes given personal names by their users. Another term for the implements of injection was an OUTFIT which lives on in current drugspeak in the attenuated form of FIT. The effects of the drug used were variously described as a RUSH, HIGH, or TRIP (originally used for LSD — ACID — but later for any kind of drug-induced euphoria). When in a drugged state one was STONED, OUT OF IT, RIPPED, SMASHED, TRIPPING, or HIGH. Bad drug experiences, especially those induced by LSD or some other hallucinogenic were a BAD TRIP, BUMMER, or a DOWNER. The after-effects of drug-taking were referred to as COMING DOWN, or GETTING STRAIGHT. Users were variously JUNKIES, HEADS, HIPPIES, and, later, FREAKS and DOPERS.

Then, as now, drugs went by a variety of lingo names. These included: ACID for LSD; CRYSTAL for a mixture of cocaine and methedrine usually sold in CAPS or capsules; SPEED for methedrine alone or some other amphetamine that produced similar reactions. Marijuana went by a variety of bewildering and continually changing names, some of which were DOPE, GRASS, POT, MARYJANE, GANJA while the more concentrated and expensive hashish was universally known as HASH. These drugs were consumed mostly by smoking in a BONG (pipe) or in the roll-your-own form of a JOINT, NUMBER, or the much earlier term, REEFER. Later the Americanisms SPLIFF and TOKE for a marijuana cigarette inevitably took hold. Drugs in general were often referred to as SHIT, as in the-then widely heard, now sometimes parodied, HEY, MAN, GOT ANY SHIT?

Many terms from the lingo of the drug subculture, beginning in the 1960s, have become part of the larger Australian vernacular, some even becoming part of proper speech. For instance, BUST, HIT, DEAL, JOINT, OUT OF IT, STONED, HIGH and JUNKIE. RIPPED TO THE TITS is one of the more arresting of these phrases still heard from the odd burnt-out hippie or middle-aged person. To be WASTED means under the influence of drugs and arrived in Australia during the 1960s, still being heard occasionally, sometimes with the extended meaning of being exhausted.

In the 1990s one may DO A LINE OF COKE or HAVE A SNORT, usually referring to the nasal inhalation of cocaine powder through a tube of some kind. Angel dust, crack cocaine and ecstasy (EEs) are relatively recent drugs to arrive on the Australian market. But UPPERS, DOWNERS, BENNIES, PURPLE HEARTS, and many other such abused pills, have been around for a long time, probably since the 1950s, though the names they are known by are more recent. So has marijuana which goes by many old and new names, including WHIZZ, STICK, CONE and BUCKET. There is also a touch of rhyming slang in the world of drug-users where JOHNNY CASH can stand for HASH. In the late 1990s CANDYFLIPPING is also in use as a euphemism for GETTING HIGH.

SURFIESPEAK

SURFIEspeak developed quickly and colourfully in Australia. It also changes rapidly. As with most in-group activities, the little lingo of surfing is liberally spiced with technical terms that mean little or nothing to the uninitiated — which, of course, is much of the point. In the early 1960s terms for surfing manoeuvres and positions included ANGLING (tacking across a wave); BACKING OUT (missing a surfable wave); a FLYAWAY was a fast twist out of a wave, TO WALK THE PLANK was to walk up and down the BOARD. A WIPE-OUT was to be smashed on the sea-floor by a wave or suffer some similar disaster involving the loss or destruction of one's surfboard. WIPE-OUT has moved into general colloquial use to some extent, sometimes being used to mean drunk or to refer to a disaster of some kind. This process also saw other surfing terms move — usually only briefly — into the wider Lingo and was made easier by the 1960s surf music fad which produced instrumentals and songs with titles like 'Bombora' (a word in use from at least the 1870s, probably derived from a New South Wales Aboriginal language and meaning a large, often dangerous, wave; HANG FIVE and the unforgettable 'My Blond-Headed, Stompy-Wompy Real Gone Surfer Boy', sung by Patricia Amphlett, then known as 'Little Pattie'.

Other terms referred to the equipment itself. A BIG GUN was a large board; POP-OUTS were mass-produced surfboards, a TOP RACK was the car board rack while a SKEG was a surfboard fin, a term that, by the 1980s, had come to be a generalised insult used in youth-speak. Another word that is in current Lingo is DING then meaning a hole in the fibreglass surface of the board, now referring to a dent in a car or, more generally, to a minor road accident. Various types of SURFIES had names like HIGHWAY SURFER, one who had the board on the roof of the car but never went in the water; a GREMMIE was a learning, usually overconfident surfer; a HEAVY was a girl; a HODAD was a beach bum; and a GIDGET was, and still is, a female surfer, usually with the sexist connotation of ineptitude while a GROMMET is a young or inexperienced surfer.

Clothes are always important items in signalling group membership. Approved SURFIEwear in the 1960s included BAGGIES, long, baggy trunks, usually with a spot of colour; MAZATLANS were sandals sold with tyre treads; PENDLETONS were over-sized, bright wool shirts and a WOODIE was a wood-panelled station wagon (these were soon overtaken by large Holden panel vans known as SIN BINS or SHAGGIN' WAGONS). Faded blue jeans with tight, straight legs were ALL THE GO and hair was blond, preferably bleached with peroxide.

Popular SURFIE magazines provide graphic examples of SURFIE-speak at work, as well as indicating the tensions among various Sydney youth groups from time to time. In these sources we see that Americanisms have become part of the Greater Lingo. Some examples are MOTHER-FUCKER, an Americanism of long standing that we have taken to with some relish since the late 1970s and early 1980s, along with others like SCUMBAGS (US slang for a used condom). Interestingly another Americanism, WIMPS can be combined with a classic Lingoism, GUTLESS, to give a most effective update on the older and still useful GUTLESS WONDER. SLUGGOES are swimming costumes; WESTIES are denizens of Sydney's Western suburbs, and WAXHEADS are SURFIES. More recent surfisms include SICK PITS for well-formed TUBES; SNAPPED for being badly dumped; LEGGIE for a leg-rope; WETTIE for a wetsuit; CRANKING for a very good surf; and A STICK for a surfboard.

In the late-1990s SURFIES are still a distinctive and substantial subgroup in Australian society, their little lingo continuing to evolve and to identify them as different. Unlike most youth groups, SURFIES have survived the toll of generational change, having been with us for almost 40 years. Other youth subgroups have not been so long-lived, often because they are challenged, sometimes to extinction, by new youth groups. SURFIES now have their own nemesis in the form of BOOGERS — that is, bodyboard riders to the rest of us.

BOOGERS are generally in the pre-adolescent age range of 12 to 15, usually, according to SURFIES, gay, and convinced that they have a very COOL lifestyle. Surfers and SURFIES are the sworn enemies of the BOOGERS who refer to those who ride the long boards as

WETBRAINS or STAND-UPS. Unsurprisingly, surfers and SURFIES are similarly disdainful of the bodyboarders, calling their favoured wave vehicles POOL TOYS, SHARK BISCUITS, GUT-SLIDERS, DOORMATS, ESKY-LIDS, and a host of other derogatives. To BOOGERS a good surf is EPIC or GOING OFF while a poor surf is SHAGGY, SICK or MUSHY. Being dumped is CRASHING, an ARS is an air roll spin, a difficult and potentially DEADLY wave manoeuvre, as is a DROP-KNEE LIP LAUNCH. A curved wave, usually known as a TUBE to surfers and SURFIES, is usually a BARREL to BOOGERS.

GAY-SAY

Terms for what has traditionally been considered sexual deviance abound in the Australian vernacular. Bisexuality (AC–DC) and terms for lesbians (DIKE, LEZZO, BUTCH) are well outnumbered by the terms for male homosexuality. While gay has become the accepted mainstream term, the vernacular is still full of other, less positive terms, such as POOFTER, POOF, QUEER, QUEEN, QUINCE, FRUIT, CAT, FAG, FAIRY, PONCE (also meaning PIMP), PUNCE, and the now totally outmoded HOMO.

A number of slightly more colourful terms may also be heard. These include BACK-DOOR MERCHANT, BUM BANDIT, DIP-SHIT, SHIRT-LIFTER, FRECKLE-PUNCHER and PILLOW-BITER. Male homosexuals are particularly well represented in rhyming slang — BAKED BEAN for QUEEN; BUTCHER'S HOOF for POOF and GINGER BEER for QUEER, as in the saying HE'S AS QUEER AS A BEER. QUEER AS A THREE-DOLLAR BILL is one of a number of colloquial similes applied to homosexuality. The number and variety of such derogations is a testament to the deep and abiding homophobia of Australia's masculinist culture. But persisting within this official framework has been a strong tradition of homosexuality, now openly celebrated in such events as Sydney's Gay and Lesbian Mardi Gras, and in many less spectacular events and activities across the nation.

The gay culture, long a clandestine network, by necessity developed a sophisticated little lingo for communication. This includes, though is not limited to, such words as SOD, an abbreviation of sodomite; MOLLY, a term in use at least as early as the 1720s. By the early 19th century the term TOMMY was being used. These terms, like those of the underworld, arrived in Australia from the earliest days where the 'unnatural vice' of homosexuality was thought to be widely practised among convicts. There is no doubt that homosexuality was common in the penal system, though the obsession with it that many administrators and officials of the time seem to have suffered from has probably over-emphasised its importance. Nevertheless, there seems to have been no shortage of terms used either by homo-sexuals themselves and/or by non-homosexuals, such as MISS NANCY (surviving in Lingo as NANCY or NANCY BOY), MARGERY, MARY-ANN, MADGE-CULL and, what was once the great Australian insult, POOFTER.

POOFTER appears to be a genuine Australianism, a Lingo elabora-tion of POOF (from the French *pouf*), first noted in London during the 1830s. As with some other persistent Lingoisms, POOFTER appeared in print first in *Truth* (1903). It has been used with wild abandon in all sorts of creative combinations, such as COMMIE, or COMMO POOFTER BASTARD; POOFTER-RORTING to describe homosexu-al procuring, and that unhappy proof of our inability to cope with difference, POOFTER-BASHING. So vile an insult is POOFTER that the term is also used to describe those who indulge in artistic or intellec-tual pastimes, regardless of their sexual orientation. As an overall description of those things the Lingoist finds beyond the pale, the catch-alls POOFTERISM and POOFTERISH are available.

Later in the19th century came the term GUSSIE and the 20th cen-tury has contributed many more, such as POONCE (from Yiddish), TRISS, CAT (perhaps a shortening of a more or less polite 19th-centu-ry term for homosexuals, catamite, though CAT may also be used as Lingo for a prostitute). QUINCE, used in such phrases as YOU'RE GET-TING ON MY QUINCE, indicating irritation, is also one of many Lingo words for the posterior or anus. This probably explains why it is also applied to homosexuals. A MARS BAR is apparently police slang for a homosexual male.

This hardly exhausts the terms used to describe homosexuals in Lingo, all of which are unrelievedly pejorative and include, but are not restricted to: DUNG-PUNCHER/PUSHER; POO-JABBER; POO-JAM-MER; POO-PUNCHER; POO-PUSHER; POO-SHOOTER; POO-STABBER; TURD-TAPPER; TURD-PACKER; DOUGHNUT-PUNCHER; FRECKLE-PUNCHER; CHOCOLATE-PUNCHER; ARSE-BANDIT; BUM-BANDIT; POO-PIRATE; TURD-BURGLAR; WINDJAMMER; PILLOW-BITER, and FAG. Related usages are to RIDE THE TAN TRACK; DIRT-TRACK RIDER; RIDE THE CHOCOLATE CANYON, and to DRILL FOR VEGEMITE. Then there are rhyming slang terms, and others already mentioned. I'LL BET HE PASSES COUNTER-SUNK TURDS may sometimes be observed of a gay man.

Non-heterosexual practices also feature in the broader Lingo, as in sayings like HE DOESN'T MIND WHETHER HE USES THE FRONT DOOR OR THE TRADESMAN'S ENTRANCE (said of a bisexual), the anus is referred to as the TAN TRACK or the USED FRUIT CHUTE, a FAG-HAG (from the USA) is a woman who associates with gays.

Well established by the 1940s, the term CAMP to describe a homo-sexual is uniquely Lingo. CAMP is an effeminate man, not necessarily homosexual. A notable lingoism using this term is CAMP AS A ROW OF (PINK) TENTS. Australian homosexuals used CAMP to describe them-selves up to the 1970s when the current GAY began to be used in its place. It has been suggested that GAY originated in Australia during the mid-1920s, and it was used during World War II as an AIF term for officers (HOCK was the AIF term for homosexual at that time), though it seems more likely to have been borrowed from US slang.

There are far fewer terms in Lingo for lesbians. These include LES, LEZZO, DIKE and reportedly in use among youths and lesbians, LEMON. FEMME and BUTCH are also used, though they are not restricted to Australia. Baker claims that CHARLIE (presumably from CHARLIE WHEEL-ER, SHEILA) and LOVER UNDER THE LAP, were also used for lesbians.

Many, though not all, of these terms are used by homosexuals themselves in the same way that Jewish people turn anti-Semitism back on the prejudiced by incorporating it into their humour. But the little lingo of homosexuality is as broad and as diverse as that of any other lifestyle or occupational group. The term SQUARE, for example, was once widely used in an extension of its more general colonial sense of legal, to indicate that the person so-described was not homosexual or STRAIGHT in current parlance. A BOY (MARK FOY in rhyming slang) was a young sexual partner, often shortened to MARK. An ASPRO was a term for a male prostitute derived from ARSE PRO (ARSE prostitute) and in Sydney during the 1940 such persons were reportedly known as COLLEGE STREET SOLICITORS. TO DO THE BEAT is TO CRUISE an area in search of sexual partners, also called a TRADE, while BOG was original-ly a GAY term for toilet, though it is now a general colloquialism. LILY is the police and TBH is an abbreviation of TO BE HAD, meaning that someone is sexually available. NTBH means they are not. ROSELEAFING is a GAY term for a form of oral sex usually termed RIMMING in straight Lingo. In the later 1990s Perth GAYS refer to suburbanites as BREED-ERS and the places where they live as BREEDER-BELTS.

Any joining together of humans to take part in a common activ-ity soon generates a sense of shared purpose. One of the first fruits of this is the growth of a distinctive language used and understood only by the members of the group. Whether these groups are leisure groups, age groups, even gender groups, their lifestyles will be dis-tinctive in one or more ways and these distinctions, these essential differences, will be reflected in their little lingoes. The examples in this chapter have been no more than a selection of these innumerable little lingoes that exist in even such a small national population as Australia's. Nevertheless, it has hopefully given the reader some idea of the richness and inventiveness of those who speak the lingo, their own, as well as that spoken in the broader community.

7

DISHING IT OUT:
BLOKES, BOOZE AND
BAD LANGUAGE

The class of female under notice has, to use an Australianism, a
chiv as tough as the rear end of a native bear, and a
hide like a dugong.

TRUTH, 20 APRIL 1902

Even the most casual survey of the vernacular will confirm both the muscular virility of the vocabulary and its strongly male orientation. Oaths, imprecations, maledictions, curses, insults, invective, vulgarities and associated abuse form a significant portion of the Lingo. A statistical glance quickly reveals that somewhere approaching 20% to 25% of Lingoisms are some kind of insult or negative. Traditionally, and still to a large extent it seems, men have been the main hurlers of these insults, a form of verbal violence mirroring the physical violence implicit in masculinism, especially in its Australian forms of mates and BLOKES. This masculinism is intimately connected with the use of Lingo with alcohol, with insult, with sexism, and with general crudity that many have found vulgar and offensive. In spite of this, or more probably because of it, Australian men in particular continue to wield the Lingo in the traditional manner, notwithstanding the rise of the SNAG (see below) and political correctness.

Before looking in a little more detail at these aspects of Lingo and national character it is as well to point out that misogyny, homophobia, racism, and invective are neither uniquely Australian, nor especially obnoxious here. All these can be found in abundance in the vernaculars of other cultures and nations. Australians have a tendency to believe the worst about themselves, and even to take a perverse pride in shortcomings real and imagined, a trait noted in the 1950s by the literary historian A.A. Phillips in coining the term cultural cringe. Once the cringe caught on, it became something of a self-fulfilling prophecy. In the 1990s especially, we have excoriated ourselves to a slightly odd frenzy about these matters to the point where almost any acknowledgment of difference is likely to be howled down with charges of racism, homophobia, or sexism.

So prevalent have these masculinist terms become that they have been largely drained of their meaning. Aboriginal leader Noel Pearson's 1997 accusation that the Howard Government were 'racist scum'— soon withdrawn — could only be a high-profile public utterance in a culture where the grave significance of the term racism had become severely devalued by both overuse and inappropriate application. This is not to say that racism is not a serious and institutionalised problem here, only that the term has been so readily hurled at those who have begged, even if only slightly, to differ, that it is now no more than a common rhetorical device. The term sexist has suffered a similar fate and homophobia is following fast behind. (A similar thing happened to the term fascist after the 1960s.) Firing off all the big linguistic guns has EMPTIED THE SHOT-LOCKER and left us without much of an armoury for sophisticated verbal duelling. This defeat of semantic clout at the level of official discourse has sharpened an already extensive tradition of colloquial speech that combines masculinism, misogyny, physical violence and verbal abuse in a characteristically Australian way.

BLOKES

BLOKE is an intriguing term that illustrates both the longevity and the flexibility of Australian folk speech. As already noted, BLOKE was originally a cant or FLASH term derived from the 18th-century British underworld and was well established in convict and general underworld parlance here from the earliest days of settlement. It meant then a male, often a gentleman and often the target of criminal activity, especially pickpocketing. From this usage it seems to have expanded into a catch-all term for a male person in which sense it is also still used in Britain.

C.J. Dennis made effective and defining use of the word BLOKE in his 1915 classic *The Songs of a Sentimental Bloke* and ever since then the word has had an affectionate place in the Lingo, strongly influenced by popular notions of Australian egalitarianism. Someone is A GOOD BLOKE, A FAIR DINKUM BLOKE or A DECENT BLOKE, never a BASTARD BLOKE, or a BAD BLOKE.

But BLOKE does have another meaning that is quite at odds with its egalitarianism. THE BLOKE is also a term for the boss or the leader of a group, sometimes the proprietor of a business. Especially in the country, someone wishing to speak to the person in charge would ask to SEE THE BLOKE, an Australian adaptation of naval slang for the commander of a ship. The word has been in use in this sense since at least the 1840s, providing another instance of the flexibility, or just plain perversity of Lingo. Nevertheless, even in this usage, the term is unequivocally male, denoting authority in a male-centred society.

Closely associated with the ethos of the BLOKE is aggression and violence. Violence is an inescapable element of Australian masculinism. Many examples of this have been cited elsewhere in this book, including STOUSH, BLUE, IT'S ON and IT'S ON FOR YOUNG AND OLD, among others. Another lingoism associated with violence is the term KING HIT. This first punches its way into print during World War I but was, according to Sidney Baker, being spoken and delivered for some time before as an item of LARRIKINese. Definitions and some usages of the term refer to a KING HIT as a pre-emptive punch or blow, often an unfair or unexpected one. While this may be so, the term is used of a type of blow involving the clenching of the assailant's hands into a club of hard flesh that is brought down on the unfortunate receiver's face or upper back. (It is interesting to note in this context that periods of institutionalised aggression, otherwise known as wars, have generated a sizeable component of the Lingo, as detailed in chapter 4.) More terms concerned with the pugilistic include to KNUCKLE, as in TO KNUCKLE SOMEONE, a FIVE-FINGER SANDWICH, and to be STONKERED or to be DECKED, as in I SHOULD'VE DECKED THE BASTARD, DECK being another Americanism that we have made our own. (Though DECK or DECKO meaning to look does seem to be one of ours.)

Many insults, often the most deadly, refer exclusively to men and are most frequently delivered by men. Insults are discussed in more detail in chapter 10, but a few of the more torrid examples serve to make the point here: FUCKWIT, DICKHEAD, CUNT (earliest reference in English was in AD1230 in the name of a London street — Gropecuntlane where the c-word had clearly not begun its descent to the bottom of the Lingo ladder) and the even more serious DEAD CUNT, applied to an undesirable, often malevolent, male. The rhyming slang terms DROP-KICK — PRICK, DROP-KICK AND PUNT — CUNT and the relatively recent DIP-STICK (DIP-SHIT is a common variant) which is also rhyming slang for PRICK (as is DROP-KICK), can be used by themselves as fairly grievous male insults.

Australian men also have a sizeable swag of misogynistic terms for insulting the opposite sex. A plain woman may be described as

A BUSH PIG or, if unusually ugly, A BUSH PIG FROM HELL. The British term for a lewd, slovenly woman or a prostitute, SCRUBBER, probably borrowed from the many British police shows on Australian television, is also in use here. A selection of other misogynisms would include the predictable and often venerable SLUT, BITCH, SLAG, BIKE, ROOT (as a noun, and also now used in this sense by women of men), and many more. A frequently encountered form of male-to-male abuse attributes femininity to the other man as in DON'T BE A GIRL'S BLOUSE (SISSY) or DON'T BE A BIG GIRL'S BLOUSE. Often just the term GIRL, uttered with a contemptuous curl of the lip, will be sufficient to invite a BLOKE to GO BERKO and perhaps LAY ONE ON YOU; anything to avoid the suspicion that his wife or other female companion HAS HIS BALLS IN HER PURSE.

Accompanying insult is the proliferation of Lingo terms for male and female reproductive organs, together with the mostly male deployment of such terms as insults as well as vulgar descriptors. Male and female genitalia are the source of many colloquial terms (see 'The Vernacular Body'). Some of these are simply slang for the various parts of the human anatomy associated with reproduction, defecation and urination. Most people know the most common of these words. Far more interesting are the broader uses to which many of the terms for our privates are put.

BALLS! is an expression of distaste or disbelief while a BALLS-UP is an organisational failure, as in THE BIGGEST BALLS-UP SINCE KING KONG FLOATED UNDER THE HARBOUR BRIDGE ON HIS BACK. Such an event would STICK OUT LIKE DOGS' BALLS, being especially noticeable or obvious. BOLLOCKS is another term for BALLS, especially favoured in Britain, though also used here, as there, in the phrase TO GET A RIGHT BOLLOCKING, meaning to be severely reprimanded or to lose out especially badly. KNACKERS are also testicles, though the word is frequently employed in a negative sense to mean exhausted, worn-out, or simply beaten. A COCK is one of many terms for penis and is also used as a derisive term for someone considered to be a fool or in some way incompetent. Not surprisingly its application is restricted to males. Closely related is the term COCK-UP— an organisational failure, as in THEY COULDN'T ORGANISE A COCK-UP IN A BROTHEL. Another term for penis is DICK which may also be used as a male insult , often as DICKHEAD, and something no longer useful or broken may be said to have HAD THE DICK, or more politely, to have HAD THE RICHARD.

Vernacular aggression is not limited to the verbal. There is also an extensive Lingo of signs. This consists of various signals made by the body and in Anglo-Celtic Australia, at least, is almost totally restricted to gestures of the hand. In the 1950s the perpendicular thumb meant GET FUCKED. This was gradually replaced during the 1960s and 1970s by the V sign made with the index finger and the middle finger. Since the 1980s, though, the single vertical digit has been used much more. The SCREW YOU sign is another 'brutish imported Americanism', as one disgruntled (male) letter-writer wrote in the *Weekend Australian* in May 1996 and, like many other lamented importations, is widely used by the community.

The dominance of BLOKE with its characteristic combination of aggression, attachment to the physical, to gambling and to strong drink, has occasionally been challenged. Sometime during the late 1960s and early 1970s a term long used in Australia as a nickname abbreviation for Oscar became the descriptor for the crude, GROG-SODDEN, BEER-GUTTED sort of BLOKE who lived next door. The OCKER is generally said to have obtruded himself into public view through the popular satirical television series 'The Mavis Bramston Show' (1965–68) in the form of a character played by the late Ron Frazer. By the early 1970s OCKER was threatening BLOKE as a central Lingoism and was being celebrated in a range of Australian films, such as *Stork*, *Alvin Purple* and *The Adventures of Barry MacKenzie*, as well as in sundry other cultural forms, including the plays of David Williamson, like *Don's Party* and *The Removalists*. The popularity and all-encompassing nature of this new blokism, almost forgotten today, can be glimpsed in the rapidity with which the term spread and the number of variant forms it produced — OCK, of course; OCKERISM; OCKERDOM; OCKERINA (a female OCKER) and even OCKERISED. National treasure Phillip Adams in one of his earlier incarnations as an AD MAN, latched onto this Lingoism and its connotations for a fitness campaign on behalf of the Victorian Government in 1975. The cartoon character NORM was created as a televisual representation of the essential OCKER in an attempt to show unfit, beer-swilling males how repulsive they looked. Unfortunately, the campaign seems to have backfired somewhat as NORM quickly became a generic Lingo term for unfit BLOKES, used and worn with a certain degree of perverse pride by the very people it was supposed to make aware of their physical shortcomings. Both OCKER and NORM are not much heard today, though the BLOKES wearing thongs, stubbies™ and singlet, pulling on A COLDIE seem as prevalent as ever, even despite that more recent challenge of the SENSITIVE NEW AGE GUY, or SNAG.

A similar term to OCKER is — or was — ALF, a derogatory abbreviation of the male forename, Alfred. Popular in the 1960s and 1970s with much the same generic clout as OCKER, the oafish ALF seems to have slumped into sullen silence, another casualty of generational change.

CRUDE, RUDE AND LEWD

Speakers of English have long been notable users of bad language. It was complained of and proscribed (well, the Puritans tried to silence it) centuries before any speaker of the language sighted these shores and has been condemned with regularity ever since. Australian English seems to have inherited this linguistic trait and to have extended and refined its range and deployment. Crudity, rudeness and straightforward obscenity are the single element of our vernacular most frequently decried by critics. They generally argue that slang, colloquialisms, the vernacular, the informal language of everyday life, is clichéd and, therefore, empty of meaning. What a load of garbage! We certainly make full use of slang in all its forms, particularly that of swearing, but our speech contains subtleties of usage and implication that show such criticisms to be inaccurate.

Take SHIT, for example. Apart from its fundamental usage as a term for faeces, the word SHIT can be deployed in a variety of ways to convey a multitude of meanings, either by itself or in combination with other words. SHIT can be used simply as an expression of disgust or despair, as in SHIT! or to describe something or someone considered inferior or unpleasant, as in THAT'S SHIT, or HE'S A SHIT. It can be used as an adjective, as in WHAT A SHITTY JOB. It can be used in a variety of creative combinations, such as SCARED SHITLESS; SHIT ME DEAD; SHIT IT IN; SHITHEAD; SHITKICKER; SHITHOUSE; SHIT-HEAP, or the discomfiting SHIT A BRICK! It can describe one's mood — SHE'S GOT A SHITTY ON, having SHIT ON THE LIVER, a condition graphically visualised in these lines referring to the boss from the sugar cane-cutting folk song 'The Cane Cutter's Lament':

> *I'll never cut cane for that bastard again*
> *On the banks of the Isis River.*
> *The cane was bad, the cutters were mad*
> *And the cook had shit on the liver.*

The term SHIT can refer to one's condition in relation to alcohol consumption, as in SHIT-FACED. BULLSHIT and THAT'S A LOAD/BUCKET/CROCK OF SHIT are common terms for lying or skiting, as is BULLSHIT ARTIST, or simply BULLSHITTER (sometimes euphemised to BULLSHIFTER) to describe one who is speaking lies and/or nonsense. A related usage is DON'T SHIT ME, to indicate that the speaker believes he or she is being told an untruth of some kind.

SHIT also features in some of our most creative colloquial combinations, such as the now sadly little-heard SHITS WERE TRUMPS, an indication of great fear; UGLY AS A SHITHOUSE RAT and BUILT LIKE A BRICK SHITHOUSE. A task of great difficulty may be described as PUSHING SHIT UPHILL WITH A SHARP STICK. One can be UP THE SHIT and UP SHIT CREEK (see Up below), often WITHOUT A PADDLE, both expressions indicating despair and failure. One may just have SHIT FOR BRAINS or be quite ignorant and KNOW JACK-SHIT. Simple disorganisation is covered in ALL OVER THE PLACE LIKE A MAD WOMAN'S SHIT.

While these, and the following crudities, are hardly the sole preserve of BLOKES, it is still men who make the most use of them. Even in these linguistically liberated times when women are entitled, able, and encouraged to swear, the traditional reluctance of men to swear in front of a woman ensures that use of this language is still largely heard in male company. When a male does transgress, his fellows are likely to remonstrate with such embarrassed phrases as STEADY ON and BREAK IT DOWN, FELLA.

Following is a selection of vulgarisms, together with some observations on their characteristics and usage.

ARSE, ARSEHOLE

One may GET THE ARSE or THE BIG A — that is lose one's job or position as in THEY WIPED ME LIKE A DIRTY ARSE. Equally unfortunate is the person who GETS IT IN THE ARSE, an indication that he or she has been badly served. ARSE may be licked, as in ARSE-LICKER, kicked, as in ARSE-KICKER or kissed as in KISS MY ARSE, an expression of refusal. An ARSEACHE, of course is A PAIN IN THE ARSE. One may also be AN ARSEHOLE, a RIGHT ARSEHOLE (especially if one is a boss), a SMART-ARSE or simply AN ARSE. This meaning is extended in colourful comparisons, such as HE WASN'T A MUSICIAN'S (or whatever's) ARSEHOLE, an expression of contempt for the abilities of the person so described.

Then there are various other applications, such as SLACK-ARSE, to describe someone who is SLACK or negligent; SILLY-ARSE, for someone foolish. The SHORT-ARSE is a person of small stature; the TEAR-ARSE, one who cares little about the consequences of his or her actions, and the FART-ARSE, one who FART-ARSES ABOUT very busily but gets nowhere. A TIGHT-ARSE is a parsimonious person, often described as being TIGHT AS A FISH'S ARSEHOLE. One's TASTE MAY BE IN ONE'S ARSEHOLE or one may be unfortunate enough to reside IN THE ARSEHOLE OF THE WORLD, or even of the universe (sometimes said to refer to Canberra, pronounced 'Canbra', and popularly considered a reality vacuum).

A disorganised situation may be described as being FROM ARSEHOLE TO BREAKFAST and one may also be KNOCKED OR KICKED FROM ARSEHOLE TO BREAKFAST in certain unfortunate circumstances.

Strong disagreement can be articulated directly with IN A PIG'S ARSE (more economically, simply as PIGS), IN YOUR ARSE or, more uncomfortably still, UP YOUR ARSE. And it is always quite possible to uselessly RUN/BUZZ AROUND LIKE A BLUE-ARSED FLY, or to have AS MUCH RIGHT OF WAY AS A HATFUL OF ARSEHOLES WALKING DOWN THE STREET — BACKWARDS. A person may also be in such great need of liquid as to be DRIER THAN A SANDGROPER'S ARSEHOLE (very dry, indeed), or to HAVE YOUR TEETH PUNCHED SO FAR DOWN YOUR THROAT THAT YOU'LL HAVE TO CLEAN THEM THROUGH YOUR ARSE.

Someone in straitened circumstances may be ON THE BONES OF THEIR ARSE or RAGGY-ARSED and may be so cheeky as to be described as having MORE ARSE (cheek) THAN A PADDOCK-FULL OF COWS. On the brighter side, though, the SUN MAY SHINE OUT OF ONE'S ARSEHOLE, or one may think that it does. If one is inclined to such self-delusion it is likely that he or she will frequently find themselves falling ARSE OVER TIT. Lastly, it is always possible for someone or something to DIE IN THE ARSE.

BASTARD

The TRAPS FOR NEW PLAYERS involved in the use of this essentially Australian Lingoism are enough to drive the uninitiated insane. As mentioned earlier, when US troops arrived in force here during World War II it was found necessary to provide them with a detailed printed explanation of the finer points of bastardry. No doubt the Americans got themselves into linguistic HOT WATER anyway, which is hardly surprising given the subtleties involved in the deployment of this beloved crudity that we also share to some extent with the British.

An OLD BASTARD; ME OLD BASTARD MATE; SILLY BASTARD; MAD BASTARD, and similar phrases are expressions of (sometimes conditional) approval and affection. But when combined with ROTTEN, MEAN, LOUSY, they become terms of strong disapproval. A RIGHT, BASTARD and A REAL BASTARD are deeply felt insults, only made more vehement by such accretions as DIRTY, STINKING, LOWDOWN BASTARD, and the like. Something unpleasant or unexpected may be A BASTARD; POOR BASTARD is a genuine expression of sympathy while to be as HAPPY AS A BASTARD ON FATHER'S DAY is to be not very happy at all.

BUGGER

Additional to its use as a slang term for one who BUGGERS, BUGGER may also be an expression of annoyance, as in BUGGER IT, BUGGER ME, a term of dismissal, as in BUGGER OFF or GO TO BUGGERY and a reference to lack, as in BUGGER ALL. I'LL BE BUGGERED is an exclamation of surprise that can also be used to express unwillingness to do something, as in I'LL BE BUGGERED IF I'M GOING TO DO THAT, or BUGGER THAT FOR A GAME OF TOY SOLDIERS — an indication that the speaker does not, or did not, wish to participate in a particular activity. One may BANG LIKE A BUGGERED TAPPET, describing excessive fornication or be OUT TO BUGGERY, meaning a long way off the mark or a long way out. Finally, someone or something may be simply BUGGERED — no good for anything at all or simply A SILLY OLD BUGGER.

PISS

This is a word of wondrous simplicity, encompassing in four letters a vast range of possible applications. These range from the basic, or root vernacular meaning of urine (PISS), the act of urinating (PISSING) to the hydraulically related terms for alcohol (PISS) and its effects (PISSED). Extending the latter connotations of the word, the Lingoist has available the following: PISSED AS A FART; PISSED AS A NEWT; PISSED AS A PARROT. It is also possible to be PISSED TO THE EYEBALLS, that is, to be extremely inebriated. One who frequently attains these states may be known as a PISS-ARTIST, or a PISS-POT (which was, in 18th-century English, a term for doctor). The fluid associations of this term are also continued in describing heavy rain as PISSING DOWN.

But these urinary and alcoholic references are not the end of this term's colloquial convenience. One who proceeds without aim or organisation, or with insufficient sense of responsibility may be said to be PISSING ABOUT. Something described as PISS-POOR, PISS-WEAK or PISSY (as in A PISSY LITTLE THING) is thought to be of inferior quality or intestinal fortitude while one who is FULL OF PISS AND WIND is indeed void of content. A person who is PISSING INTO THE WIND will achieve little other than an unpleasant shower.

PISS is also useful to suggest actions, as in PISS OFF, and to describe emotional states, as in PISSED OFF. It may be applied in terms indicating contempt, such as YOU WOULDN'T PISS ON HIM IF HE WAS ON FIRE and NOT WORTH A PINCH OF PISS or, more colourfully, NOT WORTH A PINCH OF CAT'S PISS.

Some peculiarities of PISS are difficult to account for. Why PISSING IN SOMEONE'S POCKET should be a means of currying favour remains mysterious. If this or any other action, however, is easily accomplished, it is A PIECE OF PISS.

These are not the end of this word's vernacular utility, of course. The Lingo is continually inventing new convolutions and permutations and as more than enough has been said on this PISS-ANT subject it is clearly time to PISS OR GET OFF THE POT.

By definition, Lingoisms related to sexual activity are crude, rude and lewd, at least to some people. But there are so many words and phrases available in regard to matters sexual that the subject requires at least a little discussion of its own. The slang terms available to describe sexual intercourse are almost as numerous as those related to alcohol and include: ROOT; SCREW; FUCK; NAUGHTY; NOOKIE; GIVE HER ONE; DIP YOUR WICK, PUT LEAD IN YOUR PENCIL; GET IT UP; HAVE IT AWAY (also a Britishism), and so on and on. To BONK, apparently a coy creation of the tabloid press, has become popular with youth in the 1990s, a term with a refreshing tone of breezy informality that contrasts strongly with the perjorative nature of many older terms for HORIZONTAL FOLK DANCING.

Beyond the general Lingoisms for masturbation, such as STROP-PING and WANKING, this act seems to inspire us to poetry — well, rhyme at least — JERKIN THE GHERKIN; RUB THE GRUB; TUG THE SLUG; BEAT THE MEAT and PUNCHIN' THE TRUNCHEON, are all descriptions of male masturbation. PULLING THE PUD fails the rhyme test, but presumably persists through alliteration. Cunnilingus of various kinds may be referred to as A SIXTY-NINER; A FURBURGER; TO GO DOWN, and MUFF-DIVING. Fellatio is MUNCHIN' THE TRUNCHEON, but may be also referred to as BLUE-VEIN SALAMI. Many of these rhymes are shared with US and British usage.

DON'T GIVE A CONTINENTAL is said by some dictionaries to be derived from the name for paper money issued during the War of Independence by the American Continental Congress and so, to the British at least, worthless. But this almost obsolete phrase is much more likely to be a polite form of DON'T GIVE A FUCK, deriving from the reputation of the Continent for liberated, even excessive sexual behaviour. In other words, much the same folk reasoning as lies behind the term FRENCH LETTER for a condom. (The French call them English letters, by the way). In Lingo, condoms are FRANGERS; FRENCHIES; SPORTING EQUIPMENT; FROGS; WINTER TREAD; RUBBERS; A GLOVE; A WET CHECK (presumably derived from the proprietary name 'Wet Chex'), WET SUIT; RAINCOAT, and FANTASTIC PLASTIC.

An unusual formation parodies the proverb TOO MANY COOKS SPOIL THE BROTH — TOO MANY COCKS SPOIL THE BROTHEL. These are only some of the Lingoisms related to sexual activity, but the point would seem to have been made and is a useful introduction to a discussion of the closely related forms of the vernacular insult.

GALAHS AND DRONGOES

Ned Kelly may not have invented insults, but he definitely knew how to dish them out when he described the Victoria Police in his Jerilderie Letter as: '...a parcel of big, ugly, fat-necked, big-bellied, magpie-legged, narrow-hipped, splay-footed sons of Irish bailiffs or English landlords...'. Kelly was speaking squarely within a powerful Australian cultural tradition.

One of the great joys of the Australian SLANGUAGE (probably coined by W.T. Goodge) is the colour and variety of insults available. If someone CALLS YOU ALL KINDS OF A BASTARD you have been roundly and soundly abused. Expressions of verbal malice may range from the mildly disparaging to the outrageously insulting. Depending on the degree of exasperation engendered in the speaker, an offender may be described as a DUFFER (very mild, even affectionate) or a FUCKWIT (fairly serious insult). In between lies an enormous and subtly graded range of possibilities that include the following: ARSEACHE; ARSEHOLE; BOOFHEAD; BUSH PIG; CLOWN; CRAWLER; DEAD LOSS; DEAD HEAD; DERRO; DICK; DICKHEAD; DRONGO; FACE-ACHE; GALAH; PAIN IN THE NECK/ARSE, or simply, A PAIN; POON; PRAT; PRAWN; PRICK; RIGHT BASTARD; SHITHEAD; SHIT FOR BRAINS; SILLY ARSE; TWAT and WANKER. Late 1980s additions to this list include SPACE CADET, someone who acts oddly and WUSS (WUSSIE), someone who is considered weak or reluctant, much like another Americanism that we have adopted, WIMP.

One classic Lingoism in this category is NONG, a shortened form of NING-NONG, derived from British dialect form 'ning nang', meaning a fool. NONG seems to have burst into general usage during World War II and continues to do good service as a useful expression of doubt about a person's mental ability.

Not only is there a great range of available insults that express the magnitude of the stupidity or wrongdoing, but there are also subtle gradations in the types of stupidity, thoughtlessness, hopelessness, incapacity and sheer ineptitude that may come in for verbal censure. A person may be: A FEW BOB SHORT OF THE POUND; A GUTLESS WONDER; A HOPELESS CASE/CAUSE; A MONGREL; A MUG; A NERD; ALL OVER THE PLACE LIKE A MAD WOMAN'S KNITTING; AS MUCH USE AS TITS ON A NUN; AS POPULAR AS A TURD IN THE FRUIT SALAD; FULL OF IT (BULLSHIT, that is); FURTHER BEHIND THAN WALLA-WALLA; HOPELESS; LOWER THAN A SNAKE'S BELLY and LOWER THAN A SNAKE'S BELLY IN A WHEEL RUT; MAD AS A MEAT-AXE; NOT IN THE RACE; NOT THE FULL QUID; NOT WORTH A BUMPER; OFF HIS/HER TROLLEY; OUT OF IT; RUNNING ROUND LIKE A CHOOK WITH ITS HEAD CUT OFF; SILLY AS A CUT SNAKE; SILLY AS A TWO-BOB WATCH; SLOW AS A WET WICK; SLOW AS THE SECOND COMING; THICK AS PIG SHIT; TROPPO; UGLY AS A HATFUL OF ARSEHOLES; UGLY AS A SHITHOUSE RAT; UP HIM/HER SELF; WITH THE BIRDIES; WITHOUT A CLUE and MAD AS A GUM-TREE FULL OF GALAHS...

And THAT'S JUST FOR STARTERS: a person may also be described as having: a SCREW LOOSE; BELLY RASH (from crawling to the boss);

having COME DOWN IN THE LAST SHOWER; DIED IN THE ARSE; KANGA-
ROOS IN THE TOP PADDOCK; A SMELL LIKE A GREEK WRESTLER'S JOCK-
STRAP, or AN AFGHAN CAMEL-DRIVER'S ARMPIT. Additionally, one may
be simply totally beyond redemption, as in these less than flattering
comparisons and descriptions: COULDN'T FIGHT HIS WAY OUT OF A
BROWN PAPER BAG; COULDN'T ORGANISE A COCK-UP IN A BROTHEL;
WENT OVER LIKE A LEAD BALLOON; IF BRAINS WERE MADE OF DYNAMITE
YOU WOULDN'T HAVE ENOUGH TO BLOW YOUR HEAD OFF; IF BRAINS
WERE MADE OF ELASTIC YOU WOULDN'T HAVE ENOUGH TO MAKE A
GARTER FOR A CANARY'S LEG; COULDN'T GET A JOB ON A SHITHOUSE
CART; WOULDN'T GET A KICK IN A FIGHT; WOULDN'T KNOW A BRASS
BAND WAS UP HER/HIM UNTIL THE BASS DRUM WAS BLOWING IN
HIS/HER EAR or WOULDN'T KNOW IF HE WAS ARTHUR OR MARTHA.

Even such a simple basic term as silly can be used in a number of
combinations expressing subtle gradations of insult. 'Silly', an excellent old English word originally meaning simple, still retains some
sense of this in its various applications, such as IT KNOCKED ME SILLY,
indicating amazement and incredulity, and the affectionate and mild
chastisements like SILLY-BILLY and the slightly more cutting SILLY BAS-
TARD. The word also appears in a number of insulting Lingoisms,
such as SILLY AS A BRUSH; SILLY AS A CHOOK WITH ITS HEAD CUT OFF;
SILLY AS A CUT SNAKE; SILLY AS A HATFUL OF ARSEHOLES (WALKING
DOWN PITT STREET BACKWARDS WITH THEIR SHOES OFF); SILLY AS A
TWO-BOB WATCH, SILLY AS A WET WEEKEND, and TO PLAY SILLY BUG-
GERS, meaning to avoid reality, procrastinate, or treat something in
an unduly frivolous manner. Then there is the simple, but effective,
SILLY ARSE, capable of being applied in a wide variety of circumstances
with minimal offence.

These are only some of the many insults available to the discerning speaker of the Lingo. Related closely to insults are other negative
aspects of our informal speech, particularly terms concerned with
inefficiency, obsolescence, failure, and uselessness. These include,
though are certainly not limited to: ALSO-RAN; CACTUS; CROOK; GONE
TO BUGGERY; GONE TO GOWINGS; GORMLESS; KNACKERED; NOT IN THE
RACE, RATSHIT; ROOTED; SCREWED, STUFFED and OXYGEN THIEF, one
who is A WASTE OF SPACE.

DRONGO, a very Australian insult, was the name of a racehorse of
the mid-1920s. Named after an Australian bird (*Chibea bracteatus*),
commonly known as the DRONGO, the four-legged version was totally unable to win a race. This prolonged ineptitude was so spectacular
that punters began to refer to any horses that failed to win (rather a
lot) as a DRONGO. The term spread very quickly from this racegoers'
little lingo into the Great Australian Lingo. So apt has the word been

for describing monumental uselessness and stupidity that there is a whole cycle of folk tales about the drongo, usually involving the Drongo's comic misunderstandings of instructions from the boss, as in the following example:

> One mornin' the boss asks the Drongo to hang a new gate on the barn. Off goes the Drongo with 'is tools and the gate. Come lunchtime 'e 'asn't been sighted, so we went out to look for 'im. We found 'im standin' by the dam. The boss was 'oppin' mad. 'What do you think your doin'? I told you to hang that gate!'
> 'Sorry, boss', says the Drongo. 'I couldn't find no tree ter' hang it on, so I drowned the bastard.'

BLOODY, BLOODY, BLOODY

No account of the Lingo would be complete without some consideration of 'the great Australian adjective', a term that is probably a *Bulletin* coinage of the 1890s. BLOODY has earned its reputation as characteristically Australian through long and comprehensive study by all manner of experts and would-be experts. While Australians certainly use the term with great frequency it is also the most commonly heard term in British slang (though the f-word seems to be rapidly gaining there) and is hardly silent in US slang, or in that of other English-speaking nations. Indeed, if Hollywood films of the last few years are any indication, the Americans are now barely capable of uttering a sentence without recourse to at least one FUCK. Movies, of course, are pure fantasy.

BLOODY was early established as the colonial oath of preference. Alexander Marjoribanks, travelling in Australia in the 1840s noted that it was 'the favourite oath' and that 'One may tell you that he married a bloody young wife, another, a bloody old one; and a bushranger will call out "Stop, or I'll blow your bloody brains out."' Marjoribanks, a keen observer and listener, also heard a BULLOCKY punctuate the air with 25 BLOODIES in 15 minutes, calculating that, at this rate the bullocky would use BLOODY around 18.2 million times in his life. Here, as in the vast majority of accounts, BLOODY is explicitly or implicitly spoken by males.

The reputation of our national expletive also has a lot to do with its celebration in verse by a number of popular — male — poets. W. T. Goodge first put BLOODY to paper (actually 'blanks' rather than the word itself) in his 1899 classic 'The Great Australian Adjective'. This poem, with its opening lines: 'The sunburnt _____ stockman stood/And in a dismal _____ mood,/ Apostrophised his _____ cuddy;/ The _____ nag's no _____ good . . .' was, and still is well known, even in the British army as Robert Graves noted in his little-known 1930s study of bad language, *Lars Porsena, or The Future of Swearing and Improper Language*. Goodge did at least one later version of 'The Great Australian Adjective', referring to George Reid and Alfred Deakin, political leaders of the early years of Federation. Not quite as good as the original, these lines deserve quoting again as they reflect what many Australians still think about politicians as matters Constitutional come again to the fore:

> *This Mister_____ G.H. Reid*
> *And Mister_____ Deakin*
> *Are not too_____ slow indeed*
> *They're _____ good at speakin'.*
> *They're talking every _____ night*
> *At various _____ places,*
> *I'd sooner see a _____ fight*
> *Out at the _____ races.*

Goodge's inspiration was followed up even more influentially by C.J. Dennis who produced in 1909 'The Australaise', much to the delight of the Australian troops who were occasionally heard to use such terms, as the Gallipoli poem quoted in chapter 4 suggests.

When large numbers of Australians toured Europe from 1915–19, their allies were able to listen to their speech habits at close quarters and to make observations upon colonial ways. The poet John Masefield, then a war correspondent for British newspapers, wrote home to his wife an apocryphal, but revealing, anecdote. According to Masefield, an Australian patrol entered the strategically important town of Bapaume in early 1917 only to find it empty of *Boche*, as the Germans were often called then. The officer in charge of the patrol reported back to his colonel:

> *'They've hopped the bloody twig. They're out of it.'*
> *Colonel: 'Who? The Boche? Out of Bapaume?'*
> *Officer: 'Yes, the bloody place is empty.'*
> *Colonel: 'You're a bloody liar.'*
> *Officer: 'Bloody liar be damned. You give me the bloody battalion and I'll take the bloody place right now!'*

Masefield, who lamented the wide currency of BLOODY among the DIGGERS, was probably guilty of some psychological colonialism here, as British troops were almost equally noted for their bad language. The story, however, reveals the firm hold that BLOODY had at this time and how closely others associated the word with us. It also reveals something of the Australian attitude towards authority, especially uniformed authority, an attitude quite at odds with that obtaining in the British army at the time.

In World War II BLOODY was still in popular use and was again celebrated in verse, this time by that ubiquitous poet, Anon, who has bequeathed us 'Bloody Darwin' which goes in part:

This bloody town's a bloody cuss
No one cares for bloody us
Can't even catch the bloody bus,
In bloody, bloody Darwin.

The bloody beer is bloody dear
Two bloody bob for a bloody beer
And is it good — no bloody fear
In bloody, bloody Darwin.

The bloody dances make me smile,
The bloody band is bloody vile
They only cramp your bloody style,
In bloody, bloody Darwin.

And so on...

Other words could, of course, be substituted for the famous adjective, and often were both by Australian DIGGERS and troops of other nationalities. Much as we might like to claim this one as our very own, there are numerous British and US versions. Of course, we can be certain that they stole their BLOODY, BLOODY BLOODYs from us.

Certain uses of BLOODY seem to be characteristically Australian. These include the still-common MY BLOODY OATH, an exclamation of intense agreement, as in DO YOU WANT ANOTHER BEER — MY BLOODY (sometimes BLOOD) OATH I DO. The use of the term as a description of an unpleasant situation or experience is also encountered, as in THE PARTY WAS BLOODY, meaning that IT WAS BLOODY AWFUL.

TAKING THE LORD'S NAME

Interestingly, unlike the vernaculars of many other nations, Australian Lingo does not contain much blasphemy. Even the notably profane LARRIKINS only came up towards the end of the 19th century with the mild and slightly whimsical curse, GOD'S TROUSERS, not surprisingly now well and truly obsolete. Whether this reluctance to take the Lord's name in vain is to do with being God-fearing or simply uninterested is difficult to determine. Certainly we are, nominally at least, a Christian country, though very large numbers of us profess no religious faith. The church has never played any central role in national political life here, unlike older countries, a fact that probably explains why we do not get the cathartic sense of transgression that must be involved for a Catholic Spaniard in uttering I SHIT ON THE TWENTY-FOUR BALLS OF CHRIST'S APOSTLES, or for a Catalonian Catholic saying I SHIT ON THE FIVE WOUNDS OF CHRIST. JESUS FUCKING CHRIST and HOLY SHIT is about as bad as it gets here, with JESUS WEPT, CHRIST ALMIGHTY, SWEET JESUS and FOR CHRIST'S/GOD'S SAKE being uncreative ALSO RANS. This is in stark contrast to the linguistic habits of many Christian Mediterranean cultures where blasphemy and obscenity are combined, as noted above, in sometimes spectacular fashion. As this book is primarily about Australian English we can examine such importations no further.

While we have little to distinguish us in our taking of the Lord's name, Australians have home-grown or borrowed a number of terms that express a dislike for the display of religious belief. These include calling excessively PREACHY people GOD-BOTHERERS, BIBLE-BASHERS (used elsewhere, but first recorded in Australia), BIBLE-BANGERS or DO-GOODERS. In this respect the late and eminent H.C. Nugget Coombs left characteristically laconic instructions about his funeral arrangements in 1997: 'Bach at the beginning, Waltzing Matilda at the end, and no god-bothering in between.' Someone may be described as CHURCHY if they are thought to visit such places more frequently than the absolute minimum rites of passage — HATCHES, MATCHES AND DESPATCHES — require. In recent years the growth of evangelical Christian fundamentalism has led to terms like SHE'S SEEN THE LIGHT and HE'S A BORN-AGAIN whispered with a knowing nod of the head. While these terms are not insults, they are not compliments either, and suggest a certain grassroots unease with enthusiastic displays of faith and the potentially WOWSERISH attitudes that such redeemed souls might adopt. Significantly, these social developments have occurred in the same period as the rise of political correctness.

GROGGING ON

The beery male comradeship of Australian drinking customs has been frequently commented upon and often lamented. Despite increasing concern and propaganda about the damaging health and social effects of alcohol and decreasing consumption, THE GROG remains a vital element in the leisure pursuits of many Australians. It is still considered poor form in many drinking establishments not to join with other drinkers in a round of SHOUTING. Terms like JIMMY WOODSER and HE'S DRINKING WITH THE FLIES echo this disapproval of the solitary imbiber. The link between drinking and companionship, traditionally male companionship or mateship, has always been a strong one in Australian society, celebrated in literature and folklore. Innumerable bush songs, verse, traditional toasts and popular songs, like the famous 'The Pub With No Beer' and their parodies, refer to alcohol and its effects, mostly on men. In the enlightened present, women are coming to figure more prominently in the social rituals and representations of drinking, though the effects are decidedly non-sexist. Whoever is doing the drinking, though, and whether the results are pleasant or painful, alcohol is an integral part of Australia's past and present. It is not surprising, then, to find it so well represented in our Lingo.

The liquid itself may be described as BOOZE; GROG; PISS; PLONK; ALE; VINO; AMBER FLUID, or TURPS; THROAT OIL; SHERBERT; A JAR (OR TWO . . .); A COLDIE, referring to a can or bottle chilled in the FRIDGE, the latter also known as FROSTIES and STUBBIES, not to be confused with the men's shorts of the same name. A can of beer is also called a TINNIE while different brands of beer have their own Lingo names: Fosters is A BLUEY; A GREEN is a Victoria Bitter, A WHITEY is Carlton Draft; Swan Lager is a BLACK DUCK; and Queensland's Fourex is known as BARBED WIRE from the jagged appearance of its trademark — XXXX.

Terms describing the need for a drink are numerous, including DRY AS A POMMY'S TOWEL; DRIER THAN A DEAD DINGO'S DONGA; and BURKE AND WILLS MUST HAVE PASSED THROUGH HERE — THEY DIED OF THIRST TOO. Sometimes — often unwisely — we COULD MURDER A BEER; DRINK IT BOILING, or even SUCK IT THROUGH A SHITTY RAG. At other times the grog is so strong or unpalatable that IT WOULD KILL A BROWN DOG AT TEN PACES. The problems associated with overproof and downright dangerous concoctions are also numerous in colloquial speech: SLY GROG; HOCUSSED (drugged); GROG; BLOW-ME-SKULL-OFF; the offensive GIN'S PISS; METHS, or WHITE LADY (methylated spirits); SHYPOO GROG; STAGGER-JUICE; SNAKE-JUICE; PLONK; RED NED; BOMBO; CHATEAU CARDBOARD (all terms for poor quality wine). BREWER'S GOITRE means a BEER BELLY, or BEER GUT. KIRUP SYRUP is a famously devastating home-fermented drop from Western Australia where the northern regions boast a drink called a SHOOTER. Consisting of layers of Kahlua, Baileys Irish Cream and Cointreau, the SHOOTER is quaffed in one go, sometimes helped on its way down with the unnecessary advice to 'shoot it down and take off'.

Indulgence in alcoholic consumption has given us a variety of descriptive terms, including the tongue-in-cheek HAVING THE ONE and HAVING A GLASS (or THREE), as well as HAVING A ROUND, or A SHOUT. Other terms include GETTING (or GOING) ON THE

GROG/BOOZE; HAVING A SESSION, GOING FOR A GARGLE; and BENDING
THE ELBOW. BINGEING is excessive consumption of alcohol, usually
in a short period. Over a longer period it may be called a BENDER, or
the 19th-century term SPREE. Hardly ever heard today is the term
SHIVOO, an Anglicisation of the French *chez vous*, meaning your place
and widely used at least as early as the 1830s. It was still current in
the 1940s, but seems to have since lurched into obsolescence.

The place where most drinking is done may be described as THE
RUBBIDY-DUB (from rhyming slang for PUB and first in print in 1898),
or simply THE RUBBIDY, or RUBBY; as a WATERING HOLE, or simply as
DOWN THE ROAD. Once in the pub, SHOUTING; BUYING A ROUND;
GETTING THEM; A DRINKING SCHOOL and BEING IN THE CHAIR, are all
terms associated with the Australian drinking custom of everyone in
the group taking their turn to buy the drinks for everyone else.
Flouting of this ritual, established since at least the 1850s, can lead
to serious consequences such as being asked to STEP OUTSIDE for PIK-
ING, or JIBBING on a ROUND. Less serious physically, but more damaging socially, one who does not take his or her turn to buy may earn
the reputation of NOT SHOUTING IF A SHARK BIT HIM. A related term
is a SCOTCHMAN'S SHOUT, used of someone who only buys his own
drinks when in company. Actually, the custom of shouting is fairly
widespread in Britain (usually known as GETTING THEM IN, or BUYING
A ROUND, terms that are also occasionally used in Australia) and elsewhere, though it seems to be more seriously observed here.

The effects of our occasionally over-enthusiastic imbibing show a
great variety of invention and colour, including: FULL; FULL AS A
BOOT; LEGLESS; MOZART, or BRAHMS AND LISZT (rhyming slang for
PISSED); NON COMPUS; OFF YOUR FACE; ON THE TILES; PARALYTIC;
PISSED; PISSED AS A PARROT; PISSED AS A FART; PISSED AS A NEWT; PISSED
TO THE EYEBALLS; RIPPED TO THE TITS; SHICKERED; SHIT-FACED
(American); SMASHED; TIPSY, or simply GONE, and the now, sadly,
abandoned BLITHERED. A TWO-POT SCREAMER, though, is one who
cannot hold his, hardly ever her, GROG and becomes roaring drunk
on a few drinks. A number of terms for inebriation have crept into
alcoholic use from the drug-culture lingo of the 1960s —
STONKERED; SMASHED; OUT OF IT, and HIGH, are some examples of
this crossover. While those with a jaundiced view of Australian popular culture might see such terms as further evidence of our essential
vulgarity, bear in mind that the celebrated CLEVER DICK, Ben
Franklin, identified 227 American slang terms for drunkenness.

Predictably, the after-effects of the GROG are the subject of some col-
loquialising: the JIMJAMS; the DTS; THE FANTODS; THE SHAKES (JOE BLAKES
in rhyming slang). Also associated with over-indulgence is the flaccid

phallus problem known as BREWER'S DROOP, probably invented here (the term, not the problem), though intelligible elsewhere. One may say on the following morning that one HAD A BIG NIGHT, or HAD A LATE NIGHT, or some other euphemism, such as I'VE BEEN BETTER. To alleviate the pain one may wish for THE HAIR OF THE DOG, or a HEART-STARTER.

As over-indulgence in alcoholic beverages may induce vomiting, the Lingo is well stocked with terms for this, including PUKE; SPEW; CHUCK; CHOKE; BARF (from the 1980s?), BARK, a TECHNICOLOUR YAWN (popularised, along with some of our more colourful colloqui-alisms— some probably invented — in the Barry MacKenzie films of the early 1970s, perpetrated largely by the comic genius of Barry Humphries), TO EXAMINE THE INSIDE OF THE TOILET BOWL; TO THROW UP; A LIQUID LAUGH; PUKE, PERK; RIDE THE PORCELAIN BUS; MAKE LOVE TO THE LAV (or THE 'LOO); TALK TO THE WHITE TELE-PHONE; THROW A MAP; or LAUGH AT THE GROUND. One of the most widely used of these is CHUNDER, thought to be derived from rhyming slang CHUNDER LOO = SPEW which originated from a Norman Lindsay cartoon advertising Cobra boot polish that involved a cartoon figure named Chunder Loo of Akim Foo. The advertise-ment ran in the *Bulletin* between 1909 and 1920. One who displays an element of predictability, especially stupid predictability, may be said to be LIKE A DOG RETURNING TO ITS VOMIT.

Depending on your point of view, a final note of optimism, or pessimism about the masculinism of the Lingo: it is now common-place in Australian vernacular to use the US-derived GUY (original-ly meaning a male) to describe either sex. This is often especially so in plural usages, as in C'MON, GUYS, referring to a group of males and females. The androgynous use of GUYS follows the US usage, noted at least as early as the 1980s. The British-derived MATE, once the verbal symbol of the cherished mateship, is also now used in a gender-neutral way. Perhaps this linguistic sea-change signals the replacement of the BLOKE or OCKER by the SNAG and the end of our strident masculinism, as predicted in a number of recent books. The extent to which masculinism is embedded in Australian culture, though, suggests that mateship is still a GOOD BET for the foresee-able future. Australia's highly stable social make-up is confirmed by the results of the 1996 Census. The average Australian experience is of a nominally Christian mum and dad living in the suburbs with two and-a-bit KIDS, owning or paying off the house, driving back and forth to work which is still, for dad at least, predominantly in the blue-collar manufacturing sector. After three decades of alleged-ly extensive socio-economic shifts, we do not seem to have changed much at all.

8

SPORTS AND RORTS

The umpire…was grossly insulted by some
of the 'barracking' rowdies.

AUSTRALIAN TIT-BITS, 26 JUNE 1884

Sporting events and gambling have always had a close association
in Australia, as they usually have elsewhere. A good deal of our
colloquial speech is involved with these activities and a substantial
segment of our national mythologising is related to both. Some of
the speech practices carried out in the Lingo generally have special
application in the world of sport, especially those sports closely associated with popular images of Australianness, namely Australian Rules
football, Rugby League and, to a lesser extent, Rugby Union.
Despite the large numbers that support it, Association Football, or
soccer as it is known in Australia (but not officially in Britain, where
it is football) does not have the nationalistic cachet of the handball
codes. The summer game, cricket, another hangover of colonialism,
also has an avid following and strong connotations of nation, especially in the annual battles with England for the 'Ashes'. There are
terms for each of these sports, their tactics and rules, as there are for
certain forms of gambling, particularly illegal gambling. Some of
these terms have entered into the Great Australian Lingo as well.

SPORTS

Nicknaming is especially widespread in sports where prominent athletes are given nicknames that are widely used. While many of these
names originate from professional sporting commentators and journalists, only those that meet with popular approval survive. A few

examples of past and present sports stars and their nicknames includes: BOY CHARLTON the swimmer; DEMON JACK Spofforth and Don THE DON Bradman, both cricketers; GELIGNITE JACK MURRAY the motor racer; THE GREAT WHITE SHARK for Greg Norman the golfer; THE LITHGOW FLASH for Marjorie Jackson the athlete; THE MARRICKVILLE MAULER for Jeff Fenech the boxer; NEWK for John Newcombe the tennis player, and DEEK for Robert De Castella the marathon runner. Many other nicknames and sporting usages are coined by journalists. While these may be used on the pages of sporting magazines and columns, like those earlier colloquialisms coined by writers of the *Bulletin* (ABORIGINALITIES and DRYBERA for Canberra) and *Truth* (TELEWAG, to chat on the telephone) they had — and have — little or no purchase in the wider Lingo.

Sporting nicknames tend towards the affectionate diminutive, such as THOMMO (cricketer Jeff Thomson), to name only one of many. This habit has been taken to ridiculous extremes by television sports commentators who, as well as saddling players with such appellations, have also begun to call each other by such nicknames. One exception to the diminutive tendency was the addition of a letter to Ian Chappell's surname by adoring Australian fans — he became CHAPPELLI, a hangover of the need to distinguish between Ian and cricketer brother Greg on scoreboards. The initial of the first names were added to the surname — Chappell G. and Chappell I. It is also worth noting that this Lingo nicknaming is hardly, if ever, applied to women athletes, even those who may be known by such journalistic dubbings as THE LITHGOW FLASH (Marjorie Jackson). The famous swimmer, Dawn Fraser, is not known as Dawnie or Fraso. Champion runner Cathy Freeman is, thankfully, never called Free-o.

A selection only of nicknames current for AFL players in the mid-1990s includes such colourful items as: CAPTAIN BLOOD — Jack Dyer; VEGEMITE — Peter Ware; GOD — Gary Ablett; MAD DOG — Peter Wilson; THE LIP — Lou Reynolds and THE GOLDEN GREEK — Steve Malaxos.

As well as being immortalised in the prose vernacular, some sporting personalities have added to our poetic colloquialisms. Wally Grout, the cricketer, lives on as the rhyming slang for a SHOUT. When one GOES FOR AN EDGAR one is going for A SHIT, rhymed after the jockey Edgar Britt. When one HAS THE JIMMY BRITTS, however, one is upset, rhymed after the US boxer, Jimmy Britt (1879–1940).

Sportspeak is hardly restricted to naming practices. Examples of FOOTYtalk include: SON, a player; THE METTERS SCOREBOARD, used for all scoreboards; ABSOLUTE BLINDER, an outstanding performance; SCREAMER, a good mark, and THE HIGH DIDDLE, to score a goal while

A GRAB is a good mark in AFL. A term used in Western Australia and the Northern Territory is LEMONS, meaning the three-quarter time break for on-field refreshments during an ARL game. Sometimes these and other well-known terms are themselves reduced to their initials among aficionados and even occasionally in the wider community. Thus A RED HOT GO becomes RHG, an ABSOLUTE SHOCKER becomes AS and STD stands for SPAT THE DUMMY.

Football has also developed its own little lingo for aspects of play, tactics and just about everything else connected with the various games, all of which involve the kicking and passing of an egg-shaped leather ball. In Australian Rules these include the following, some of which also relate to other football codes: TO RABBIT, is to illegally trip an opponent; AN ANGEL BRUISER or CLOUD-BURSTER is a very high kick; A BALL BURSTER is a powerful kick; and A MARCH CHAMPION is a player who looks promising in the pre-season, but fails to live up to that promise when the FOOTY proper gets under way. In Rugby League and Union there are likewise mini-vocabularies peculiar to each variety of football. The SCRUM, for example, is an adaptation of the British dialect term for a tussle, 'a scrummage' and reflects the origins of Australian (and US) football in THE OLD DART or the mother country as England used to be called in more imperially conscious times.

Given the widespread reverence for the FOOTY it is not surprising to find a whole range of terms from the various clubs. Many of these are local lingoes, such as THE BYAS for the Glenelg (South Australia) Rules team, though as the main codes have become increasingly commercialised, those old club names that have survived have become more widely known. Sydney League clubs have included THE BLUEBAGS, or just BLUES (Newtown), THE RABBITOHS (South Sydney, or just SOUTHS), THE ROOSTERS and THE SAINTS (St George). The Parramatta Rugby Union team was known as the TWO BLUES, from the two shades of blue of the team colours. Manly–Warringah Rugby Union club was known as THE GREEN RATS, a reference to the battling spirit of the World War II RATS OF TOBRUK. Randwick Union team was known as the GALLOP-ING GREENS, usually by sports journalists, rather than supporters who preferred the more laconic WICKS. Melbourne's Australian Rules clubs include, or included THE TIGERS (Richmond) and THE BULLDOGS (Footscray), THE MAGPIES or just THE PIES (Collingwood, now defunct) and THE ROY BOYS (Fitzroy). The North Sydney League team was known as THE BEARS for many years, apparently from the businesses that sponsored the team, including the Big Bear Hamburger Shop. Some of the more colourful names for clubs, such as THE HYPHENATES for Sydney's Canterbury–Bankstown usually called THE BERRIES) are, again, coined by sporting journalists. Some of these catch on, most do not.

The increased commercialism of the various football codes has seen the demise and/or amalgamation of many local and regional clubs. Interestingly, names chosen for the new teams, at least in the AFL, often use the earlier titles, such as the Sydney Swans, West Coast Eagles, Brisbane Bears (now called the Brisbane Lions) and Adelaide Crows.

As their players will know, all sports have distinctive words and phrases, spoken and understood by their participants. Few of these specialised terms reach the broader vernacular, though the processes by which the little lingoes are formed and operate are much the same. Rhyming slang exists in the golfing term LADY GODIVA, meaning the club known as a driver, usually rendered simply as LADY. A KELLY is the axeman's term for his instrument, from a brand name and in use from the early 20th century. An axe was also known from slightly earlier as DOUGLAS, again based on a (US) brand. Lawn bowls has its own repertoire of jargon for the balls, the greens, and the way the ball veers either to the left or the right as it travels (BIAS). Gymnasts use MAG (powdered magnesium) to dry the sweat from their hands when convoluting themselves around bars, rings, and other instruments of torture associated with this sport. The BLOOD BIN is a term now used in various contact sports for an off-field location for bleeding players to have some time out and some binding of their wounds before returning to the game.

BARRACKING

BARRACKING is an essential sporting term, in use from at least the 1870s and is applied nowadays mostly to football. It means to loudly and often aggressively verbalise support for one's team. This is what the Americans call rooting, a term that has a much different meaning in our Lingo. BARRACKING was originally not only about support for the home side, but also about insulting and hopefully demoralising the opposition and, if an unwelcome decision was made, the referee as well. BARRACK in this sense has been with us since at least 1880, derived from either Irish or Cockney slang (possibly both), itself derived from the French *baragouin*, meaning gibberish. During the last half or so of the 20th century, BARRACK has tended to lose its antagonistic overtones and is now used mainly to indicate that one is supporting or encouraging one's team.

BARRACKING has long been an exhilarating weekend activity, especially in relation to the main football codes of Rugby League (League) and Australian Rules (AUSSIE RULES, or just RULES), a game sometimes referred to in those States that do not play this game to any great extent as AERIAL PING-PONG or CROSS-COUNTRY BALLET). Along with Rugby Union, a minor code in Australia, these games have been known generically in Lingo since at least early in the 20th century as FOOTY, sometimes even THE FOOTY where the indefinite article is used in the same way as in 'the church'. Soccer, however, despite being a game of football, is never referred to as FOOTY. Supporters of Rules are likely to refer to the Rugby codes as SNIFFY BUM or MOBILE WRESTLING.

An entire mini-language of BARRACKING has evolved, refined over generations of passionate support for one's FOOTY TEAM, FOOTY CLUB or FOOTY SIDE. A few selected football examples recorded in 1917 give something of the flavour:

> 'Yer couldn't pass the sugar before the tea gets cold.'
> Little man to big man: 'Garn, you're overgrown; you forgot to get yurself pruned this year.'
> Big man replies: 'Get away, yer little sawed off. Pity yer mother didn't put some superphosphates in yer grub when you was young; mighter made yer grow a bit.'

A selection of current BARRACKING terms includes such items as BOUNCE, shouted when a ball may fall into the hands of the opposing team. Probably the most famous Aussie Rules cry of all is UP THERE CAZALY (also UP THERE CAZZER), after famed Victorian Football League (the VFL) player Roy Cazaly (1893–1963), yelled at a player going for a high mark in Australian Rules football. So powerful was the symbolism of this incantation that it became a battle cry for Victorian troops in the Middle East during World War II. The term was given another airing in the late 1970s when a song of the same name became a big hit. Other more or less universal 'barracking' terms include MOZZING a player which means to try and put him off by yelling something off-putting such as 'chewie on your boot'.

BARRACKING is often the occasion for outstanding artistry in the use of Lingo, as reported some years ago by the historian late Ian Turner at a tense moment in the last quarter of a St Kilda–Richmond contest:

> ...the Tigers, having been down five goals, were now drawing ahead, a St Kilda supporter — thirtyish, short-back-and-sides, running to fat, white shirt and clasping a can of Carlton Draught — addressed himself to the umpire: 'You rotten, bloody, commo, poofter, mongrel bastard...'

None of this is to suggest that the need to abuse the opposition and the umpire (UMP) or referee (REF) is restricted to football fans. Since the 1970s the term SLEDGING has come into play to indicate vehement insults directed at the opposing team in cricket. According to Ian Chappell the term originated in Adelaide during either the

1963–4 or 1964–5 Sheffield Shield season. A cricketer who swore in the presence of a woman, was, in accordance with the peculiarly Australian double standard, accused of being AS SUBTLE AS A SLEDGE-HAMMER

About the same time the song 'When a Man Loves a Woman' happened to be on the hit parade, sung by Percy Sledge and so, it is said, a man who swore in front of a woman was given the nickname Percy or Sledge. SLEDGING, as an item of cricketing little lingo began then. Often the etymologies given for colloquialisms are even more entertaining than the items themselves, as a number of examples throughout this book indicate.

The term and the practice of SLEDGING, though, was first brought to the wider attention of the general public in the 1980s when cricketers, understandably, began objecting to the increasing nastiness and profanity of the crowds as they attempted to play the game. As well as verbal abuse, the fans were also hurling bottles, cans, and other projectiles at players and referees. This unhappy development seems to have been controlled through stricter policing, wire enclosures and heavy fines, but the word escaped into the Greater Lingo and is now fairly widely used as a synonym for abuse or invective. Cricket, has its own lexicon, of course, which could make a complete study in itself, the finer points of which would include comprehending terms such as LEGGIE which has two meanings. The word may refer to a ball bowled so that it changes direction, also known as a LEG BREAK, or it may refer to a bowler who is good at LEG BREAKS, a LEG SPINNER.

Since the arrival of SLEDGING, a new sporting embarrassment has arisen. In the mid-1990s football was embroiled in dispute and embarrassment about SLEDGING that involved racist and ethnic slurs against players, especially Aboriginal players. A code of conduct that attempts to suppress such abuse when perpetrated by players has been developed and has been implemented. The behaviour and expressions of fans, though, cannot be so easily controlled and racial abuse remains a common feature of football 'barracking' in all codes. Although SLEDGING, and other unpleasant crowd behaviour also occurs at cricket matches, it rarely takes a racist tone, perhaps because there are still very few prominent cricketers of non-Anglo-Australian background in the Australian teams?

HORSES AND COURSES

The vagaries and argot of the turf were brought forcibly to the attention of the non-racegoing public in the mid-1980s through the FINE COTTON RING-IN, a celebrated and notorious case of horse substitution, the consequences of which are still working their way through the legal system. A RING-IN, included in Vaux's 1812 cant dictionary and then meaning to defraud, is now a Lingoism with the related meanings of a latecomer, (also a BLOW-IN) a stranger, or a substitute. It has been used in this sense within the racing fraternity since at least the 1890s, though the term POSSUM is also used for the same dishonest practice.

Like other sports and gambling games, horseracing has an extensive linguistic repertoire of its own, the use of which marks out the true punter from the hordes of MUG PUNTERS or amateurs. Here are some examples: to BET LIKE THE WATSONS is to make large bets, and said to be derived from the surname of a pair of brothers, legendary for their betting; to GO FOR THE BIG LICK is to try and win a large amount of money on a race; to be WITHOUT A MINTIE (the chewy peppermint lolly) is to be without the means to bet while HICKEY HOCKEY is racing rhyming slang for a jockey.

Many of these and other terms, recorded by the redoubtable Sidney Baker between the 1940s and the 1960s, were well established by the 1890s. BOOKIE, a term referring to one who keeps a book, that is, lays odds on a race and is prepared to take bets, is used in Britain and the USA, but is recorded earliest in Australia. DEAD BIRD was used for a sure winner from at least the 1880s; a long shot was exactly what it is today, as is a RANK OUTSIDER. An UNDERTAKER was a person who laid odds only against horses certain to lose, or DEAD 'UNS. This evolved into the later term an UNDERTAKER'S JOB, meaning a horse that is not being run to win, that is, running DEAD. A MUDLARK, MUDRUNNER, or simply a MUDDER is a horse that runs well in wet conditions. The subtleties of this little lingo are comparable to some of those already noticed in the larger Australian Lingo, in terms like BASTARD, for example. In racing a DEAD BIRD was certain to win, yet a DEAD 'UN was, and is, certain to lose.

Racing and general gambling slang of the 19th century included a few other convictisms and cant terms surviving from the earlier period. Words like CASER (a crown or five shillings); MAGSMAN (confidence trickster) and FAKED, meaning arranging to cheat. Another racecourse term derived from thieves' slang is a SKINNER, meaning a horse that wins a race at very long odds and is therefore beloved of the bookmaker. In use well before the 1890s when it is first attested, the word is still used today. Some terms were taken over from goldfields slang. One such was SHICER (from British slang for someone considered worthless) and applied in Australia to a worthless mine. By the 1890s SHICER had come to mean a criminal type of person, surviving into the present as SHYSTER.

Yet other racing expressions moved into the general vernacular, including CRONK meaning crooked or bad (now largely unheard); TO POKE BORAK, meaning telling ridiculous lies in racing slang, had the meaning of tease or stir; DIVVY means to share out; A GOOD THING, a certainty can be a DEAD CERT or a PRETTY SAFE BET; A LONG SHOT is to take a chance, and A MUG is a person who bets badly or is easily gulled by the unscrupulous. THE DRUM, meaning accurate information about a horse, as expressed in the racing lingoism RUN A DRUM, means to run as expected, while A DRUMMER is A TIPSTER. TO PUT THE MOCKER(S) ON a horse means to NOBBLE it and to do the same to someone or something means, in the wider Lingo, to bring about the failure or disruption of a course of action.

A rare example of racecourse little lingo as spoken towards the end of the 19th century is provided by 'The Welsher's Confession' which also gives an eyewitness account of the year that Carbine won the Melbourne Cup, 1890:

We — that is, my mate and I — had been doing the double all the day. While the race was being run we changed hats, bags, signs, coats, in fact everything. The Cup was the race we all looked for to get a haul. I laid the field with odds better than anyone else. It was Carbine's year and the bookies were frightened of him. I was not, for I was sure I had him 'in my bag', and I had been training for about a week and was in rare buckle for running.

Well we yelled out the odds, and the shekels rolled in fast, and my bag was heavy with silver. I said to my mate, 'We ought to bag £40 a-piece.' Just then a 'demon' came up, and I squared him with two quid. The bell rang for the horses and the start was ready. I was ready also, I promise you. Just then a man with a wooden leg comes up and asks 'What price Carbine?' 'Tens' I said and he gave me a quid. I wish to goodness I'd never have seen him.

Away they started. Such yelling and yelping of the backers. 'Off' says I to my mate. 'No you don't', says a voice from behind, and I was pinned to the fence by the wooden leg of the man I had laid ten to one about Carbine. 'I'll keep you here' says he, 'till the race is over.' Lor' love me, I've got the pain in my stomach still that his wooden leg caused. 'I'll give you two quid', says I. 'Give me ten,' says he, and I out with the cash and off for a 'spiel'. My mate ran hard, but I could not. 'Take the bag,' says I, 'I am done.' The pain in my inside was awful. He runs back, collars the bag and off. 'Carbine! Carbine!' the crowd yelled, and I was running groggy. Then there was a yell and I felt like a dog on a racecourse. They caught me fair, and when they found the bag gone they chucked me into the Saltwater River. I had a fine suit and a bell-topper on. When I crept out on the other side I was in shreds, and frightened the police would arrest me for indecent exposure. Then I could not walk. That wooden leg had crushed my bread basket so. So I laid down on the bank and a 'copper' comes up and 'pinches' me. Well Old Panton, the 'beak' in Melbourne, he gives me a month, and

Lor' I wanted it, for I had two ribs broken, and my 'chivvy' was altered awful. We netted £30 a-piece over Carbine, and when I came out of gaol had a good spree on the strength of it. If you want to be a spieler — that is, a good one — you must have a hide that would kill a rhinoceros, and brass that would build a monument to the memory of your cheek. You must be a good runner, a grand liar, a thief, and a blackguard generally. But be virtuous when charged with the offence, and your cheek will pull you through. And above all, avoid laying odds with wooden-legged men...

The contrived nature of this anecdote makes it especially useful as an indication of the racecourse parlance of the time. It also highlights the still-existing tendency of the betting fraternity to depersonalise the sport with terms like PRICE. In the late-1990s this specialised racing usage had threatened to pass into more general sports journalism where individual cricketers, footballers, or teams may be referred to as A CHANCE, as in 'ablett is a chance to score', and so on.

MUGS' GAMES

Backing the gee-gees was only one sure way of DOING YOUR DOUGH at 19th-century racecourses. Contemporary sources refer to a bewildering variety of gambling games played at and around racecourses. These included the card game banker (still played), bay and ray, involving mechanical horses; bonanza cloth; Boston-whist (introduced from the USA in the 1890s); chuck luck (said to be a Chinese game played with two dice); dumps (in which a wooden ball is used to knock down two pegs placed in the ground); fan-cloth (dice game); garter (involving a tape); gold and silver bank (dice), nap (cards); knock-em-all-over (skittles); lengths (a coin is set in a stick which is set in a circle drawn on the ground. The stick must be knocked over and the coin knocked out of the circle); making the pig (dice); marble peter (involving marbles and a box with a hole drilled in it); marvelle (a form of roulette using marbles); penny-in-the basin (throwing a coin so that it will remain in a basin); ringing the bull (usually played in PUBS and using a metal ring suspended from the ceiling. This ring is then thrown so that it, hopefully, catches on a hook set in the wall); round the horn (one die and a numbered card); sanc balls (coloured and numbered balls); skittle-pool (played on a table similar to a pool table and using three octagonal pins, a wooden ball and a cue); spinning jenny (using a revolving, numbered board); square cube spinning; under and over (two dice), a form of Yankee sweat. Poker was also played, though at this time was sometimes known as bluff, for reasons obvious to anyone who has ever played the game seriously. A pinch-board was a roulette table believed to be arranged to swindle players.

Some games involved live animals other than horses. Duck-in-the-hole was a pastime in which a hole was dug sufficiently deep to allow a live duck's head to poke up. Players threw sticks at the duck's head, trying to hit it. Said to be very difficult to do, this was probably the reason for the disappearance of the game at the end of the 19th century, rather than any sensitivity to animal welfare. Another racecourse favourite was usually called the monkey sweep. Numbered tickets corresponding to numbered balls held in a revolving box were sold to punters. The box was turned or shaken, the lid opened, and a monkey would draw one of the balls, that being the winner. Similar sweeps were said to be conducted with other animals such as turkeys, ducks and geese. How any of these animals might draw the winning marble remains a mystery.

Other games typically enjoyed by gamblers included pak-a-pu or Chinese lottery, a very similar game to modern lotto-type gambling with the odds stacked just as highly against the punter. This game has also left its traces in Lingo where sayings include to GO UP LIKE A PACK-APOO TICKET (inflammable) and to be MARKED LIKE A PACKAPOO TICK-ET (difficult or impossible to understand). In Melbourne the CABBAGE PATCHERS are said to use a latter-day variation of these terms — GOES OFF LIKE A PACKET OF POO TICKETS describes someone who is liable to hasty and ill-considered actions. As well as pak-a-pu or packapoo hazards, a dice game played in two main versions, one known as here goes (said to be Dutch) and a British version known as 7 the Main; there was fan-tan (played on a metal board or cloth with coins); Chinese grab and Yankee grab (both dice games); pitch and toss; odd man out; two-up (all games played with coins) and, inevitably, the three card trick, and all the variations of the pea and thimble trick.

Many of these diversions are still to be found in one form or another in the sideshow alleys of country shows and fairs, as well as in the grander metropolitan agricultural shows, such as Sydney's ROYAL. The 19th-century racecourse term for a place or stand where sideshow games were played — a JOINT — is still used by SHOWIES (show people) today, as is the word for the area of land where the joint is erected, THE PITCH. Fan-tan and pak-a-pu are illegal today, but are said to be still favoured by members of the Chinese community. In his autobiographical account of mainly Northern Territory life, *Sitdown Up North*, Ted Egan refers to 'a great Chinese gambling game' popular in Darwin where it is known as PAI KEW and has its own argot, including such terms as IN FRONT, GO BACK, BEHIND and TAKING THE BANK.

A favourite recitation and song, 'The Spider from the Gwydir' highlights the close connection between showgrounds, the chances of being parted from your HARD-EARNED, and the Lingo.

By the sluggish River Gwydir lived a wicked redback spider,
He was just about as vicious as could be.
And the place that he lived in was a rusty Jones's jam tin
In a paddock by the showgrounds at Moree.

Beside him lay a shearer snoozing; he'd been on the grog and boozing,
Drunk that night and all the previous day.
Now listen closely fella and this story I will tell yer
Of what happened on that bright and sunny day.

Along came a spieler with his dainty little sheila
Collecting wood to build themselves a fire.
Said the spieler to the shielah 'I'll bet this mug's a shearer,
If he's not you can christen me a liar'.

'Now you just keep nit, honey, while I fan the mug for money,
And we'll have some little luxuries for tea'.
But she said 'Now don't be silly, you go home and boil the billy,
You can safely leave this mug to little me'.

And as she went to take his money this story then gets funny
As she put her hand near to that rusty tin.
That spider leaped and bit her where her mother never kissed her,
And that sheila sure kicked up a din.

Then the shearer, weak and haggard, off down the track he staggered
And promised he would give the booze a rest.
But he never knew that spider down beside the Gwydir,
Had saved him fifty-seven of the best.

SPIELER, meaning a swindler, often a cardsharp, was common among circus people and other travelling entertainers by the 1870s. It was joined in the following decade by BUTTONER, a person who assisted show people by encouraging volunteers to come forth from the audience. Both these words seem to derive from British circus usage. (Australian circus little lingo is discussed in chapter 9.)

The scope in gambling for cheating and chicanery was, and is, almost unlimited, so it is not surprising to find many gambling terms related to less than honest practices. These included: CARDSHARPER which is still in occasional use and has probably given us SHARPIE, a sharp person, one who is not to be trusted. CARDSHARPS were also known as ROOKS, a term that lives on in phrases such as THAT USED-CAR DEALER ROOKED ME. As well there were other varieties of cheat including a LUMBERER, a TIPSTER who swindles; a MAGSMAN; a CONFIDENCE TRICKSTER. Other cheats were those who FAKED; GARROTTED (hid cards at the back of their neck); LAMBED DOWN (also used in the bush), or organised CATCH-BETS in which a decoy bet was made to entice a FLAT, or PLUNGER (both fools and EASY MARKS) to place a losing bet. A SELL was a swindle, also used more broadly to mean a poseur (a POSER, a BIG-NOTER or PSEUD also used in British colloquial speech) or an unreliable person. To stack the cards has an obvious meaning, probably more familiar as stack the deck or the practice of stacking the meeting with one's own supporters, said to be widespread in political life. A TAKE-DOWN was a swindle, living on as A TAKE and I'VE BEEN TAKEN. TATS were loaded dice; a TUG was a CON MAN prepared to be violent and a WELSHER was one who took bets without any hope of covering them — then MADE HIMSELF SCARCE, as in the account quoted above. WELSHERS, of course, are still with us today in many other walks of life.

Something or someone referred to as SNIDE was false or worthless and a GREY was a two-headed or two-tailed coin, used in various games, though nowadays best known in TWO-UP (see below). Cheats when discovered usually had need to run quickly away, a practice that generated such arresting terms as GUY-A-WHACK, DO A GUY, CLEAR OUT and SHIROCK. Those found to be consistent swindlers were known as BLACKLEGS and were warned off the course. SHEEN meant bad, probably counterfeit, money.

Terms for those who were the victims of such cons were almost as diverse as the technical language of swindling, including MUG, used so effectively in 'The Spider from the Gwydir', a shortening of MUGGINS, a simpleton or a fool. MUG is another colloquialism that has a number of subtle meanings, depending on the context. MUG PUNTER has already been mentioned in the context of horseracing, but that is not the end of this word's usefulness. MUG can also mean a face, related to another of its uses—kissing, first recorded in Australia, though not exclusively ours. In the combination MUG LAIR, the primary meaning of stupidity is extended into an insult and in this form the term is still used today. We still refer to any losing, failing, or dubious activity as A MUG'S GAME. MUG is also used in the little lingo of circus folk to refer to townspeople. Other terms for those to be gulled included two with connections to football and cricket: a MARK is also used to mean the taking of the ball in Australian Rules, while a BUNNY is also a cricketing term for a poor batsman.

Modern gambling habits are far less exotic than those of the past. The racecourse has been tamed and betting regulated by the Totalizator Agency Board in New South Wales, a bureaucratic mouthful swiftly Lingoised to THE TAB. Governments routinely use lotteries to fund public works and to fund other essential activities. The Opera House Lottery ran in Sydney for many years to subsidise the building of the Opera House by the harbour. Queensland's GOLDEN CASKET lottery was established in 1916 to pay for soldier repatriation, or REPAT as it has been known ever since. Governments with an eye to the revenue potential of gambling have also allowed casino gambling in most States and Territories where highly commercialised and regulated versions of roulette, Blackjack (TWENTY-ONE or PONTOON in Lingo), poker and a variety of other games are provided in an atmosphere of shopping mall entertainment. In all of these establishments, as in many social clubs in some States, such as the RSL and League clubs of New South Wales, are found poker machines, known during their pre-electronic days when operated by a mechanical lever as ONE-ARMED BANDITS, an Americanism. The dread arm of officialdom even extends to the street-corner newsagent where the Pools, Lotto and other similar hard-to-win games of chance are accompanied by various kinds of SCRATCHIT (also known as SCRATCHIES) gambling games, starting at a dollar and including a SCRATCHIT form of the gambling game beloved, in stereotype at least, of elderly ladies and the Catholic Church —bingo, also known as housie and housie-housie. It is common for groups of friends or workmates to band together into SYNDICATES to play lotto-type games and to buy lottery tickets, all still hoping for the big win or, as revived by advertisers of one of these modern games of chance a few years ago, a MOTZA probably derived from Yiddish and still on middle-aged Australian tongues in the late 1990s.

Something of the sideshow and carnival atmosphere of the race-tracks of the past can still be captured at WEEKEND RACES, or PICNIC RACES. And once a year most workers down tools to watch the Melbourne Cup (FIRST TUESDAY IN NOVEMBER), often enjoying a convivial lunch complete with funny hats. They may even HAVE A PUNT or join in the informal SWEEPS that are commonly run at workplaces throughout the land.

Since the deregulated, monetarist 1980s increasing numbers of Australians have been doing their gambling in the sophisticated arenas of stocks and shares—the markets and in international high finance. Some have MADE A PILE; many DID THEIR DOUGH in the spectacular corporate and financial collapses that followed the fall of the stock market in 1987. The high-flying entrepreneurs of the 1980s are either still in gaol, have DONE A SKASE and left the country or await various forms of judicial decision on the legality or otherwise of their activities. Chief among these, of course, is self-made tycoon, Alan Bond. Despite his financial and legal difficulties Bond is still held in some — slightly diminished — affection by the public and is known universally as BONDIE.

Writing of yesterday's gamblers is an appropriate place to record briefly the demise of a once-important aspect of working-class life — the SP (Starting Price) BOOKIE. Towards the end of the 1960s a young man began work in a large Federal government bureaucracy. At the next desk was a middle-aged FELLA named Wally who was continually on the telephone. He got more telephone calls than the rest of the office staff combined. It was amazing how busy the poor BLOKE was. One day Wally was out when his phone rang. The young and innocent NEW STARTER answered it.

'Is Wally there?' rasped a voice at the other end.
'No, he's out".
A pause.
'Tell him Jack rang and wants twenty on number three to win in the two o'clock at Flemington.'

Wally was, of course, an SP BOOKIE, one who takes bets outside the government-controlled system of the TAB (TOTE, by the way, is an Australian first). Wally has either retired a rich man by now or he may be still DOING THE GOVERNMENT STROKE, but at Her Majesty's expense. Whatever his fate, his existence was a good example of the refusal of many people to bow to officialdom in their gambling habits. Although outlawed, it was always possible — and probably still is — to find a BLOKE in a PUB RUNNING A BOOK on the SP. The appeal of the illicit also applies to another favoured Australian game of chance, TWO-UP.

TWO-UP

TWO-UP or SWY is the Australian version of a quite ancient European gambling game, known in Germany as *zwei* (two) and also played in a Scots version. A form of the game has been with us since the earliest days of colonisation when it was referred to as CHUCK-FARTHING. TWO-UP persisted as one of dozens of gambling games played throughout the country during the 19th century. It became the characteristic gambling game (though hardly the only one) of the Australian soldiers of World War I. The men of the AIF were so keen on the game that they would risk injury and death by playing in exposed situations. After the war a German aviator who flew observation missions over Australian lines told an Australian soldier that the Germans came to believe the Australians were very religious people. The soldier scratched his head and looked puzzled until the German explained that whenever he and other pilots flew across Australian lines they kept seeing groups of men with their faces upturned to heaven. The Germans were mightily impressed by this display of piety. When the Australian soldier finished laughing he explained to the German flyer that they were, of course, watching the pennies spin as they played SWY.

The importance of TWO-UP in Australian mythology is indicated by its uneasy status as a mostly illegal gambling game for 364 days of the year. But on THE ONE DAY OF THE YEAR — Anzac Day — it is tacitly allowed by the police that traditionally TURN A BLIND EYE on crowds of merry DIGGERS and others noisily staking large amounts on the fall of a couple of pennies at country races and at the back of city PUBS.

The little lingo of TWO-UP is convoluted and extensive, an indication of the importance and longevity of this game in Australian popular culture. A few examples are given here, though an extensive treatment is given by Sidney Baker in his *The Australian Language*: The term SCHOOL, meaning a game of TWO-UP, was originally a reference to spontaneous games at lunchtime or SMOKO and was part of 19th-century gambling slang. An organised game with COCKATOOS to keep NIT (lookout) was called an ALLEY. In later years though, the alley has largely been replaced by school as in the famous Thommo's Two-Up School in Sydney, and moving from venue to venue night after night. It is said that those IN THE KNOW can still track down Thommo's to risk their DOUGH on the toss of two coins.

To SPIN is to throw the coins so they revolve in the air, the motion preferred by the members of a SCHOOL. The cry COME IN, SPINNER, is the signal that all bets are in and it is time to spin the pennies. The SPINNER is the person who tosses the coins. To HEAD-EM is to play TWO-UP and also to throw the coins so they land HEADS UP. Bets are won or lost on whether the result is two heads (SKULLS, NUTS, NEDS); two tails (TWO MICKS), or one of each (ONES). A KIP (or STICK, BAT, or KYLIE) is the wooden bat or spatula-like device used to throw the pennies into the air. Early KIPS (also called LANNETS) are said to have been masterpieces of carpentry often with secret compartments used to hide double-headed (NOB, JACK) or double-tailed (GRAY) pennies until the moment of launching by a HARDHEAD (crooked two-up MERCHANT).

The RING is marked as a circle on the ground about three metres in diameter. The SPINNER stands at the CENTRE or GUTS of the ring accompanied by the CENTREMAN or SPINNER'S STAKEHOLDER who collects the bets, called STAKES. Pennies minted in the reign of Edward VII used to be preferred because of their weight and clear stamping of the HEAD and TAIL, though this does not seem to be so important today when a sanitised version of TWO-UP has become a licensed game at casinos and racing clubs throughout Australia. There is even an annual World Two-Up Championship held in Kalgoorlie. Nowadays it is held in the plush surroundings of the local racing club, rather than the original corrugated iron and dusty bush SCHOOL at the edge of town.

9

WORKING WORDS

If for yacker you're a demon,
You can do <u>their</u> share as well.

THE SHEARER, 19 AUGUST 1905

EARNING A CRUST

The workaday world has been and is still a major part of life for most Australians. Many aspects of work have added to the vernacular. Often these are little lingoes, or specialised occupational terms, and even languages that are mostly incomprehensible to those who do not belong to the particular trade, profession, or industry group. But because work of one sort or another has been and, even in these times of high unemployment, continues to be a common experience of many Australians we have developed a considerable vocabulary about work and also, not surprisingly, to its avoidance.

The affectionate diminutive is a feature of much of the lingo of labour, with such terms as SICKIE (a sick day, probably about World War II) and COMPO (a compensation PAYOUT for injuries sustained on the job, c. 1930, though probably coined earlier) being widely known and used. In the car industry a faulty car (known as a LEMON to most of us, or by far worse terms) used to be called a MONDAY OR FRIDAY CAR because it had in all likelihood been built on either of those days when there were so many off on SICKIES that there was too small a workforce to ensure quality control.

Although not heard so frequently in these times the SMOKO (first in print 1865, but certainly earlier in popular parlance) is both an Australian invention and a typically economic lingoism describing a short break from work, long enough to roll a FAG (or SMOKE, CIGGY, BURN, NAIL, the latter becoming popular since the linking of smoking with lung cancer and meaning a coffin nail) and smoke it. Other terms peculiar to Australian work include LEAVE LOADING, LONG SERVICE for Long Service Leave (a unique Australian benefit), and the acronymic POETS DAY (that is, Friday, a usage that seems to date from the 1960s), the meaning of which is said to be PISSING OFF EARLY, TOMORROW'S SATURDAY. To KNOCK OFF is not an exclusively Australian term for finishing work, but is recorded earliest here in the 1860s. When work resumes, it may be referred to as STRIKING A BLOW.

STIRRING, or STIRRING THE POSSUM, while not restricted to the workplace, is often practised on the job by those with AN AXE TO GRIND, or just a desire to needle, niggle and annoy their fellow-workers and/or the bosses. STIRRING may take various forms. It can be simply bantering, name-calling, sending up or TAKING THE PISS. More seriously it can involve jokes, hoaxes, and even mild forms of sabotage. STIRRERS are not an exclusively Australian phenomenon, though the term seems to be recorded earliest here. We Australians are blessed or cursed with plenty of STIRRERS, due perhaps to the ingrained distrust of authority that persists throughout our history and folklore. STIRRING THE BASTARDS UP has long been practised here and shows no signs of going away.

Some terms, while not exclusively Australian, have an antipodean piquance in their usage and their meaning. A SCAB is a strikebreaker or one who refuses to join his mates in industrial action. He, less frequently she, is held to be THE LOWEST FORM OF LIFE. A CRAWLER is a sycophant who KOWTOWS TO THE BOSSES or LICKS THEIR ARSE and is widely reviled in any workplace. He or she is someone who BROWN-NOSES and is usually considered to be LOWER THAN A SNAKE'S BELLY or A LOW DINGO. Also associated with industrial unrest is the term GO SLOW meaning WORK TO RULE, that is, as inefficiently as possible. The term is used elsewhere, but is recorded first in Australia early in the 20th century. A SHITKICKER (redolent of the Australian ethos, though not exclusively ours) is someone who performs the most menial occupational tasks. In the world of banking during the 1970s, specifically the then Bank of New South Wales (now Westpac), the lower levels of middle management were known to the workers as RSK, REGIONAL SHITKICKER. HEADKICKER is a term widely used to describe BLOODY-MINDED managers and vicious bosses, of which we still seem to have more than our fair share in the world of work.

A widespread and venerable work custom is the workers' perquisite (PERK or PERKS) or right to take for himself or herself the clippings, scrapings, dustings, or other leftovers and rejects of an industrial process. This contentious practice has been extended in many countries to include the unsanctioned use of time, equipment, materials or other items belonging to the employer. Such a grey area between custom and legality has given rise to a number of related Australian terms. In New South Wales the clandestine use of the office photocopier to run off a few hundred fliers for the primary school fete or operating the factory lathe to turn some much-needed items for the local FOOTY club is known as a FOREIGN ORDER. In Victoria similar perks seem to go under the name of A FOREIGNER and further west it is sometimes known as A FOREIGNY.

There are a number of often-heard YARNS about foreign orders, one of which inevitably involves an old WHARFIE who every day walked his wheelbarrow past guards at the dockyard gate. Each day the security guard religiously checked the wheelbarrow and the WHARFIE for pilfered goods. This went on for months until the WHARFIE retired. A few months later the guard met the retired WHARFIE in the PUB and in the guilt-free and convivial atmosphere of the BOOZER asked him, ON THE QUIET, to let him in on what he had been stealing all those months. The WHARFIE sipped his beer, smiled and answered: 'Wheelbarrows'.

YAKKA is that quintessentially Australian word for work, HARD YAKKA being what many like to think made the country great. Perhaps derived from Aboriginal speech YAKKA has been used in Australia from the early 19th century. A SOFT COP, an EASY TOUCH and a GOOD POSSIE are terms describing a good job. There are plenty of other terms that describe work of a particular kind, including BOGGING, seeming to be originally a West Australianism referring to working underground in a mine, though now used generally to mean shovelling or otherwise loading BLUE METAL, known in some places as AGGREGATE. BOGGING is probably related to a convictism for working and must not be confused with BOG IN, meaning to eat heartily, or the BOG, the LOO.

A very important aspect of work is the time involved, especially arrival and departure. The Victorian practice of BUNDYING ON still operates in many places. The BUNDY CLOCK, and similar devices of industrial time discipline, was a large clock attached to a machine that stamped the time on a card. Each worker would have his or her own card, placing it in the machine at arrival and departure. Regardless of whether you were coming or going the ching the bell made was exactly the same. THE BUNDY has still not been entirely displaced from the workshops and factories of Australia, although more sophisticated systems are now used, such as Flexitime (giving rise to the

Lingoisms FLEX DAY (a day off from work due to accrued flexitime), FLEX OFF (to finish work) and just FLEX and the NINE-DAY FORTNIGHT with its two-weekly OFF DAY, DAY OFF or DAY-IN-LIEU. Interestingly, the use of TIME for a prison sentence, now widespread in the English-speaking world, seems to have originated in Australia from the earliest days of transportation and a suggestive linking of the notions of bondage and the labour.

Aversion to work also features in Lingo, as in phrases like HE'D RATHER PICK UP A BROWN SNAKE THAN PICK UP A RAKE. Someone who WOULDN'T WORK IN A BARREL OF YEAST or WOULDN'T WORK IN AN IRON LUNG is very lazy. A BLUDGER, from the 1970s a DOLE BLUDGER is someone with a serious affection for indolence. Such behaviour may result in GETTING THE ARSE or the A, meaning to get the sack, also referred to as THE BIG A. Other terms for losing one's job include to be ARSEHOLED; GET THE FLICK; GET THE PUSH; GET THE SHOVE; GET THE SPEAR (a shearing term, it seems); to GET YOUR MARCHING ORDERS; to GET THE ORDER OF THE BOOT, and to get A DCM, that is DON'T COME MONDAY. At the other end of the process, a NEW STARTER is just what the term implies. Often such innocents are subjected to mostly well-meaning initiation pranks and hoaxes, such as being asked to GO FOR A LONG WEIGHT or to find a LEFT-HANDED SPANNER. The variations on these little tricks are almost infinite and are often industry-specific.

Most occupations, trades and professions have their own little lingoes spoken by practitioners. Each of these is a study in itself, though some have or are contributing words to the general stock-in-trade of the Great Australian Lingo.

MINING GOLD AND BLACK GOLD

Goldmining has been an important part of the Australian economy since the middle of the 19th century. A large vocabulary of words and phrases has developed over this period, sometimes borrowing from the gold industry elsewhere in the world, sometimes inventing new words to suit Australian conditions and practices. A hard layer of sedimentary rock, probably shale or slate was known as BLACK JACK; a SLUG meant a nugget of gold while a SWAMPER was someone travelling on foot towards what they hoped would be a golden hoard. The serious activity of searching for gold was CHASING THE WEIGHT; FRACTEUR was a term for the explosive gelignite, after the waterproof material used for lining boxes of gelignite; WINZE was a passage leading downwards in a goldmine; a RISE was an upward passage from a level mine passage, and a GRUB STAKE referred to the practice of supplying prospectors with provisions in exchange for a share of the profits. This term is also used in the USA and probably arrived here with the influx of Americans attracted from the Californian fields, continuing our long linguistic entanglement with US slang. (One oddity of this relationship, characteristic of the vernacular, is our borrowing the term KANGAROO COURT which is an Americanism. No-one seems quite sure why.) Be that as it may, in the 1890s KANGAROOS was the name given to Western Australian gold-rush mining shares and their dealers, so-called because of the ability of these stocks to jump in and out of existence. This is definitely one of our own many adaptations of this useful word.

Later gold-rush terms included TRIBUTES, tributing being a system that allowed parties of miners to work privately on parts of underground mines. Payment was made under agreement, based on the amount of gold the miners won and after paying the company back for the materials and costs involved in recovering the gold. SHYPOO meant cheap, or of dubious, quality, a word of unknown origin applied in terms like SHYPOO SHARES (penny or virtually worthless stocks) and SHYPOO SHOWS (fraudulent mines). It was also heard outside the gold trade in such terms as SHYPOO BEER and SHYPOO JOINT (a beer house). A related term of about the same vintage, in the last years of the 19th century, is a SHYSTER MINE. Again the sense of fraudulence inherent in this goldmining use of the word remains in its general Lingo usage — SHYSTER, one who is a fraud, a person of little worth. Another related gold-mining term that was to be heard in the wider Lingo in future years was SHICER (SCHEISSER and other spellings), said to derive from British slang meaning a worthless person. It was widely used on the goldfields to mean a worthless hole or mine. From the number of such negative terms in gold-rush lingo it seems that there was no shortage of disappointed DIGGERS.

The early days of goldmining produced the term DIGGER in the sense of someone who does just that in search of gold. This was already in use by the end of the 1840s and before the really big gold rushes got underway. The word remained with us and there were many proud to wear it on the goldfields. This great coming-together of humanity from around the world with the common aim of striking it rich, rapidly generated a distinctive little lingo as the everyday form of conversational exchange. Raffaello Carboni's eyewitness account of the Eureka Stockade, published in 1855, just a year after the event itself, is spiced with the speech of the diggings. Early in his engagingly eccentric book, the Italian-born DIGGER describes his first encounter with the licence-hunting goldfields police, universally detested both for the job the authorities of the day asked them to do and for the manner in which they collected the hated licence fees.

It seems that Carboni bribes the policeman with THE OLD ALL RIGHT:

> One fine morning (Epiphany Week), I was hard at work (excuse old chum, if I said hard: though my hand had been scores of times compelled in London to drop the quill through sheer fatigue, yet I never before handled a pick and shovel), I hear a rattling noise among the brush. My faithful dog, Bonaparte, would not keep under my control. 'What's up?' [Carboni calls]. 'Your licence, mate,' was the peremptory question from a six-foot fellow in blue shirt, thick boots, the face of a ruffian armed with a carabine and fixed bayonet. The old 'all right' being exchanged, I lost sight of that specimen of colonial brutedom and his similars, called, as I then learned, 'traps' [foot police] and 'troopers.' [mounted police] I let off work, and was unable to do a stroke more that day.

At this time terms like TRAP and JOE were used to describe the police. TRAP was a convictism derived from earlier British slang for a person who trapped OFFENDERS while JOE probably, though not certainly, came from the middle name of the-then Lieutenant-Governor of Victoria, Charles Joseph La Trobe.

The technical aspects of goldmining gave us CRADLE, a device for washing gold dust from sand, ROCKING THE CRADLE being a generally used term for this do-it-yourself form of mining. Later, in the arid West Australian goldfields, the DRYBLOWER was invented for the same purpose, using a current of air to separate the dross from the precious metal. Paddy Hannan's account of his monster find at what is now Kalgoorlie (KAL) in 1893 makes it clear that DRYBLOWING was a well-established practice on the Western goldfields by that time:

> The flats and gullies all about our reward claim became alive with diggers dryblowing and finding gold...Where the ground was too wet for dryblowing, the men dried the earth by fires and so could work their claims.

The West Australian balladist E.G. Murphy took the pen-name Dryblower both in recognition of the-then atmosphere of the gold rush and also as a deprecating reference to his poetic spoutings, many of which contained liberal servings of then-current Lingo, as in 'His Quest':

> *It was out beyond the Bulong track we met him swagging in,*
> *He was middle-aged and ginger, haggard-eyed and famine-thin;*
> *And while he munched some damper and a pannikin of tea,*
> *He asked us if we thought he'd catch the Perth express at three.*

There was not a watch amongst us, but I reckoned, by the sun,
'If he cut across the leases it could easily be done';
But Mickey brought a clock to light he'd pinched at Hogan's store,
And arst him 'Wot's your trouble, what's your worry-'urry for?

'You've done the rattler in today, you ain't got Buckley's 'ope,
But there's one goes down at night-time when the stony-brokers slope.'
The swagman sighed a trifle and unstrapped his scanty swag,
Then drew a crumpled letter from a dirty linen bag.

It is clear that the letter bears bad news from home...'A bloke
wot boarded with us has skedaddled with my wife...

A neighbour sent this letter and he's give me the tip
Where I'll find the pair who made me chuck my job and take this trip.'
'Any nippers?' chipped in Mickey, with a scowl upon his brow.
'But if or not, I'd belt the 'ide from off the bloomin' cow'.

The men hope that the treacherous couple have not taken the SWAG-
GIE's money and wish him well in seeking his revenge. But, to their
surprise, the SWAGGIE says he is not worried about the loss of his wife.
Puzzled, they ask the man:

'Then wot on earth's yer 'urry?' argued Mickey with a sniff,
If you ain't goin' after boodle and yer ain't goin' after biff?'
'Just this,' the stranger answered as he rose from off his log,
'When the pair of blankers bolted, spare me days, they took me dog!'

A DOLLY was a machine for crushing gold out of rock, by using grav-
ity, a heavy rock, an iron grill and a good deal of faith. TO DOLLY was
to perform this operation and a DOLLY POT was the container beneath
the iron grill into which the crushed material fell. YANDYING, a word
derived from the Yinjibarndi language for a shallow dish or similar
receptacle, came to describe the process of separating gold in a dish,
also referred to as PANNING. A YANDY was the name given to the pan
or dish used for this purpose. The West Australian gold rushes also
developed that essential forerunner of the FRIDGE, the COOLGARDIE
SAFE.

Another kind of gold was also mined from the earliest days of
European settlement. The first coalminers were convicts but, as in
many other countries, a distinctive industry and accompanying way
of life has evolved around the difficult, fraught and often tragic business of winning the black gold from the ground. Strongly rooted
in British coal traditions and values, Australian coalmining includes

many terms often derived from the Welsh and English mines. A DARG used to mean the amount of coal in one skip, though today DARG usually refers to some other agreed measure or time of work, usually negotiated between management and miners; a SPRAG is a temporary brake for a skip which may be stopped by SPRAGGING it. This term is also known in the larger Lingo, usually meaning to catch or to apprehend someone or something, probably passing from the mining industry via the great melting pot of slang created by the Australian soldiers of World War I. CRIB is, as in Britain, the miner's meal, carried in a CRIB TIN. While the methods used in mining coal have changed dramatically, many of the older terms are used in what is still a close-knit community of coalminers and their families, held together by a common tradition of struggle and by the many tragedies of a dangerous way of earning a living.

Some other specialised coalmining little lingoisms include: BRATTICE (hessian-like curtains proofed with bitumen and hung along the HEADINGS (main thoroughfare of a coalmine) to direct the airflow; a JIM CROW is a double-hooked tool for bending railway lines; a TOMMY DODDS was a device for keeping the endless rope that provided the motive power to haul the SKIPS of coal off the mine floor; SKIPS are wheeled along the SKIP-RAILS and the CAGE is the lift that lowers the miners DOWN BELOW and raises them back UP TOP again at the end of the shift.

UP THE COUNTRY

'I'll take you up the country and I'll show you the bush', goes the line from the bush song 'The Old Bullock Dray'. Opening up the country, exploration, pioneering, squatting and later, free selection, were the central experiences of 19th-century Australia. The yarns, ballads and other folklore from that period and from those experiences have become our defining images of Australianness. THE BUSH is either from the Dutch *bosch*, probably cargoed here via South Africa in the mouths of the earliest transportees or derives from Scandinavia via Middle English. With its Arcadian images of freedom, its beauty, its strangeness and its hardships, THE BUSH forms the bedrock of 'the Australian Legend'. As well as the songs and legends of bush life, these experiences also generated a large lexicon. Some of this rural language has become part of the vernacular we still use today. Other more specialised terms remain in the little lingoes of particular trades, skills, and groups associated with bush life, including shearers, fencers, overlanders, horse breakers, swagmen, and many more who live and work on the land.

Many of our traditional similes, even though still in robust urban use, retain a hint of THE BUSH. AS LEAN AS A WHIP; AS DRY AS A SUNSTRUCK BONE; AS TIGHT AS A CALF'S (or FISH'S) ARSE; AS DRY AS A CAMEL'S HEELS; SILLY AS A CUT SNAKE and RUNNING ROUND LIKE A CHOOK WITH ITS HEAD CUT OFF, are just some of many that conjure up the great outdoors. Despite our heavily urbanised reality in Australia there is no doubt that THE BUSH has provided us with some especially colourful contributions — and still does. Just as importantly, the laconic sense of humour characteristic of bush life has established the recognisable tone of much of our colloquial speech. Folklorist Ron Edwards reported a few outback similes that he had heard around the Laura region of northern Queensland in 1985. They included describing a wine cask as a HEADACHE IN A BOX and a person wearing a very wide-brimmed hat as A WALKING ROOFING NAIL.

Older bush slang conjures up images of the hard-travelling, hard-working and hard-drinking lifestyles that we have long associated with swagmen, shearers, rouseabouts, and the like. TO KNOCK DOWN is to spend your money, as in KNOCK DOWN A CHEQUE. In the bush song 'On the Road to Gundagai' the shearers left Roto for Sydney 'with a three-spot cheque between us as wanted knocking down'. Their SPREE was over in a week and then they SHOULDERED THEIR MATILDAS and went back on the track to nurse their hangovers and search for more work, the classic pattern of bush working life. To GO ON A (the) SPREE was to go on a BINGE of drinking, gambling, and womanising, and derives from 18th-century cant. Judging by the frequency with which the term turns up in bush ballads and songs the SPREE was a fairly frequent occurrence, often associated with the end of a shearing season or the harvest, as in 'The Old Keg of Rum':

And when harvest time was over,
And we'd get our harvest fee,
We'd meet and quickly rise the keg
And then we'd have a spree.
We'd sit and sing together
Till we got that blind and dumb
That we couldn't find the bunghole
Of the Old Keg of Rum.

A variation of KNOCK DOWN is to be LAMBED DOWN (1870 in print), a difference of word, but not of effect. LAMBED DOWN generally meant that a man had been conned into parting with his money, usually through the dual blandishments of the GROG and a prostitute.

Like many colonialisms these terms appear in bush songs and ballads, forms of verse and song that often deal with workers such as shearers, drovers, BULLOCKIES (famed Lingoists), and a whole host of associated figures of Australian myth .'This bloke I know came rolling home as shickered as he could be', begins one bush song about the unfortunate results of arriving home with A SKINFUL. SHICKERED, from the Yiddish for drunk, has been in use since at least the early 19th century in various forms, including ON THE SHICKER. It was probably preceded by SHICK or SHUCK as a general term for excessive imbibing.

MAKING DO has been a constantly necessary skill of bush life and could cover a multitude of activities from improvising tools, furniture, and other essentials to obtaining the means of subsistence, not necessarily in a strictly lawful way. 'You've only to sport your Dover to knock a monkey over, that's cheap mutton on The Wallaby Brigade', goes a line from 'The Wallaby Brigade'. SPORT for show or for display is from 18th-century cant, a DOVER was a favoured brand of knife while a MONKEY was a sheep. This method of GETTING A FEED got an even more famous swagman into terminal trouble in Paterson's 'Waltzing Matilda', itself a mini-treasury of colonial bush lingo, one of the reasons for its enduring popularity as the unofficial national anthem.

'The Wallaby Brigade' is one of many songs and ballads about itinerant bush labourers or SWAGGIES who HUMPED their DRUMS, BLUEYS or SWAG (derived from 17th-century cant for a shop) from place to place in search of work. Although MATILDA is now one of the best-known terms for this bundle of belongings, Henry Lawson, who would have known, was at pains to point out in 1893 that this term was unusual: 'A swag is not generally referred to as a "bluey" or "Matilda" — it is *called* a "swag"' and 'You do not "hump bluey" — you simply carry your swag.' Lawson might have made much the same comments about an even more romantic term for a SWAG — SHIRAL(L)EE, a word of unknown origin and of probably restricted provenance that was effectively used by D'Arcy Niland in his book of the same name.

Lawson was a determined anti-romantic about THE BUSH, at least in his short stories, if not in much of his poetry. 'The Bush Undertaker', among others, deals with an unhappy, isolated alcoholic soul, known in bush lingo as a HATTER. These men lived and worked alone in the bush, often going mad as a consequence, experiences with which Lawson was well able to empathise. On the romanticisation of bush speech, Lawson also made some other salutary observations:

The manager is not called the 'super'; he is called the 'overseer' — which name suits him better...Station-hands are not noble, romantic fellows; they are mostly crawlers to the boss — which they have to be...Men tramping in search of a 'shed' are not called 'sundowners' or 'swaggies' — they are 'trav'lers'...No bushman thinks of 'going on the wallaby' or 'walking Matilda' or 'padding the hoof'; he goes 'on the track', when forced to it...You do not 'stow grub' — you 'have some tucker, mate'.

The work of rearing, handling, and disposing of livestock has always played an important role in bush life and many country lingoisms reflect this. TRAVELLING STOCK is an Australianism dating from at least the 1870s and meaning to take livestock through the country, usually to or from a market. Drovers TRAVELLED cattle or TRAVELLED sheep, as in the bush ballad 'The Shearer's Dream' which begins 'One night while travelling sheep, my companions fell asleep . . .' To HANDTHROW a steer is to throw an animal to the ground ready for branding, also known as SCRUFFING. MOKE and PRAD (from British dialect) were both common terms for horses and were in use from the early years of European settlement. PROG was in use during the 1870s to mean food and it is used in one of the contemporary Kelly ballads on the subject of the gunfight at Stringybark Creek, describing the policemen sent to catch the bushrangers as about to '...wire into the prog'. Intriguingly, PROG also survived in Newfoundland with the same meaning.

Bullock drivers — BULLOCKIES — were legendary for their profane language, a skill celebrated in a backhanded way in the recitation 'Holy Dan'. Dan is known to the other bullockies as 'Holy Dan' because he never swears, no matter what the provocation. Dan's bullocks are dying and as each one dies Dan simply turns the other cheek, reckons this must be the will of the Lord and prays for deliverance from the pestilence. Eventually, however, even Dan's monumental patience is tried too far. His second-last animal dies:

> *Then Dan broke down — good Holy Dan —*
> *The man who never swore.*
> *He knelt beside the latest corpse,*
> *And here's the prayer he prore:*
>
> *'That's nineteen though has taken, Lord,*
> *And now I plainly see*
> *You'd better take the bloody lot:*
> *One's no damn good to me!'*

The other drivers laughed so much
They shook the sky around;
The lightning flashed, the thunder roared,
And Holy Dan was drowned.

The modern-day equivalents of BULLOCKIES, the TRUCKIES are noted for their facility with the Lingo. On long-distance hauls the trucks are checked at weighing stations along the highways. The much-despised inspectors who staff these establishments were known in the 1980s as MERMAIDS because they are, according to the TRUCKIES, CUNTS WITH SCALES.

Dogs were, and still are, the inevitable accompaniment of bush life. Valued as working animals and as sentinels, four-legged friends, were a stock element of the literary yarns of Lawson and others, even of the anti-romantic Barbara Baynton. Dogs also seemed to feature in just about every early Australian film as they chased the horses or the cows, apparently in total disregard of the director and script — when there was either. The DROVER'S DOG, in particular, is a beast of considerable stature in Australian Lingo. Bill Hayden's bitter quip on Bob Hawke's 1983 election victory to the effect that even A DROVER'S DOG COULD HAVE WON IT, is well known and is often quoted or referred to in everyday speech. Canine companions of the bush also figure in a number of colloquialisms. One is an extended simile for a thin person —HE WAS LIKE A DROVER'S DOG, ALL PRICK AND RIBS. In all likelihood the dog of the following phrase probably did not belong to a drover — IT SMELT SO BAD IT WOULD KILL A BROWN DOG AT TEN PACES — drovers' dogs are tougher than that. Another variant, used to describe something considered excessively rank, is IT'D GIVE A BROWN DOG THE SHITS. The wild dog, the dingo, features prominently in Lingo, usually in negative terms like A LOW DINGO, or in ways suggesting a certain spartan level of existence — a DINGO'S BREAKFAST, for instance, is a PISS AND A GOOD LOOK ROUND. Dogs also appear metaphorically in bush talk in the term for bully beef — TIN DOG, a staple of the bush worker's cuisine, as was the occasional rabbit, or UNDERGROUND MUTTON.

In 1859 the owner of Barwon Park property (Victoria), Thomas Austin, received a gift of two dozen wild rabbits from his brother in England. The rabbits were to provide a quarry for the shooters of the district. Soon the animals spread, and spread...Within a decade they were a serious pest in Victoria's Western District, hopping across the Nullarbor Plain by the early 1890s. Eradication of the cute, but economically and environmentally disastrous, bunny, was an ongoing nightmare for the rural sector until the scientists of the

Commonwealth Scientific Industrial Research Organisation (CSIRO — SIRO for short, also CICERO) concocted myxomatosis — the MYXO or MYXY — a disease which effectively eradicated rabbits for many years until they developed a degree of immunity by the end of the 1980s. In 1996 the rabbit calicivirus was officially released into the rabbit population to replace myxomatosis — after it had already escaped from its 'safe' experimental island off the coast of South Australia. RABBIT CALICIVIRUS is now an established element of Australian speech, especially in rural areas.

That essential implement of bush travel, the BILLY or billycan, has a central place in the lingo of the bush, and more widely in the national mythology. The term itself has a number of apparently folk derivations: one version is that it is an adaptation of an Aboriginal word *billa*, said to mean water; another is that it comes from the Victorian GOLD-DIGGERS' use of the cans that contained a popular French soup called *boulli*. The real origins of the word are more prosaic; it comes, as do many lingoisms, from a British dialect term, in this case the Scots 'billypot'. Regardless of its origins, BILLY is often heard in bush talk: BILLY TEA, BOIL THE BILLY, SWING A BILLY, and so on. The BILLY is also part of the enduring romance of the bush, found in such titles as Lawson's 'While the Billy Boils' collection of short stories and in numberless bush songs, such as 'My Old Black Billy' and in this tongue-in-cheek verse:

> *You can sing of your whisky and sing of your beer*
> *There's something much nicer that's waiting me here.*
> *It sits on the fire beneath a gum tree,*
> *There's nothing much nicer than a billy of tea.*

MONEY TALKS

Moving away from the bush and into the city we hear an elaborate argot in the work language of stockbrokers and their associates. Nineteenth-century brokering terms included a BACK-HANDED TURN, meaning an unprofitable bargain. Directors of public companies were referred to as GUINEA PIGS. A TAPE-WORM or WIRE-WORM was someone who telegraphed the prices of various stocks to clients in the country, while TWIST-ON-THE-SHORTS was a term used to describe a dishonestly overvalued market in which the shorts have been forced to settle for a heavy loss. Other terms included those still with us and now sanctified as officialspeak of the finance world, such as BEAR, BULL, BOOMING, CORNER and to UNLOAD, hopefully, now as then, at the right moment.

Interestingly, until at least the early 20th century, stockbroking and related financial transactions were considered in the same category as gambling and games of chance in general. Professor Scott ('The Australian Lightning Calculator') pointed out in his 1895 treatise *The Doctrine of Chance*, the mysteries of investment, speculation and gambling, including horseracing, making a book, Chinese lotteries and various other related arts. Among many intriguing techniques, Scott describes the cover system of gambling in shares. His description makes clear that stockbrokers were considered to be essentially bookmakers, an epithet that few would like applied to them in these sophisticated financial times. The cover worked by staking one per cent of any amount on the rise or fall of selected stocks. If they fell below the amount paid, say five pounds, the broker collected the money. If they rose the speculator claimed the difference between the five pounds and the new value. No stock is actually purchased. As Scott points out, 'When analysed, it is simply betting upon the rise and fall of the market, the broker being to all intents and purposes a bookmaker.' This seems remarkably similar to the current fad for futures and other derivatives spawned by the financial excesses of the 1980s. Scott goes on to use some of the past and present language of gambling:

> In sharebroking the operation of the 'bulls' and 'bears' are [sic] similar to the general 'cronk' (crooked) work of the turf; the 'lame-duck' (the loser, who waddles away) finds his counterpart in the 'welsher'.

Modern stockbrokers, of course, are thoroughly respectable professionals whose playing of the stock market is governed by highly scientific techniques, such as RISK MANAGEMENT and HEDGING. Those who deal with stocks, shares, bonds and the bewildering array of DERIVATIVES, FUTURES and other vehicles still depend on the BOOMING of a BULL MARKET and generally despair of the BEAR MARKET with its threats of a SHARE BUST. Since 1983, financially unsophisticated Australians have had to come to grips with a deregulated economy and so learn a lot of sometimes painful lessons about money. THE BOTTOM-OF-THE-HARBOUR SCHEMES and SCAMS of the early 1980s were just the first of a continuing series of financial disasters, bank runs, SWISS LOANS and defaulting financial institutions. Accompany-ing and associated RORTS, included those of the high-flying entrepreneurs of the excessive 1980s who are either serving TIME or have DONE A SKASE.

ACCA YACKER

The popular concept of academics as an occupational group inevitably revolves around corduroy jackets, pipe smoking and profound discussions pursued in erudite language.

While there are no doubt a few academics around who still fit this stereotype, many university teachers in this country carry out their tasks with much the same attitudes, values, successes and failures as any other professional group. Because they come from many different backgrounds and carry out a variety of functions with different philosophical points of view, academics are an unusually disparate occupational group, often more given to disputation than to cooperation. But, like all other groups academics have their own special terminology that is intelligible on all campuses. ACCA YAKKER includes self-descriptions like ACCA for an academic; ASPRO — Associate Professor (and not to be confused with the little lingo term for a male homosexual prostitute); SL (ESEL) — Senior Lecturer; and PROF — Professor. Within the wider university community the following contractions and acronyms are universally used by students, teachers and administrators: TUTE — tutorial; DEET — Department of Employment, Education and Training, though since 1996 DEETYA, Department of Employment, Education, Training and Youth Affairs; E.F.T.S.U. , often pronounced EFTSU — equivalent full-time student unit; VC — Vice Chancellor; DVC — Deputy Vice Chancellor; OFF CAMPUS — away from the university.

Universities also have their own little lingo names. UQ is the University of Queensland; UT is the University of Tasmania; ENID BLYTON UNIVERSITY or EDITH COWABUNGA — Edith Cowan University; the University of New South Wales in the Sydney suburb of Kensington is known as KENSO and at an earlier stage of its evolution, was fondly dubbed KENSO TECH; Melbourne University has long been called THE SHOP. In Perth, the University of Western Australia retains its status as the premier tertiary institution in popular parlance where it is almost always called THE UNIVERSITY (though never by staff at other Perth universities). Before the Institutes of Technology began changing into variously named universities from 1987, the 'I' in their titles occasionally generated intriguing acronyms, often impenetrable to the uninitiated. The Western Australian Institute of Technology, for instance was, fairly straightforwardly and predictably WAIT while the Queensland Institute of Technology was known as QUIT. Most inventive, if convoluted, was the New South Wales Institute of Technology — NEWSWIT, now known as UTS (University of Technology Sydney). The generic abbreviation UNI has become part of Australian parlance since opening up university places to greater numbers of Australians in the 1970s.

FAT CAT CHAT

Bureaucrats, public servants, or FAT CATS (CRATS is the mid-1990s Canberraspeak) are notorious for mangling the language in the interests of obfuscation and policy. While most of this non-communication goes on in formal memoranda and reports, bureaucrats also have their own lingoes. These vary from office to office, but always feature TLAs — three-letter abbreviations or acronyms, such as EIS (Environmental Impact Statement); WPB (waste paper bin or basket, as in FILE IT IN THE WPB), also known as THE ROUND FILE in many bureaucracies.

It has long been known that bureaucrats commit heinous crimes against the basic tenets of written communication. Every decade or two there is an attempt to weed out jargon and sense-obscuring constructions from the language of FAT CATS — but it always creeps back in. The overwhelming need to fend off the public and rival officials, together with the imperative to remain detached, inevitably means that bureaucratese will be bland, euphemistic, and sometimes plain nonsensical. This was well illustrated by the findings of a report by the Language and Literacy Council (July 1996) into the use of plain English in the Australian Public Service. The report, *Putting It Plainly*, noted that, despite the introduction of a plain English policy into the Federal public service as long ago as 1984, the survey of 23 Federal government departments carried out in 1995 shows that most of these did not have any formal guidelines on writing in clear language. So poor was the level of written communication emanating from the bureaucracy that the compilers of the report felt the need to recommend action at the highest level. A kind of linguistic inquisitor should be appointed within the Prime Minister's Department with responsibility for cutting out the GOBBLEDYGOOK, DOUBLETALK and deeply entrenched jargon perpetrated by the nation's public servants. To date, such a position has not been created. If it ever is, its incumbent might find the jargon generator of some didactic value.

The jargon generator is a long-standing device that satirises the tendency of bureaucracy towards GOBBLEDYGOOK. It has been around for a very long time, one of its surfacings into formal print being in Sir Ernest Gower's *The Complete Plain Words* in 1948. In mid-1996 it turned up on the FRIDGE door of an Australian university staffroom and circulated elsewhere in various photocopied forms. Now known as 'The Systematic Buzz Phrase Generator', an impeccable proof of the very tendency which it parodies, this useful device was said, apocryphally, to have originated with an official in the US Public Health Service:

0. integrated	0. management	0. options
1. overall	1. organisational	1. flexibility
2. systematised	2. monitored	2. capability
3. parallel	3. reciprocal	3. mobility
4. functional	4. digital	4. programming
5. responsive	5. logistical	5. concept
6. optimal	6. transitional	6. time-phase
7. synchronised	7. incremental	7. projection
8. compatible	8. new-generation	8. hardware
9. balanced	9. policy	9. contingency

You simply think of a number of three digits and write down the corresponding words from each column. So, 058 yields up 'integrated logistical hardware'; 314 gives 'parallel organisational programming', and so on. The real worry is that there is probably at least one BURO (bureaucrat) using such a device to compile written 'communications'.

TECHNO-BABBLE

As well as adding immeasurably to our ability to manipulate and to store information, the computer revolution has greatly magnified our language. Sometimes referred to as TECHNO-BABBLE, computerspeak has confused and bewildered many more individuals than it has enlightened. Words such as BIT (from binary digit) and BYTE (eight bits), CACHE, BAUD, and innumerable others, have been rocketing electronically, verbally and in print form since the 1980s. This new language seems to grow each week as the phenomenal advances in computer communications and associated technologies demand new terms for new concepts, techniques, devices, or some new combinations of these.

A few examples that have mostly come and gone in the computer cosmos include: NESTED LOOPS, a KLUDGE (pronounced kloodge and meaning a jerry-rigged configuration of devices); WYSYWYG (what-you-see-is-what-you-get); DTP — desktop publishing. As these few items suggest, computerspeak is often boringly functional, unless you are a COMPUTER PERSON, that is. One of the few interesting coinages is that of DOS. This apparently came from its experimental name Q-DOS (kudos — get it? COMPUTER PEOPLE are full of wicked little puns) which actually stood for Quick and Dirty Operating System. When this system was taken over by Microsoft in the early 1980s the name was changed to MS-DOS for Microsoft Disk Operating System, a point often noted by the rival Apple Macintosh (MAC) users.

So prevalent and overblown has TECHNO-BABBLE become that a US company developed a Generic Description Table (known in the lingo as an ANAESTHESIA-INDUCTION MATRIX). This table is a computer-age extension of the jargon generator mentioned above. The Generic Description Table, like much computerspeak, simply extends this concept and makes it more complicated and wordy, yielding up terms like Centrally Balanced Analysis Chain or Globally Digital Data-Demand Environment. None of these phrases means anything, though someone may market something sounding very much like it next week.

These and many other terms are spoken by computer professionals and those TECHNO-PSEUDS who wish to appear knowledgeable about such matters. As befits such a large and complex organism as the computer industry there are many subgroups, all with their own languages. They include HACKERS, those who HACK into computer systems, usually for curiosity or for altruistic motives. The term is said to have originated in the late 1950s at the Massachussetts Institute of Technology (MIT) among experimental technophobes. Those with criminal intent, of whom there is no shortage, are called CRACKERS, a hangover of the criminalism SAFECRACKER. So vast is the lexicon of HACKING that there are a number of dictionaries devoted exclusively to terms peculiar to this pastime. One favourite HACKER GAME is FREAKING (also spelt PHREAKING sometimes FUN FREAKING) which describes the practice of sending false tones or other information to a telephone line in order to obtain free use of the line. Those who carry out such practices are called FREAKERS. Lowest on the hierarchy of hacking are CARDERS, those who obtain other people's credit card numbers by breaking into the computers of financial institutions.

An intriguing example of how the Lingo is being exported into the global ELECTRONIC HIGHWAY began in late 1989. On 16 October of that year NASA's computers caught a VIRUS. This one was a self-replicating NASTY that deleted NASA computer files as soon as staff logged on to their terminals. Before it started destroying untold amounts of highly secret and highly expensive information the VIRUS displayed on the computer screens the following message:

Worms against nuclear killers
WANKED
Your system has been officially WANKed
You talk of times of peace for all
and then prepare for war.

NASA's computer specialists reportedly were at their wits' end trying to discover the source of the HACKERS who had done this. One clue was in the term WANK, a popular Australianism for male masturbation that also means any questionable or futile activity. Although this term is also a feature of current British vernacular speech, it eventually turned out that the HACKERS were, indeed, Australian.

Closely connected with HACKING and growing exponentially (now I'm doing it) is the language of the Internet, the global communications network of personal computers. NETSURFING is an Internet neologism meaning to browse the information superhighway, though the more recent term WEB seems to be gradually overhauling NET in the race for what to call this chaotically ballooning communications system, with WEB MASTER, WEB SITE and WEB SPIDERS (those who crawl the WEB, also known as WEBSTERS) giving some idea of the semantic critical mass involved. TLAs are common in Netspeak, a consequence of the system's origins as a Pentagon fail-safe communication network and, for many years prime uses, in government and academic circles. These include FAQs (Frequently Asked Questions, pronounced facks) and URLS (Unknown Resource Location). Other terms refer to characteristics of the NET, such as exchanges of information and opinion, some of which erupt into FLAME WARS when users insult each other in cyberspace. FLAMING is generally considered poor NETIQUETTE. But as the system is, so far, almost totally unregulated, it is very common. Then there are BULLETIN BOARDS, NEWSGROUPS, USEGROUPS and the practice of SPAMMING, essentially electronic junk mail posted (despite the proliferation of new terms in computerese, this quaint old word is still used) indiscriminately around the system. As the little lingo of the NET grows, so inevitably does its sense of itself against other forms of communication. In the usage of the INTERNETTER and E-MAILER, the old-fashioned and hopelessly slow postal service is known as SNAIL MAIL.

VIRTUAL VERBIAGE

Some modern forms of folklore that use technologies such as the photocopier, the facsimile machine (FAX) and the computer are concerned with Lingo in one form or another. While these terms are not usually specifically Australian, due to the international nature of modern communications, they are spoken, written, and otherwise transmitted, in Australia. The following abbreviated example of this kind of reprographic lingo usually appears on official letter-heads of corporations or government departments. It gives an EARFUL of the popular responses to the stresses and strains of working life.

Internal Memorandum

SUBJECT: Introduction of the Use of Departmental Codes
The Management wishes to bring to the attention of all
personnel that some individuals have been using abusive
language in the normal everyday performance of their work
duties.

The following code has been devised to permit freedom
of expression, originality and understanding between fellow
work-mates, and at the same time provide clarity in an inoffensive way of communication whilst within the hearing
distance of customers and other persons outside the
Department.

From the time of receiving this memo all personnel are
hereby directed to use the following codes in all inter-depart-
mental communications. Any failure to do so will result in a
504 to those responsible for a breach of this directive.

500 Series — ARSE.
501 — Stick it up your arse
502 — You're an arsehole
503 — Kiss my arse
504 — You play ball with us or we'll stick the bat up your
arse.
505 — You're nothing but an arse licker.
600 — Series — SHIT.
601 — I don't give a shit
602 — This place gives me the shits
603 — You give me the shits
604 — Shit a brick
605 — This person shits me up the wall
606 — Do you know what shits me?
607 — Fat shit
608 — Beats the shit out of me
609 — Who gives a shit?

This item continues in like vein through a variety of abusive
possibilities.

Closely related to these photocopied items, and often identical
with them, are those missives transmitted to and from workplace
e-mail addresses. Usually compiled from BULLETIN BOARDS and similar Internet sites, these are often extensive glossaries of workplace and
general Lingo. A couple of mid-1996 examples included a list of FULL
DECKISMS containing almost 800 entries compiled since 1987.
Because those with the most access to this emerging form of

communications technology tended to be technocrats of one kind or another, these lists typically contain occupational little lingoisms, like A 10K BRAIN ATTACHED TO A 9600 BAUD MOUTH, a reference to the size and speed of the insulted one's intellect. Others of this type include A 3.5 INCH DRIVE, BUT DATA ON PUNCH CARDS, 3K RAM FREE, NO EMS and A ONE-BIT BRAIN WITH PARITY ERROR, A RETURN WITH NO GOSUB, and so on. These are incomprehensible to those who are not part of the USER-GROUP of computerologists. As well as these specialised jargonisms, these six- to seven-page lists also contain more general Lingoisms, such as A FEW INCHES SHORT OF A FOOT, A LAP BEHIND THE FIELD, A HAMBURGER (or A FEW FRENCH FRIES) SHORT OF A HAPPY MEAL, and I WOULDN'T PISS IN HIS EAR IF HIS BRAIN WAS ON FIRE. Coming from occupational groups that value high intelligence levels and the application of such intelligence, the concentration of these FULL DECKISMS on brain power and stupidity is not surprising, though there are also extensive repertoires of similar insults more widely available, as shown in chapter 10. Examples of these insults also appear in lengthy e-mail files, sometimes with an eclectically international collection of entries. The extent of these lists and the frequency of their circulation raises a question as to whether those whose jobs allow the compilation and transmission of these lists have enough work to do...

LEGO LINGO

Cadets at the Australian Defence Force Academy (ADFA), like other student groups, have their own in-group language. They even call it LEGO LINGO, a reference to the in-group name for the cadet accommodation blocks at ADFA — LEGOLAND — so-called because of the close resemblance of these structures to the well-known children's building blocks, Lego™. LEGO LINGO was collected by Bill Cowham and published in a book of that title in 1988.

The ADFA cadets refer to themselves as CORDIES, a CHECKIE is a minor offence, the commandant is known as the COMM, drill sergeants are DRILLIES, ENDEX means the end of an exercise, signalled by the delightful phrase MAG OFF, PACK OFF, FUCK OFF. Officers are THE PUTSCH and widely reviled, of course. The FID is the field, from the army abbreviation fd. It is clear from just these few examples and from the larger body of cadet slang that those future leaders of the armed forces are adept speakers of lingo — theirs and everyone else's.

Another military grouping near by is Duntroon, the Royal Military College (RMC). Its cadets also have a little lingo, some of which they speak in common with the CORDIES, such as the pig Latin-like DENTHOR ARGABAG (rotten garbage), referring to a woman of exceeding plainness. As well, Duntroon lingo, like that of ADFA, is shared with the general youthful male population. Liberally sprinkled with swearing, scatology, and an impressive variety of terms related to sexual activity, Duntroonspeak also has a considerable vocabulary of its own. This includes terms like: FOURTHIE, a fourth-year cadet, actually in the first year of his four-year course at the college and GROGAN (or GROGE), a woman, often considered of plain features (GROGAN in Lingo is a piece of SHIT or TURD). There are a variety of variations and extensions of this term in Duntroonspeak, including GROGANING and GROGAN HUNTING (to go in search of female companionship). A GROGANER is a cadet engaged in GROGANING. The importance of sexual activity in the life of the cadet is highlighted by a couple of columns of terms related to sexual activity, almost all of which are notable not only for their general vulgarity, but for their overwhelming objectification of women.

Some terms of cadet communication are borrowed from other little lingoes, especially those of youth and lifestyle groups. An example of this is the borrowing of the SURFIE term for a young or new surfer, a GROMMET. In Duntroon lingo, in the early 1980s to mid-1980s at least, this word was used to describe civilians in general or any cadet who had SURFIE leanings. Another example is SKEGG, in the late 1970s to early 1980s, deprecating youthspeak for a SURFIE or someone who pretends to be one by dressing in appropriate clothes and sporting the appropriate hairstyle. This term was used at Duntroon with much the same meaning as GROMMET.

Like all lingoes, large and little, that of Duntroon cadets changes quite rapidly. Within a few years of graduation it is said that old cadets might not recognise many of the terms that have since come into currency. Similarly, the new cadets may often scratch their heads at the parlance of their predecessors. This process is well illustrated by the Duntroon traditions and legends associated with THE SEVEN WONDERS OF DUNTROON. These are areas of the campus that have specific associations and names. They have changed markedly over time, as the objects and personalities associated with them have disappeared. THE SEVEN WONDERS are also complicated by the fact that there may, at any one time, be more than seven! Bruce Moore's study of the language and sociology of Duntroon between 1983 and 1985 lists the then-wonders as THE BELL THAT NEVER TOLLS; THE BOOMERANGS ABOVE THE MESS; GENERAL GRAVE'S BRIDGE; GENERAL BRIDGE'S GRAVE; THE MAST WITHOUT A SHIP; THE ROOM WITHIN A ROOM; THE STEPS THAT LEAD NOWHERE and, number eight, THE TANK THAT HOLDS NO WATER. At various times between 1930 and the 1980s there have been another 20 Seven Wonders, known to various generations of cadets. These have included THE KOKODA TRAIL; THE CAVERNS OF GLUM; THE BARRENNESS OF MRS HERITAGE; GILLIE'S SHOUSE (that is, SHITHOUSE, a venerable and valuable general Lingoism); COSTELLO'S TOOL; PARNELL'S PIMPLE, and THE LEANING WALLS OF THE TACTICS ROOM.

Many of these WONDERS have legends associated with them. As is often the case with legends, as with proverbs, these may contradict each other. For instance, the wonder known as THE BOOMERANGS ABOVE THE MESS was said by cadets to be a wonder because the boomerangs were crossed the wrong way. The wrong way was variously explained as the boomerangs in the mess being above the emblem on the wall rather than below it, or being placed left over right whereas the the correct position on the Corps badge was right over left. And so it goes on. Clearly cadet life at Duntroon is complex and the lingo it has produced most sophisticated indeed. For an insight into that culture HAVE A SQUIZ at Moore's *A Lexicon of Cadet Language* (Canberra, 1993) which takes almost 500 pages to present and explain Duntroon cadet lingo—as spoken in just the three years from 1983 to 1985.

For an insight into the earlier lingo of this specialised group, there is a study of cadetspeak that delves back as far as the 1930s. R. Raywards's *More Than A Mere Bravo* provides decade-by-decade listing and explanation of RMC argot from 1930 to the 1970s. Of those terms that have come and gone during the lengthy history of this institution and those who have peopled it, the following are some examples. From the 1930s—ADM BLOCK (pronounced Adam) for Administration Block; BISH TIN for rubbish tin; BOGGING for panicking; BUNGLE for cheese; MIRNIP was a cigarette, derived it seems from manipulate as in making a roll-your-own smoke, though the term was also applied to TAILOR-MADES; a MUNGA MAN was a cadet who consumed a great deal of food, possibly from earlier DIGGER slang for hunger/eating, MUNGER, itself a corruption of the French *manger* ; DOG ROBBERS were plain civilian clothes, and the cadets of the 1930s referred to the college as THE CLINK, a reference to its gaol-like regulations and discipline. It is also revealed that the Lingo term—or one of them, at least—for Roman Catholics, ROCK CHOPPERS (RCs, probably derived from its earlier British use for a navvy or labourer, many of whom were Irish) was in use at RMC in the 1930s, quite a few years before it seems to have been noted in the broader vernacular where the term GREEN MAFIA was once quite common.

Other terms flourished for a decade or two, such as a SEAL (as in performing) for a cadet who worked in the mess as a waiter (1960s and 1970s); SCHLONG, derived from the Yiddish for snake and meaning to cadets of the 1970s, as it did and still does in broader Lingo, the penis; SHURD, an insult derived from blending SHIT and TURD, popular in the 1930s and 1940s. A few, mainly those rooted firmly in the physical and institutional aspects of Duntroon life such as THE SEVEN WONDERS and BC DAY (Battalion Commander's Day, being the Thursday morning kit inspection), have lived on, little changed, into the present.

As well as having their own language, Duntroon cadets are the targets of usually derogatory terms aimed at them by Canberra civilians — CORDIE/ARSEHOLE/FUCKWIT/PRICK/WANKER, DUNNY, DUNTROONY and TROONY. Not quite the TOWN AND GOWN language of Oxford, though the sentiments are probably much the same.

Before leaving LEGO LINGO one interesting item of lore and legend needs dealing with as it provides one of the very few examples of back slang. The RMC possesses an unusual mascot that accompanies teams to all sporting events to bring luck. The mascot is known as ENOBESRA (ARSEBONE) and has been with the college since 1924 when two cadets engaged in a tactical exercise found a sheep's jawbone and whimsically named it ENOBESRA, using it as their secret weapon and succeeding in the exercise. A legend was born, it seems, and ever since ENOBESRA has been celebrated and perpetuated by generations of cadets, not always to the delight of the administration. There are, not surprisingly, other versions of the origins of the bony talisman and it is unlikely that the current version is the same as the 1924 original, but the legend — and the lingo — lives on.

TOWIE TALK

Tow-truck drivers have a fearsome reputation in many parts of the country, especially in Sydney where they have been known to carry — and occasionally use — shotguns. The cause of all this (mostly) suppressed conflict and aggravation is the highly competitive nature of the towing business and the fact that each operator fanatically guards his or her (there are very few female TOWIES) own territory.

Like most other occupational groups, tow-truck operators are adept at inventing nicknames for their number. A few examples used in the Western Australian branch of the business: BUZZARD, BRUCE THE LOOSE GOOSE, WINGNUT, COCKROACH and GARRY GLITTER (so-called because his truck was spotlessly clean).

The nature of the towing business has generated a considerable lingo of TOWIE talk, including BRICK — a commission paid by panel beaters or other repairers for the delivery of vehicles needing repair, also known as DROP MONEY. So, a BRICK SHOP is one that honours this particular perquisite. A PAVING BRICK is a commission of $50 to $100 at the time of writing while a GOLDEN BRICK is a commission exceeding $100. A CHOP SHOP is a workshop where stolen vehicles are reworked to mask their origins and sold on. A PRANG is an accident, a term that is also used in the wider Lingo, though in TOWIE talk the term GONE OFF may also refer to an accident. The REDS are the ambulance radio frequencies while the BLUES are those of the police. A BASE-SUCKER is a TOWIE who remains at the base depot taking his towing jobs only from the telephones instead of being out on the roads listening to the ambulance, police, and opposition radios. A SPOTTER is one who notifies TOWIES of car accidents, also known as a VULTURE. To be asked to HAND THE RADIO IN is to be given the sack. TOWIE technical terms include QUICK LIFT, a movable table upon which a towed vehicle can be placed, a TWIN EYE BEAM, a form of independent front-wheel suspension AND HOOK-UP, the act of securing the vehicle to be towed.

CIRCUS ARGOT

Historian of the Australian circus, Mark St Leon, has studied the intriguing intricacies of circus and showground argot. Travelling shows of one kind or another have long been a feature of Australian life, as they have elsewhere in the world. Early shows seem to have been peopled mostly by performers and workers 'drawn from the provincial circuses, outdoor equestrian shows, fairgrounds, music halls, cheap salons and "penny gaffs" of southern England', as St Leon colourfully puts it in his article on 'Australian Circus Language' published in *Australian Folklore*, 1996. He mentions a few terms from that period which have survived in the Australian circus, including BENDER, a contortionist, FLYING ACT for a trapeze act and JOEY for a clown. He also notes a number of presumably Romany-derived circus terms like ALEKETEEKENOVEE, meaning he's no-good, and the command to mount the line-up board in a sideshow, FIG-A-LA-PA. Circus and show folk seem also to have been keen users of rhyming slang, much of it common in the larger Lingo, but including one or two specialised forms, such as CEMETERY ON THE RIGHT for a good house tonight.

St Leon's largest list, though, is of locally developed circus terms, including CHEAP JACK for a sideshowman, dating from the late 1890s (though also used in Britain with a similar meaning), a COMMON-WEALTH SHOW being one in which the profits and costs are divided equally among the performers and workers and in use from around 1910, and a WOOD AND WATER JOEY, referring to a circus rouseabout, dating from 1882 and the oldest term in his list. Like bullock drivers, fabled wielders of the expletive, circus wagon drivers were also noted for their creative profanity. One of history's neglected dimensions is the relationship between people's bad language and their vehicles.

Between the early 1850s and up to 1920 large US circuses included Australia on their tours. Some of the US performers joined Australian shows, contributing yet another set of linguistic influences to the argot of circus. Terms were introduced like BANDWAGON, JANE, a negative description of a female; LEG SHOW being one that depended on female performers; JUMP, a distance between towns, and RIP AND TEAR for any form of sharp practice or swindle. Nowadays it seems that the previous distinctions of education, lifestyle and attitude that made circus and show people a particularly insular group that defined itself against TOWNIES are rapidly fading. The effect of this has been to relegate this little lingo to the memories of older SHOWIES and circus folk and to the determined salvage efforts of historians like St Leon.

ICY WORDS

One very specialised and unique Australian occupational group is that of bold and, until recent years, mostly male adventurers who make up the Australian National Antarctic Research Expeditions — ANARE, of course. Unlike most workplaces we know exactly when this one began, 1947, and can hear something of the little lingo they have developed since then. Down near the South Pole, for example, a DING is a good time, a party. This word has been noted elsewhere with various other colloquial uses, none of which are related, depending entirely upon context and location for their meanings.

Another term related closely to ANARE partying, or DINGING, is that for the home-brewed beer, HOMERS, concocted to warm the innards of Antarctic dwellers and their guests. Many of these are what the hardy winter stayers (known as WINTERING) call a JAFA, reported to mean Just Another Flaming Academic, though it is just conceivable that the f-word quoted might occasionally be replaced by the seven-letter version of *the* f-word sometimes favoured by Australians in extreme circumstances. This disdainful reference to academics is a commonly encountered Australian prejudice against those who earn their living with their brains, often expressed in terms like ACADEMIC WANKERS, POINTY-HEADS and even occasionally as BOFFINS, the Britishism for mad scientists. Such intellectuals, frequent visitors to Antarctica for the conduct of apparently esoteric research, are obviously viewed by the ANARE workers, preoccupied with more pressing practicalities, as A WASTE OF SPACE, something of which they have precious little, inside at least.

The value of internal space is reflected in the development of at least one specialised term for the only personal room available. A DONGA is the ANARE name for a bedroom, also used in much warmer Australian climes like Western Australia and Queensland's Hamilton Island as the word for a small SLEEPING APARTMENT. This term is thought to have originated in South Africa where it means a small hollow in the ground. The theory is that the word came back with Boer War veterans (it first appears in print here in 1900) and, by TRANSFERENCE (lexicographer jargon for the mysterious processes of lingo) has gradually come to mean a small, often makeshift, dwelling. Care should be taken not to confuse DONGA with DONGER, pronounced the same but with an entirely different meaning.

Other examples of Australian (the expeditions of other nations have developed their own little lingoes) South Polespeak include JOLLY, meaning a trip or excursion and SLOTTED, a reference to one ever-present danger while on a JOLLY, falling into a crevasse or SLOT. There is also something known locally as THE A FACTOR (Antarctic Factor) meaning that whatever can go wrong will go wrong at the worst time and in the worst possible way, a DEAD CERT known in less frigid climes as MURPHY'S LAW.

All occupational groups that persist for a reasonable period develop their own lingoes whether they are skilled tradespeople like carpenters, bricklayers, welders, or people with a variety of skills thrown together into a common workplace. This chapter could have been easily expanded to an entire book, concentrating simply on the jargons of occupational groups. What has been provided here is no more than a small EARFUL of those things that Australians have said and are saying wherever they work and whenever they get a chance to HAVE A MAG.

10

THE ANATOMY
OF LINGO

...a ragged-trousered informality, a laconically expressed desire
for independence, an irremovable parochialism, a prolific power
to create both euphemisms and also expressions that go
beyond normal profanity...

DR ROBERT BURCHFIELD, NEW ZEALANDER AND CHIEF EDITOR OF
THE OXFORD ENGLISH DICTIONARY DISCUSSING
AUSTRALIANS AND THEIR SPEECH

What is it about the Lingo that fascinates people from one generation to another? Why are we so attached to it? What are its characteristics, its virtues and its vices? What makes it so appealing, so effective, so humorous? What makes it work? Some answers to these questions are provided here, though certainly not the definitive answers. These answers do not exist because the vernacular is a reflection of the way we see ourselves and the ways in which we adapt to an ever-changing world is always in a state of flux, a kind of floating impermanence that happily accommodates a variety of different trends, emphases, and even contradictions. Some significant features of the Lingo are worth pointing out, particularly for the light they throw and for the confusion they cast on aspects of national identity.

CHANGE AND PERSISTENCE

A fundamental characteristic of the Lingo is its ability to change over time, to adapt to new circumstances with subtle, or otherwise, changes in meaning and usage. Many examples of this process have been mentioned already, though a few further illustrations might help reinforce this important point.

From about the 1930s the term ROCK SPIDER was used to describe someone who robbed couples in parks and bush areas while they had their minds on other things. The term is also given by Baker as one who fishes from rocks. But by the 1980s the word had become a description of a peeping Tom, especially one who took advantage of high balconies in blocks of units. By the early 1990s, though, the same term was being generally applied to paedophiles.

Another example of many that might be given is the apparently recent term CLEANSKINS meaning blended or varietal wines in bottles lacking a recognised proprietary label, often simply saying what grape-growing area or region the wine is (supposedly) from. This usage stems from around the early 1990s, though the same word has a much longer history, being used in the mid-19th century to describe unbranded cattle and, from a little later in that century, to refer to a person without a police record.

Many Lingo words are flexible enough to continue functioning in subtly changing contexts over long periods. DEMON was used in the colonial era to mean a trooper policeman. By the 1920s this word was being a little more restrictedly applied to a detective, in which sense it is used in the depression song 'The Dying Bagman', quoted in chapter 6. By about the middle of the 20th century a DEMON was a motorcycle policeman and in 1997 the word was in use among Perth youth to describe the police who pursued a number of them in a high-speed car chase.

But while the Lingo is capable of adaptation and change, it can also operate as a barrier to change in other areas of the society, as in the case of metrication, an official policy that has clearly failed as far as the colloquial consciousness is concerned with the old Imperial still triumphant. In the early months of 1996 a takeaway chicken chain advertised its wares on Australian television saying that its chicken burgers were a foot longer than previously and three inches longer than anyone else's. While this was a US advertisement where Imperial is, oddly, still used, it was clearly intelligible to the mass of Australian television viewers, providing evidence for the refusal of Imperial measurements to lie down and die more than 30 years after we officially went metric.

Since then, rulers displaying Imperial measurements have been supposedly illegal and our children should all have been educated to talk in centimetres and kilograms, rather than in inches and pounds. But go into any hardware store in the land and there you will not only find a grizzled old guard and not-so-old guard fighting a determined rearguard action against metrication. Screws, bolts, nails, and all sorts of other items are measured and are weighed in the supposedly obsolete Imperial. Tape measures and rulers displaying both metric and Imperial measurements are widely sold. Although the government of the day decreed that such implements would not be available, they always have been. One reason, apart from the inability or unwillingness of many of us to change our ways, has been the inability or unwillingness of many occupations to change over to metric or to abandon Imperial altogether. The printing trade still operates in inches as well as centimetres, as do many other trades, skills, and industries where measuring and weighing are central concerns. These include plumbers, electricians, and real estate agents who still either advertise their rural selections in acres or provide a conversion to the trusty acres for those of us who have trouble with hectares.

Most compelling evidence of all for the failure of metric is in everyday speech. Australians still talk of miles, yards, feet, inches, pints, quarts, gallons, pennies and, occasionally, pounds, stones and ounces. Even the young, who should know better after being taught metric measure at primary school, and having supposedly never heard of such ancient weights and measures, have little difficulty in understanding the Imperial calculations of their elders. Sometimes they even use Imperial themselves.

Imperial survives stubbornly in many aspects of popular parlance: GIVE THEM AN INCH AND THEY'LL TAKE A MILE simply does not work as GIVE THEM A CENTIMETRE AND THEY'LL TAKE A KILOMETRE. Other examples include clichés and a number of idiomatic expressions still frequently heard like: EVERY INCH A WINNER; to INCH IN; IN FOR A PENNY, IN FOR A POUND and IT'S A POUND TO A PENNY; HAVEN'T GOT A PENNY TO MY NAME; HAVEN'T GOT TWO PENNIES TO RUB TOGETHER; QUIDS IN; WOULDN'T BE DEAD FER QUIDS; HAVEN'T GOT TWO BOB TO BLESS MYSELF WITH; DOWN TO THE LAST PENNY; GOING A MILE A MINUTE; A COUNTRY MILE; having A MILE OF CHEEK; PINT-SIZED; SHE DIDN'T HAVE AN OUNCE OF FAT ON HER; NOT THE FULL QUID; SILLY AS A TWO-BOB WATCH and to HAVE TWO BOB EACH WAY.

And, as a number of examples throughout this book have shown, although Lingo adapts quickly, some terms stay in use for amazingly lengthy periods. Such long-lasting words and terms as BLOKE, discussed elsewhere and the evocative CROOL (sometimes CRUELLED) THE PITCH, meaning to damage someone's chances or, more generally, to interfere with the smooth running of an event or plan of action. CROOL, first recorded in print here in 1899, derives from underworld slang and was probably used by the earliest transportees. It is most often encountered these days in its shorter version of CROOLED, as in THE SILLY BUGGER CROOLED ANY CHANCE WE HAD.

The apparently very Australian simile LIKE AN OLD MOL(E)L AT A CHRISTENING meaning flustered or overly excited is recorded in print here during the 1930s, but it can be traced back to a very similar earlier saying of 18th-century England.

The Australianism TRIANTELOPE, a version of tarantula, the huntsman spider, is of unknown origin. What we do know is that even in the mid-1840s TRIANTELOPE was an established usage of the OLD HANDS and that it is still heard occasionally among older Australians today, its preservation aided perhaps by C.J. Dennis's MANGULATION of the word in his children's poem 'The Triantiwontigongolope' (1921, reprinted many times since). It may even have passed to coming generations. Time will tell.

An interesting sidelight on just how colloquial speech can remain in amber is the story of New Australia. After the failure of the serious industrial conflict of the 1890s to bring about real reform, one radical labour leader, William Lane, determined to leave Australia and establish a new community in Paraguay. The settlers sailed off to the jungle and set up a number of communities, including one called 'Cosme' in accordance with Lane's utopian socialist ideals. Like most such schemes, New Australia soon began to fall apart and Lane, something of an authoritarian personality, left embittered after a few years. With the departure of the charismatic leader the Australians and their descendants gradually moved into essentially the system they had sought to escape, free enterprise. Today there are a considerable number of later generation New Australians in Paraguay, still using some of the slang of the 1890s interspersed with their everyday Spanish, including TUCKER and SMOKO, both now little heard in Australia.

EMPHASIS, HUMOUR AND COMMUNITY

Generally, Lingo is straightforward, conveying its message with precision, efficiency, and colour. Sometimes though, it does take a bit of decoding, as in the phrase BARBED WIRE CONNECTION meaning related by marriage. The allusion is to the ability of barbed wire to prick, therefore PRICK RELATIONS. A person may be said to PLAY A MEAN KNIFE AND FORK, meaning that he or she is a good eater. Rhyming slang may also demand a knowledge of the complete original, as in TAKE A BUTCHER'S meaning take a look, the full rhyming slang being BUTCHER'S HOOK which may also be rhyming slang for CROOK meaning ill (not angry, as in another usage). Consequently, both knowledge of the speaker and the hearer and an understanding of the context in which such a communication might be taking place are both crucial in understanding what is being said.

The Lingo is especially effective and useful in providing emphasis to statements and is frequently used in this way. The obvious example is in the use of swearing and related vulgarisms to indicate greater or lesser degrees of anger, irritation, or other negative emotion. But the Lingo is capable of much subtler and more flexible modification. Expressions expanding the quantity or size of something include IN SPADES; AND THEN SOME; WITH KNOBS ON; THE WHOLE BOX AND DICE; ALL THE BELLS AND WHISTLES; AND THE REST; TELL ME ABOUT IT. Expressions indicating doubt, dubiousness or outright rejection include IN YOUR DREAMS; YOU SHOULD BE SO LUCKY; YOU AND WHOSE ARMY; and YOU MUST BE JOKING. Then there are exclamations of agreement, in various shades of enthusiasm, such as RIGHT ON (a 1960s-ism); MY OATH; NO FLIES ON...(recorded in print in 1845 and also used in the USA), YOOOO BEAUTY! THAT'S THE SHOT; WOULD I, WHAT and YESS! pronounced with exaggerated sibilance and feeling, often accompanied by a non-threatening, triumphal presentation of a clenched fist. This expressive combination of verbal and body language probably originated in the USA, but is now used universally, especially in sport, which is probably where we caught it.

Closely connected with the emphatic aspects of Lingo is its humour and playfulness. In many of the examples used in this book, and in the many that are not, a love of bending the language to all sorts of ends is evident. Sometimes these ends are regrettable, especially when they voice our uglier prejudices. In many other cases, though, the Lingo can be a form of gaming in which unofficial language is played by its speakers. Sometimes this may be for the sheer pleasure of manipulating available words and phrases to produce a comic effect, as in calling THONGS (an Australianism) JAPANESE RIDING BOOTS. Sometimes the play element appears in offhanded contest to hear who can wield the words most effectively.

The playful dimension of colloquial speech is also highlighted in the folk etymologies that are constructed and debated between the numerous passionate speakers and listeners of Lingo. Many a PUB argument and newspaper column has pivoted on the various origins and derivations of words and phrases. DIGGER is one such example for which yet another etymology has already been provided in this book. Other well-known words and idioms that regularly provoke disputation are POMMY; BUCKLEY'S CHANCE; MATILDA (for a SWAG, as in 'Waltzing Matilda'), and many others. Debate on these matters, whether verbal or in print, is frequently lively and learned, obviously bringing great satisfaction to all involved. Further light is rarely shed on the disputed etymologies, though this is not the purpose of the fray. Etymological duelling enhances and enlarges the broad sense of community that is a fundamental purpose of vernacular exchange and a part of the larger cultural processes the Lingo serves.

Another of the important functions of colloquial speech is to render the obvious, the mundane, and the absurd, in ways that allow recognition or concealment. That which is considered inept, unsanctioned, or otherwise negative, is frequently impaled in Lingo. An example of governmental lunacy may be labelled CLAYTON'S LEGISLATION. On a smaller scale, perhaps the career-advancing antics of a colleague may earn him the title AN ARSELICKER.

Those matters that require consolation or the investing of more emotion than someone is prepared or is able to give may be elided, lessened, or contained, through the use of the colloquialisms that trip quickly to the tongue of the Lingoist, not unlike the use of proverbs such as WHAT CAN'T BE CURED MUST BE ENDURED. For those who are part of the Lingo speech community, such expressions are received in the spirit in which they are sent, as signals of connection and of sharing, even though the form and content of the words may suggest a lack of sympathy. This accords with the traditional manner of stoic acceptance, combined with staunch, often silent but always practical support, a characteristic perhaps best exemplified in the levels of voluntarism and community spirit evident in such movements as surf lifesaving and volunteer bushfire brigades. Such values and attitudes are found among humans throughout the world. Here they are simply the taken-for-granted ways of articulating, or more accurately, almost not articulating, these things, the much-maligned taciturnity of the Australian myth.

LINGO AND NATIONAL MYTH

Lingo is linked closely with some of our most cherished myths about ourselves as a people. Our fabled enthusiasm for CUTTING DOWN TALL POPPIES and for KNOCKING individuals, institutions, achievements, and so on, is related to a spirit of pugnacious egalitarianism and knock-about democracy. Interestingly, we rarely seem to cut down our tall sporting poppies, though just about every other kind of hero and heroine seems to be FAIR GAME. Likewise our aversion to DOBBING IN and DOBBERS (now called WHISTLEBLOWERS and officially approved) and our espousal of the FAIR GO. Closely related to egalitarianism is our uneasiness with authority which leads to a propensity to STIR THE POSSUM. Those who are felt to be NOT PULLING THEIR WEIGHT are BLUDGERS and a SCAB is one who totally outrages the codes of loyalty usually, though not only, in situations of industrial conflict. While MATE is not exclusively an Australianism (nor is SCAB), the intense male bonding and masculine notions of loyalty and sacrifice that we associate with the term are peculiarly and persistently AUSSIE, TRUE BLUE and are further acknowledged in the highly approving and laconic A GOOD BLOKE. Other Lingoisms like HAVING A YARN, BULLSHITTING, HARD YAKKA, and BASTARD in its various nuances, also resonate strongly of the Australian myth.

The most persistent elements of our myths revolve around our relationship with the bush, more especially with the romanticisation of the pastoral past. This still wields a great influence in the national consciousness, expressed in our attachment to the unofficial national anthem, 'Waltzing Matilda', the verse (though not the short stories) of Banjo Paterson, a selected number of other, always male writers such as Lawson, ridiculously rural four-wheel drive (4WD) vehicles that never leave the suburban tarmac and a host of other bucolic oddities like Drizabone™ raincoats, Akubra™ hats, and the outdoor ritual of the BARBIE. Lingo is an especially potent preserver and purveyor of this Arcadianism. Sayings like GAME AS NED KELLY or THE MAN WHO DROVE THE BULL THROUGH WAGGA [WAGGA] WITHOUT ONCE CRACKING HIS WHIP, and any number of other country colloquialisms, are evidence of the enduring effect of the great Australian myth on our speech.

At least such sayings have long been associated with the 'typical' Australia. There is some evidence that the influence of the rural past on mainstream Australian is fading. Even the examples quoted above are heard more frequently in historical re-creations or among a declining number of older Australians. Many expressions still have currency among those who live the legend in THE BUSH, the outback, THE NEVER-NEVER, THE BACK OF BEYOND . . ., especially among Aboriginal Australians. But the economic roller-coaster of the 1980s and 1990s has caused significant depopulation of rural Australia. Lingoisms like MEANER THAN HUNGRY TYSON; the OT (Overland Telegraph); COCKY'S JOY (treacle or golden syrup); SUNDOWNERS (swagmen who arrive just as the sun goes down in search of a bed for the night, not early evening drinks sessions), and so on, are understood by, or relevant to, fewer and fewer Australians. Terms about the mythic Australia, even COBBER and FAIR DINKUM are rarely spoken and, if they are, are more likely to be used in parody.

One of the worst things to do in Australia is to PUT ON SIDE or PUT TICKETS ON YOURSELF. That means to appear as if you are in some way different or, even worse, superior to those around you. So entrenched is this attitude that the reaction to it has a Lingoism all its own — CUTTING DOWN TALL POPPIES. In other countries such affectations also bring censure and dislike and would be interpreted as someone trying to place themselves above their fellows. While there is such a class element in the Australian dislike for SIDE, SKITING or BIG-NOTING this is submerged by a much stronger dislike, even fear, of difference. Someone who expresses unpopular political or social opinions will be ostracised and/or classed as a RATBAG in many circles. This SKITER may also be prone to PERFORM LIKE A PORK CHOP, be UP HIMSELF/HER-SELF, or MAKE A RIGHT ARSEHOLE OF HIM-SELF/HERSELF.

Such serious social levelling is a product of both the genuine egalitarianism of the Australian myth as well as of a deep-seated inability and unwillingness to engage with or to accept otherness. This cultural difficulty lies at the root of much ethnic slurring in Australia and also many problems of interpersonal communication often noted by commentators and artists. It is not so much a product of hate as a product of fear, a fear embedded deep in the self-perception of a little country hanging off the bottom of the world and increasingly worried about its identity as European or Asian. While the tyranny of distance is no longer a major factor in the Australian popular psyche, the burden of the past still weighs heavily on our language, disguised though it usually is by the famously sardonic Australian humour.

As well as disguising our insecurities, humour also hides our contradictions. To WHINGE is an activity that many Australians associate with British migrants — WHINGEING POMS or, a little more abrasively, WHINGEING POMMY BASTARDS. Australians are supposedly stoic and tight-lipped about adversity, BATTLING ON through thick and thin, COPPING IT SWEET, or WEARING IT (that is, THE SHIT). But in fact we have developed the art of complaining to a very high level. WHINGEING (also used in Britain) is a noted characteristic of one of our main culture heroes, the DIGGER in whom the practice has been carried to its finest form, as in the famous YARN of World War II and since, in which 'The World's Greatest Whinger' is described as complaining about every conceivable thing in all sorts of situations, including the Kokoda Trail, the outback, working, not working, and so on. In the end the yarner dies and goes to heaven where, who does he strike but the whinger, still complaining about the angel's wings he has to wear, his crooked halo and the fact that he cannot drink, swear, or be late for choir practice.

Civilians have taken up the art of complaining as the harsh realities of global economics have impinged on our previously taken-for granted way of life. Media sources are full of groups and individuals complaining that their rights have been infringed or that they have not received their fair share of something. To some extent this is an inevitable product of Australia's vast media networks and their imperative to fill screens, AIRSPACE or pages with something contentious. It is also related to the folk notion that IT'S THE SQUEAKING WHEEL THAT GETS THE OIL meaning that if you do not complain or protest, you are likely to MISS OUT ON YOUR CHOP. There is undoubtedly a good deal of commonsense in these sentiments as past experiences show. But the trend in both public rhetoric and political ideology towards various forms of economic rationalism has encouraged this ME-TOO-ISM and an accompanying concentration on the individual at the expense of the collective, something that goes dead against the mythology of the FAIR GO and the notion of a common wealth that have been unofficial belief and official policy for the best part of a century. Perhaps it is inevitable that as larger numbers of Australians perceive, too late, just how lucky the LUCKY COUNTRY has been, we should feel the need to express our disillusionment AT THE DROP OF A HAT. Certainly the large number and variety of negative and aggressive lingoisms mentioned at various places in this book proves that the vernacular contains a well-equipped armoury of complaint.

CASUALNESS

Not surprisingly for informal speech, Lingo is very casual, even offhanded. When new areas of Australia were settled during the 19th century they were often named after the first European to stumble across the valley, mountain, or cave, so we have place names like Payne's Find in Western Australia. This indicates that Payne was the first one to find gold in this particular region (or was the first one to tell others about it). In Western Australia the original European name of Kalgoorlie (anglicised Aboriginal from *Kal-guurli* or *Gubbigulgardo*),was named Hannan's Find. This rapidly became just HANNAN'S, the name by which the golden city is still called by a few oldtimers. Other place names display a determined informalisation, including THE TOWERS for Charters Towers (Queensland), THE HILL for Broken Hill (New South Wales, also known as SILVER CITY), THE ALICE for Alice Springs (Northern Territory — though earlier in the 20th century the town was usually known as THE SPRINGS) and THE ISA for Mt Isa. New South Wales is often sliced and compressed to simply NEWSOUTH, while Western Australia, South Australia, the Northern Territory, Victoria and Tasmania become, respectively, WA, SA, NT, Vic. and Tassie.

Our fondness for the affectionate, and not so affectionate, diminutive is another facet of the casual image projected by Australian vernacular. A persistent linguistic reductionism lies behind all those good nouns being sliced apart and having an 'o' or 'ie' suffix stitched on to their truncated remains. Even our interrogations have an air of contracted casualness about them. BEG YOURS? and COME AGAIN? often being heard as a request to repeat something the ear has not caught.

The apparent urge towards casual contraction, though, does not simply depend upon the affectionate diminutive. We also have terms that are shortened without affection or malice. These include, though are hardly limited to UTE for utility and TEEV for television (contrast with TELLIE) among the many other examples already cited. Once again, this demonstrates the Lingo accomplishing its ends in the most efficient manner possible.

A good example of the casualness of Lingo is found in the ritualised forms of greeting and farewell. The ubiquitous G'DAY is capable of being uttered in most social situations, even the highly formal, without fear of offence of impropriety. We have been using this derivation of the British 'good day' since at least the middle of the 19th century and it shows no signs of going away. At the other end of social intercourse is the farewell. The very casual 'OOROO and HOOROO, appear to derive from the late 19th-century use of HOORAY for goodbye. Although their usages tend these days to be associated with lower class speech, they can be used in a variety of situations with relative impunity. This is also true of the vernacular farewell that most perplexes foreigners — SEE YOU LATER. Someone using this cordial form may well have no intention of ever seeing the person so addressed again, but unless you speak the Lingo you DO NOT HAVE A HOPE of knowing that.

WISDOM

The vernacular discourses of the Lingo are the home of that literary outcast, the proverb. Australian folk speech is full of the common proverbs of the English-speaking cultures and those proverbial expressions found in the many other languages spoken here. In Australia, as in the USA, Britain, Canada, New Zealand, South Africa, and elsewhere in the world, A BIRD IN THE HAND is indeed WORTH TWO IN THE BUSH; IT NEVER RAINS BUT IT POURS; and IT'S NO USE CRYING OVER SPILT MILK.

As well as this large repertoire of traditional proverbial wisdom, there are a few uniquely Lingoistic forms of advice. These include: YOU WOULDN'T BE DEAD FER QUIDS, WOULD YA? HORSES FOR COURSES meaning to make sure that whatever action taken is appropriate; KNOW WHEN TO PULL YER HEAD IN meaning know when to keep your mouth shut; COP IT SWEET meaning to be stoical in adversity (quite different to a SWEET COP which is a sinecure or perquisite of some kind) and THERE'S MORE WAYS TO SKIN A CAT THAN SUCKING

ITS BRAINS OUT THROUGH ITS ARSEHOLE, a striking image indicating that there is always more than one method of accomplishing a task or aim. WHEN YOU'RE ON A GOOD THING, STICK TO IT — popularised for many years as the slogan for Mortein™ insect spray — is a piece of proverbial good advice still heard from time to time. YOU'VE GOT BUCKLEY'S and variants like YOU'VE GOT TWO CHANCES — BUCKLEY'S AND NONE (occasionally written, though never spoken as BUCKLEY'S AND NUNN), sometimes rendered as YOU'VE GOT BUCKLEY'S AND FUCK-ALL, are Lingoisms that have an advisory quality to them. William Buckley (1780–1856) was an escaped convict who lived with Aborigines for more than 30 years. When his story became known it is said to have generated the popular term for having no chance at all, BUCKLEY'S CHANCE. Other such collocations include PISS OR GET OFF THE POT; HE/SHE/THEY COULDN'T FIGHT YOUR WAY OUT OF A PAPER BAG (worse, OUT OF A WET PAPER BAG) and SUCK IT AND SEE.

Related to the above sayings are a good number of Lingoisms that may be used in an advisory or even cautionary manner: IT'S BETTER THAN A POKE IN THE EYE WITH A SHARP STICK (also used in Britain and the USA); UP SHIT CREEK (usually WITHOUT A PADDLE); UP A GUM TREE; AS MUCH USE AS AN ASHTRAY ON A MOTORBIKE; and HOP IN (OR GET IN) FOR YOUR CHOP, suggesting that a person should waste no time obtaining his or her share of whatever is going. Sayings such as YOU'LL BE IN MORE STRIFE THAN FLASH GORDON are similarly used, as is the terse caution WATCH IT, also available in its less threatening version as WATCH YOURSELF.

HOT TO TROT can function as a warning of the level of preparedness of one's allies or opponents, and is often heard in sporting contexts. Imprecations such as GO AND TAKE A RUNNING JUMP AT YOURSELF also have a certain advisory quality about them, but tend to shade quickly into invective and insult.

A LITTLE LINGO GOES A LONG WAY

As demonstrated at a number of points, one of the most useful and appealing qualities of Lingo is its great efficiency. Despite a relatively restricted vocabulary compared with that available in formal English, colloquial speech excels in doing a lot with a little. In this, Lingo harmonises with the pioneering ethos so strong in Australian popular consciousness, the ability to GET BY, to MAKE DO with little more than the bare necessities. Accurately or not, we Australians pride ourselves on our skills of innovation, enterprise, and SHEER BLOODY DETERMINATION to get where we are going, no matter what. Our use of the vernacular relates very closely to this frontier mentality, as a listen to even just a few terms and combinations quickly tells us.

DEAD

DEAD and its derivations figure frequently in Lingo. Not surprisingly the various usages of the term are mostly strongly negative, except in those cases where dead is used to add emphasis, as in a DEAD CERT; a DEAD RINGER; DEAD RIGHT; DEAD ON, and so on. Perhaps its most positive usage is in the form DEAD SET, indicating absolute truth. DEAD SET? is also used in the interrogative as a questioning of the veracity of information one has been given. It is used in both these senses also in Newfoundland lingo.

Such terms as DEAD IN THE WATER (incapacity, failure); DEAD LOSS; DEAD MEAT meaning doomed, currently popular with our youth, and the ultimate insult, DEAD CUNT, however, all indicate the general use of this term for ineptitude, inefficiency, and hopelessness. Some selected examples: DEADHEAD (an insult); TO LOOK LIKE DEATH WARMED UP (very ill); TO FLOG A DEAD HORSE meaning to carry out a pointless and/or hopeless exercise and the colourful comparison IT'S AS MUCH USE AS A POULTICE ON A DEAD MAN'S BUM.

FAIR

FAIR, probably originating as a British dialect term meaning complete, is used as an intensifier. Sometimes it is used to reinforce an expression of annoyance, as in IT'D FAIR MAKE YOU SICK and the famous FAIR DINKUM, an insistence that what one is saying should be treated as the truth.

The word FAIR is also used for our well-developed sense of equality. FAIR DINKUM may also signify that something is fair and above board and FAIR CRACK OF THE WHIP; FAIR SUCK OF THE SAV(ELOY)/SAUCE BOTTLE/PADDLE-POP; and FAIR GO, are also expressions that function as requests for equality and for fairness in general.

On the other hand, things may just be FAIR TO MIDDLING, an indication of minimally satisfactory performance or, if used to describe a person's state, to indicate that he or she is TRAVELLING WELL, though he or she also COULD BE BETTER.

If there are a number of things they may be referred to as A FAIR FEW. When something is really bad it is simply A FAIR COW.

FULL

The primary colloquial meaning of FULL is to be excessively affected by alcohol, as in FULL AS A BOOT. A person, however, may also be FULL OF IT, a term understood to convey the meaning that one has an excess of BULLSHIT and is insisting on speaking it, so making little, if any, sense at all.

There is also the archaic, but still oft-heard, term THE FULL QUID, a reference to mental capability or, in its more usual usage, HE'S NOT THE FULL QUID, lack of such capability, but someone may be THE FULL BOTTLE on something, knowing all that there is to know about a particular subject.

A person may be FULL of food, a condition covered by a number of colourful phrases: FULL AS A BUTCHER'S DOG (of which the venerable Britishism FIT AS A BUTCHER'S DOG is a variant); FULL AS THE FAMILY PO (a reference to the overflowing condition of the family chamber pot); the poetic FULL AS A BULL and (though heard little in these happily post-sectarian times) AS FULL AS A CATHOLIC SCHOOL, the retort to which was, of course, AS FULL AS A STATE SCHOOL.

Something that is FULL-ON is either or both very serious or very complete in its details, as in IT WAS A FULL ON PARTY. On such an occasion one may well go at it FULL BORE.

HARD

Toughness is one of the predominant associations of HARD in the Australian Lingo. This accords with its general use in the language as a term for something that is unyielding, firm. These associations are combined in the machismo of a HARD, a term for erection as in I'VE GOT A HARD-ON. Perhaps related to this meaning is to ask for sexual favours by PUTTING THE HARD WORD ON a person.

The ability to persevere and to battle on against all adversities is a much-admired Australian characteristic reflected in terms like A HARD CASE, a HARD DOER and HARDNOSE for those who can both deal it out and take it. To be HARD UP, is to be without adequate financial resources.

Giving or getting A HARD TIME is to experience difficult relationships, as in an interview with an irate superior, or with one's wife when a husband is returning late from the public house.

There is HARD LUCK, bad luck expressed in forms such as HARD CHEDDAR and HARD CHEESE, both of which convey a lack of sympathy, if not a distinct heartlessness also heard in the terms STIFF SHIT, TOUGH BIKKIES, and the like.

IN

Similarly unassuming is the word in. It is possible to BE IN THAT meaning the speaker will cooperate and/or participate. A person may HAVE AN IN — to have a contact or knowledge of a group or subject.

A man may get in, immortalised in the saying IN LIKE FLYNN, meaning success, especially in relation to the conquest of a female by a male. This term is widely believed to be derived from the fabled sexual prowess of the sometime Tasmanian and Hollywood film star, Errol Flynn.

Less happily, a person may be IN THE WRONG — mistaken or wrong-headed about something; PUT IN — to be put in line for extra work and/or responsibility, as in I'VE BEEN PUT IN FOR THE WORST JOB, or that most heinous of sins, be DOBBED IN meaning to be informed on or betrayed.

Conjuring up a distinctly uncomfortable image is the Lingoism IN A PIG'S ARSE meaning certainly not. Simply PIGS conveys the same essential meaning, mingling just the right proportions of contempt and incredulity.

OFF

OFF AND RUNNING and OFF LIKE A SHOT are common terms for getting into motion, generally with some speed. The horseracing term OFF LIKE A BRIDE'S NIGHTIE, still heard quite frequently in these linguistically sensitive times, means to move quickly and with resolve. Terms such as FUCK OFF, PISS OFF and their ilk, are serious requests to take much the same action, or else.

Copulation may still be described as HAVING IT OFF. This is interesting to compare with other terms for the same activity, including GETTING ON, GETTING IN, GOING THROUGH, and GETTING UP, all of which seem to favour the colloquial use of such ambulatory verbs.

OFF is also used in the negative sense of being unsavoury or in some way less than wholesome, as in OFF LIKE A BUCKET OF PRAWNS, or simply OFF, indicating a state or personality considered abnormal in some way. OFF YOUR FACE is another of many terms for extreme inebriation, probably related to OFF YOUR TROLLEY, OFF YOUR HEAD, and other terms indicating a loss, or simply an absence of, rationality.

ON

You can be ON, in the sense of being in a relationship with someone, as in SHE'S ON WITH HIM, you can be ON for a bet (ODDS ON, if it looks like a winner), PUT ON a bet or agree to a joint enterprise of some kind, as in YOU'RE ON. A person can be ON THE NOSE or, oppositionally, have GOOD ON YOU, well known from at least the early 20th century.

It can be on, as in IT'S ON, meaning to fight, possibly a big fight denoted by IT'S ON FOR YOUNG AND OLD. A person may be lucky enough to be ON A WINNER or unlucky enough to be HAD ON to be deceived.

On may be taken, as in TAKE ON, meaning to fight against someone or something in a serious, calculated manner as in THE GOVERNMENT IS GOING TO TAKE ON THE UNIONS, a perennially popular Australian pastime. Perversely, even though you may take on the other side, those who support your view are said to be ONSIDE, as in THEY'RE ONSIDE WITH OUR DECISION.

Another common usage is YOU MUST BE HAVING ME ON, spoken as a response to (usually) good-humoured exaggeration. The phrase can also be used to indicate disbelief and dissent in less humorous situations. You may also HAVE YOURSELF ON by failing to exercise a due amount of self-criticism and objectivity. And, as mentioned above, WHEN YOU'RE ON A GOOD THING, STICK TO IT.

A person may PUT ON SIDE, that is show off or act as if more important than others, a cardinal sin. Often this is simply PUTTING IT ON, or PUTTING ON A SHOW, to be distinguished from BUNGING IT ON which means to fight as in BUNGING ON A BLUE, in which you may have an ODDS ON chance of winning.

A distinctively Australian usage of on is to indicate the presence of someone at a particular location, in preference to the proper form of in or at, as in sentences like THEY WERE SEEN ON THE (gold) DIGGINGS, in colonial folk song: 'On the far Barcoo, where they eat nardoo, a thousand miles away', and in general conversation, HE WORKED ON THE SNOWY (Snowy Mountains Hydro-Electric Scheme).

DONE

Done, give and go (with variants) are humble words made to do a good deal of work in Lingo: DONE A BUNK deserted; DONE A RUNNER fled; DONE, exhausted; beaten; DONE IN (a) exhausted (b) murdered; DONE LIKE A DINNER convincingly beaten; thrashed! DONE MY/YOUR DASH — exhausted, finished; DONE OVER beaten, often by trickery; DONE TO A TURN comprehensively conned or tricked; and DONE YOUR DOUGH lost one's money, as in I DONE ME DOUGH AT THE TRACK. A person may also have been DONE, that is have had sex, willingly or otherwise.

A variation of this lingoism was used memorably by Paul Keating while prime minister in telling the leader of the Opposition, Mr John Howard, that he was going to DO HIM SLOWLY in parliament.

GIVE

The Lingo has also made efficient use of give, as in GIVE BIRTH TO A COPPER defecate; GIVE IT A GO to attempt something; GIVE IT A REST a reasonably polite request for someone to either stop talking or change the subject (variants: GIVE IT A BREAK; GIVE US A BREAK). You can be asked to GIVE IT AWAY, give up or leave it alone; GIVE THE GAME AWAY, to give up on something, or GIVE US A HOY! attract my attention. A reasonably polite request to someone to cease talking is GIVE YOUR OTHER END A CHANCE.

GO

To GO is to fornicate well and frequently, as in COULDN'T SHE GO!!
GO DOWN means to engage in cunnilingus; GO FOR IT means to try
for something; GO FOR YOUR LIFE is to attack something with enthusiasm; GO THE RAT means no holds barred; FROM GO TO WOE is from
beginning to end; GOER describes anyone who carries out tasks with
excessive zeal and energy, particularly those of a sexual nature.
GOING AT IT LIKE HAMMER AND TONGS is to attack a task enthusiastically. GOING FIT TO BUST, GOING LIKE A BASTARD, GOING GANG
BUSTERS and GOING LIKE BILLYO have much the same meaning. If
you are GONE you are finished, in DEEP SHIT as in YOU'RE GONE,
MATE or the related GONE FOR A BURTON, probably adapted from the
World War II RAF euphemism for death. One who has GONE FOR A
WALLOPER has gone to the toilet (WALLOPER is an older term for a
detective). GONE TO BUGGERY and GONE TO GOWINGS (a Sydneyism)
mean to have failed, lost, or been bested in some. *The Macquarie
Dictionary* (3rd edition) also has the meaning of illness for GONE TO
GOWINGS. A GONER is one who is dead, or soon will be, figuratively
or literally.

An example of the effective and efficient use of Lingo came from
an unexpected quarter on the now-famous video tapes involving a
well-known senior detective and another detective. After only a few
sentences had been exchanged, the senior detective had managed to
use FUCK and its variants impeccably. The other detective asked him
if he was happy with the payment he had allegedly received. The reply
was: YEAH, FUCK YEAH. FUCKIN' SEE THAT FUCKIN'…THE FUCKER, THE
FUCKIN' DUD'N.

Australian Magazine columnist and author Barry Oakley was so
impressed by this exquisite use of the Lingo that he asked readers for
their contributions to the GET F…SOCIETY. Subsequent issues in late
1995 brought such gems as THE FUCKING FUCKER'S FUCKED and,
from Kalgoorlie, FUCK IT, MATE, THE FUCKING FUCKER'S FUCKING-
WELL FUCKED AND WE FUCKING NEED A NEW FUCKER, RIGHT? Difficult
to better that one.

There was an intriguing and revealing sequel to this display of
verbal vulgarity from Sydney's finest late in 1996. A senior officer of
the New South Wales Police was charged with offensive language and
brought before a police tribunal. The tribunal decided that the
charge should be dropped because the officer had not uttered the f-
word to a member of the public, but to another police officer. The
matter was appealed and the New South Wales Court of Appeal
upheld the tribunal's decision, stating that swearing was 'part of

police culture'. Both the Minister of Police and the Police Commissioner were unhappy with the decision, with the minister raising his discontent in parliament and the commissioner seeking ways to bring the matter to the attention of the High Court of Australia.

NOTABLE LINGOISMS

The sheer inventiveness, colour, and willingness to play with the language is one of the most important and interesting aspects of the Lingo. This takes many forms, from the understated but effective expression of hopelessness HE DIDN'T HAVE A PRAYER, to the more overblown, yet evocative, crudities of HE LOOKED ABOUT AS HAPPY AS A CAT SHITTING RAZOR BLADES; HE'S SO TALL HE OUTGREW HIS BRAINS — THEY'RE STILL IN HIS ARSE; FLOPPING AROUND LIKE A PRICK IN A SHIRT SLEEVE and the like. Beneath these lengthier formulations, the Lingo also makes extensive use of the most humble words in the language.

IF

A number of especially colourful expressions turn on the very small word if. Unassuming though it is, if is a very important standard English word conveying the complicated meaning of something being conditional upon certain circumstances. Some of these formations present a set of circumstances and then proceed to bloom into expressions of negativity and insult: IF BRAINS WERE MADE OF DYNAMITE HE/SHE WOULDN'T HAVE ENOUGH TO BLOW HIS/HER HEAD OFF; IF BRAINS WERE MADE OF ELASTIC YOU WOULDN'T HAVE ENOUGH TO MAKE A GARTER FOR A CANARY'S LEG; IF I NEVER SAW/HEARD/…IT/HIM/HER AGAIN IT WOULD BE TOO SOON, and the topper, IF I WAS AS TWO-FACED AS YOU AND HAD A FACE LIKE THAT — I'D WEAR THE OTHER ONE.

Many if formulations are expressions of personal bad luck: IF I FELL INTO A BUCKET OF TITS I'D COME UP SUCKING MY THUMB; IF I FELL INTO A ROSE GARDEN I'D LAND IN DOG SHIT; IF IT RAINED GRAVY EVERYONE WOULD HAVE A FRYING PAN AND I'D HAVE THE GRIDIRON; IF IT WAS RAINING FEMALE MOVIE STARS I'D END UP WITH LASSIE; IF IT WAS RAINING SOVEREIGNS YOU'D BE OUT THERE WITH AN UPSIDE-DOWN UMBRELLA, AND I'D HAVE BOXING GLOVES ON; IF IT WAS RAINING TITS I'D BE HIT ON THE HEAD WITH AN ARSEHOLE; IF IT WAS RAINING VIRGINS I'D BE WASHED DOWN THE DRAIN WITH A POOFTER; IF THEY CUT A WOMAN IN HALF I'D GET THE HALF THAT EATS, and so on.

MORE

More, in the sense of excess, is used in a number of important combinations, the following being a representative selection:

MORE...THAN YOU CAN POKE A STICK AT a great number of whatever is being so described, as in MORE CHILDREN THAN YOU CAN POKE A STICK AT; MORE ARSE THAN A PADDOCK-FULL OF COWS cheeky; forward, over-confident; MORE GUTS THAN A BEDFORD TRUCK great strength and/or bravery; MORE PRICKS IN HERE THAN A SECOND-HAND DARTBOARD a roomful of unpleasant or otherwise undesirable people; MORE PRICKS THAN A SECOND-HAND PRIMUS an equally disenchanted observation; MORE ROOTS THAN A SAIGON BROTHEL a good number of females available for sexual activity, and MORE WRINKLES THAN AN OLD CHINAMAN'S FORESKIN, meaning very old.

NOT, NO AND NONE

These negative forms occupy much of the Lingo and play an important role in many of our most colourful idioms.

NO CHANCE, for instance, indicates that the speaker considers there is little, if any, hope of success. It may also indicate disagreement or dissent. NO COMEBACK(S) means no recriminations or repercussions; NO FLIES ON...indicates that the person referred to is no fool and does not stand around waiting for the flies to settle, as in THERE'S NO FLIES ON THOSE RICH BASTARDS. No-go is an indication of impossibility while NO HOPE indicates that there is no chance of success, as in YOU'VE GOT NO HOPE, MATE.

A NO-HOPER is an individual who is incompetent and/or penurious. NO JOKE means a serious truth is being told, as does its variant, NO JOKING. NO JOY means to be unsuccessful and/or to have had an unsatisfactory experience, as in WE HAD NO JOY FISHING TODAY. NO PROBLEMS (also NO PROBS) is an expression of agreement and/or anticipation of a successful outcome. NO SHOW is to be without hope of success while NO SWEAT can indicate that there will be no difficulty carrying something out, or may be used as an imprecation meaning not to worry. NO WAY is an expression of disagreement or refusal and NO WAY IN THE WORLD means more intense disagreement or refusal.

NOT A/THE FULL QUID is not possessing full mental faculties; NOT A LEG TO STAND ON is being without recourse to an acceptable justification as in HE DIDN'T HAVE A LEG TO STAND ON WHEN THE TRUTH CAME OUT, while NOT A PRAYER (or WITHOUT A PRAYER) is having no hope at all. NOT A PROBLEM is a response, common among tradesmen, indicating that all will be well, not necessarily accurate. To be NOT ALL THERE is to be stupid or mentally deficient, perhaps having NOT ENOUGH SENSE TO COME IN OUT OF THE RAIN. NOT IN THE RACE means a person is not, as in THEY'RE NOT EVEN IN THE RACE or NOT IN THE RUNNING. IT'S NOT ON expresses disagreement and dissatisfaction as do NOT ON YOUR LIFE and NOT ON YOUR NELLY. Something that is NOT WHAT IT'S CRACKED UP TO BE is something (or someone) presented in a less than frank manner and so NOT WORTH A BUMPER or NOT WORTH A FART IN A HURRICANE (or STORM or GALE).

COULD AND WOULDN'T/COULDN'T AND WOULDN'T

Closely related to these general terms of negativity are those combinations involving could(n't) and would(n't), such as HE COULD TALK UNDER WET CEMENT to describe a loquacious person or HE COULDN'T HIT THE SIDE OF A BARN WITH A HANDFUL OF WHEAT, INSIDE WITH THE DOOR CLOSED to indicate incompetence. Someone who COULDN'T KNOCK THE SKIN OFF A RICE PUDDING is weak or ineffective; one who WOULDN'T BEAT TIME WITH A STICK is lazy or slow and you WOULDN'T FEED HIM OR HER ON CORN as they WOULDN'T GET A KICK IF THEY WERE LOCKED UP WITH A WILD HORSE ALL NIGHT. Anyone who WOULDN'T GIVE YOU A SHOCK IF HE OWNED THE POWER-HOUSE is mean or stingy and WOULDN'T GIVE YOU THE TIME OF DAY. WOULDN'T IT ROOT YA!? is a classic exclamation of disgust and frustration, related to the milder YOU WOULDN'T READ ABOUT IT, said of events that seem incredible, as is WOULDN'T THAT RIP THE CROTCH OUT OF YER NIGHTIE?! The comprehensive WOULDN'T KNOW A BRASS BAND WAS UP HER 'TIL SOMEONE GAVE HER THE DRUM may be said of a stupid woman, also heard in the variant WOULDN'T KNOW A BRASS BAND WAS UP HER 'TIL THE BASS DRUM WAS BLOWING IN HER EAR. Another version of this formulation is HE WOULDN'T KNOW AN EXPRESS TRAIN WAS UP HIM 'TIL THE GUARD BLEW THE WHISTLE IN HIS EAR.

UP

Those useful phrases, combining both wouldn't and up, lead us comfortably into the remarkable flexibilities of the two-letter up. Used in a diversity of combinations, up is a simple, yet malleable, Lingoism. It has many meanings, but most colourful are those associated with sexual activity, failure or loss, and anger.

The word can be used in combinations indicating trouble, difficulty, failure or frustration, such as UP SHIT CREEK WITHOUT A PADDLE, an expression of hopelessness, doom and disaster, sometimes simply UP SHIT CREEK. UP THE DUFF/SPOUT is pregnant. UP THE SHIT is to be in DEEP TROUBLE or no longer functioning properly which may be rendered even more casually as UPTER. Upisms also embrace UP THE SPOUT, meaning finished; failed, as in THAT BUSINESS IS UP THE SPOUT and not to be confused with the maternal version above. Others are UP A GUM TREE, to be in trouble; UP A TREE, or TREED, meaning baffled or frustrated; BALLS-UP, COCK-UP, STUFF-UP, all meaning a mess, confusion, while a FUCK-UP is a big mistake, possibly a disaster. To BARK UP THE WRONG TREE is to make a mistake or to be misguided; STITCHED UP is being outsmarted, beaten or swindled, and STICK IT UP 'EM is to fight or to play hard, usually to win. Up may also be used in any situation involving conflict and disagreement and to GET UP someone means to best them, as in WE'LL GET UP THEM IN THIS GAME. When something is PLAYING UP it is not working properly. If someone is PLAYING UP they are usually not doing what they should be doing and, in all likelihood, are doing it with a member of the opposite, or possibly the same, sex.

The u-word may form part of an angry exhortation or insult, as in 'UP YOURS' — an expression of derision, as in UP YOURS FOR THE RENT, SPORT. To be UP YOURSELF is to be seriously misguided or simply conceited, possibly SO FAR UP YOURSELF THAT YOU CAN'T BREATHE or that you CAN'T SEE DAYLIGHT and need to WAKE UP TO YOURSELF. To TURN IT UP! means please stop saying or doing that or else; STICK IT UP YOUR ARSE is an expression of antagonism and disagreement and BUTTON UP! means be quiet! DEAD FROM THE NECK UP is just as it sounds.

Other uses of up include the sartorial DRESSED UP LIKE A POX DOCTOR'S CLERK dressed in a lurid, flashy style; DRESSED UP LIKE A SORE THUMB in sartorial splendour, ALL DRESSED UP AND NOWHERE TO GO, and the negative: JACK UP to refuse to do something and NOT UP TO MUCH. Something that is not satisfactory may be said to be NOT UP TO THE MARK, NOT UP TO SCRATCH, or NOT WHAT IT'S CRACKED UP TO BE.

But then if someone or something is considered legitimate or generally okay, it is ON THE UP AND UP. Regardless of how it is used, the Lingo is always ONE UP.

11

WILL THE LINGO
LINGER LONGER…?

If bullshit was music, you'd be a symphony orchestra.

CABBIE, PERTH, 1989

It happened in a little estaminet (bistro) in France during World War I. A couple of DIGGERS were carousing and conversing when a group of TOMMIES (British soldiers) entered the wine shop. As soon as they saw the TOMMIES, the DIGGERS began speaking a strange tongue: 'Yalla wally Wollongong, Bondi, Wollongong, Yambi, Nullarbor . . .', they went on.

Overhearing this impenetrable speech the TOMMIES — politely, of course — inquired what language the DIGGERS were speaking. 'Oh', said one of them airily, 'that's our language, Australian. We only speak it amongst ourselves.'

The point of this old yarn was to both STIR the TOMMIES and to establish that Australians were different to their British cousins — they had their own language, their Lingo, gibberish though all Australians would know it to be. We are still passionate about our language as the primary signifier of our difference, of our Australianness.

To listen to the Lingo is to hear a nation talking to itself — vulgarising, insulting, swearing, laughing, discriminating, giving names to people, places, objects, events, ideas. Turning every experience, no matter how unprecedented, into something that can be known, understood and so dealt with at the level of everyday necessity. Lingo is not just a funny way of talking that helps to define us as a particular group of mostly English-language speakers. Nor is it only one of the main modes by which we communicate. It is these things and more. It is the magic spell, the code, the means by which all is made, if not known, at least apparently knowable and so controllable. Lingo is also one of the ways through which the sometimes not very funny is made humorous, and so, bearable. Most important of all, Lingo lets us articulate popular notions of our past and so share the meanings we wish to make of the ongoing Australian experience. It is not surprising, then, that Australians have developed a passionate relationship with their vernacular.

But will the Lingo linger longer? Not according to the hordes of persons expressing their fears in letters to the editors of newspapers large and small. A constant theme of these complaints, often echoed in newspaper columns, is the extent to which our language is being subverted, perverted, undermined, overwhelmed and just plain BUGGERED UP by foreign imports. Most of the WHINGES are about Americanisms — TUSH; BUTT; KICK ARSE (increasingly spelt in the US way, as ass), and so on — and the culprits are usually identified as US popular songs, films, videos, television shows and, to a lesser extent, literature of various kinds.

The soundings that prompt these concerns are certainly accurate. Since the 1940s Australia has been increasingly submerged by US cultural products, a trend that has been even more noticeable since the progressive deregulation of many aspects of the Australian economy. Recent developments in communication and computer technology, especially

CD-ROM and the opening up of the Internet are also dominated by US product and ways of seeing and speaking about the world. Indeed, the fear of cultural swamping by the overwhelmingly US-produced CD-ROM revolution prompted the Keating Federal Labor Government to formulate its Creative Nation policy and funding in 1994, providing for the production and distribution to all schools of purely Australian cultural materials in CD-ROM format. While anything that provides cultural resources to an increasingly under-funded education system is a good thing in itself, whether it would have saved Australian culture is another matter. And does it really need saving anyway?

This larger question is closely connected to the fears of the letter-writers about the Australian language and its demise. They (and they frequently seem to be middle-aged or elderly) hear the distinctive Lingoisms of their generation giving way to an apparent cacophony of unfamiliar terms. These new terms are usually identified, not always correctly, as the dreaded Americanisms and the blame SHEET-ED HOME to the insidious influence of US media on the minds and the mouths of the young. In his *Weekend Australian* column of

17–18 February 1996, the indefatigable Phillip Adams called for individuals to each choose one colloquialism and, as characters in Ray Bradbury's *Fahrenheit 451* memorised a whole book against the flames, preserve their chosen Lingoism against the increasing influence of US culture. Adams claimed that 'In the past decade alone, more than 10 000 Americanisms have been incorporated into the Australian language and every one of them has made that language less Australian.' Adams's chosen word was 'the affectionate pejorative of DRONGO', now largely replaced by the Americanism DICKHEAD.

No slouch himself with the Lingo, in all its forms, Adams's fears are misplaced. As this book clarifies, what is really happening is that the vernacular is doing exactly what it has always done — changed, adapted, and survived. The Lingo does this because, like its speakers, it is a living thing, an interconnection of nerves, arteries and veins. Instead of carrying blood and electrons the channels of the Lingo carry words and phrases. Like any organism these words and phrases are forever rearranging themselves into new formations. Cells split and re-combine. Some die off, new ones are born. Our language, like everyone else's, is no exception. Those foreign bodies that are not suitable for the linguistic metabolism are either rejected or, if accepted, soon sloughed off as their inappropriateness becomes obvious.

Some examples of this are terms like SCRAM; BALONEY; LOWDOWN; CINCH; a PUSHOVER, and TO BELLYACHE among numerous other Americanisms current here in the 1940s and 1950s. The informal body linguistic, the vernacular democracy, has tried these titbits, extracted whatever nourishment they were able to provide then expelled them in the appropriate and time-honoured manner. A similar process seems to be eroding those acronymic imports of the 1980s — DINKS (Double Income, No Kids), YUPPIE (Young, Upwardly Mobile Professional) and NIMBY (Not In My Back Yard), from Britain. The Lingo moves on, garnering new, often only temporary, sustenance from many sources such as the Americanism, from British slang and occasionally from other languages. It also continually regenerates and recycles itself. Quite a few terms persist for surprisingly long periods. Some from the earliest days of settlement are still in robust use. Others drop in and out of favour, not in mainstream currency but not dead either — just sleeping until they are once more called back to consciousness by the mysterious processes of the vernacular. As well, we still display wit, colour, and originality in our invention of new forms, especially among the young who, while consuming and sometimes adapting foreign imports, are perhaps the main sources of new home-grown colloquialisms. One example of this is the mid- to late 1990s use of A BUCKLEY to mean a

202 • THE LINGO

loser, one who is considered unlucky and/or inadequate. This is a generational transformation of the older BUCKLEY'S CHANCE, well and truly in the efficient and colourful traditions of the Lingo.

Nor is the traffic in Lingoisms restricted to the internal or the one way. A number of Australian rhyming slang terms were identified in the argot of US criminals during the 1940s. More salubriously, Australian English moved into the global arena during the 1980s, carried by films like *Crocodile Dundee*, tourist promotion campaigns featuring the star of that film, Paul (HOGES) Hogan, some popular music hits and our brief but spectacular possession of the America's Cup (fleetingly re-named the PERTH PLATE). Television soaps like 'Prisoner'/'Cell-Block H', 'Neighbours' and 'Home and Away' have, puzzlingly to most of us, become significant factors in the everyday discourses of Britain and, to a lesser extent, the USA. Americans have reportedly taken to the Australianism ANKLE-BITER, meaning a child, in the belief that this is an Australian expression. It certainly is, though as it is widespread in British folk speech we probably cannot lay claim to it as our very own offspring. Still, in the popular mind at least, if the YANKS think it is an Australianism, no harm done.

Another interesting case in this context is the term LINEBALL, meaning a borderline case in which it is hard to decide the outcome either way. This term is used in US sporting speech and is increasingly heard in Australia, prompting the writers of Letters to the Editor to complain of yet another example of the Americanisation of our Lingo. But according to the lexicographers, LINEBALL, with exactly the same meaning, has been in use in Australia since before the World War I — it may even be an Australianism.

A Melbourne academic complained at a conference on 'Discourse and Cultural Practice' in March 1996 that Australian television soapies 'Heartbreak High' and 'Paradise' were now riddled with Americanisms. According to the author of the paper, 'Paradise Beach' had been DE-OCKERISED by its producers to appeal to the US market. While this may well be true, the examples given of Americanisms heard in this show included LITTLE MONKEY and RACK OFF. LITTLE MONKEY as an affectionate slang term for a naughty child has a long history in English, including Australian English, while RACK OFF (usually in the form RACK OFF, HAIRYLEGS) was adolescent Australian slang in the 1960s and is still quite commonly heard in speakers of that generation. When it comes to our Lingo emotional jingoism easily overwhelms actuality and the necessity of doing some research.

Lingo has always borrowed and adapted or, more realistically, NICKED (also British) and KNUCKLED other people's slang, especially that of Britain and the USA and it always will. When it ceases to do so, our treasured national speech will become an ossified museum piece. A couple of common items of contemporary Australian Lingo are BONK and BLT. The former originated in British slang in the 1970s while the latter, meaning a bacon, lettuce and tomato sandwich, is an Americanism from the 1950s. Another is SHONKY, imported from the USA via Yiddish and widely hurled, even by such eminences as Kim Beazley, leader of the Parliamentary Labor Party who used the word to describe the Federal Government's proposed land rights bill on 1 December 1997. The Honourable Mr Beazley might also have described his political opponents, in this matter, at least, as SHONKS, a recent and evocative adaptation of SHONKY. Such borrowings and transmogrifications are the very things that keep the Lingo, or any other language, healthy and vital.

The last word on this vexed subject must be left to Sidney Baker, still our greatest popular lexicographer, and a man of considerable wisdom:

> The extent to which a country absorbs the language of another country is not governed by lexicographers or academics...The instinct of the people as a whole governs it. They accept what they like, they reject completely words which have no useful application or which do not appeal to them, they modify others. We have used and survived English slang. We will do and are doing the same with American slang.

The Lingo has little to worry about from outside linguistic influences, then. But what about the forces within? Many people worry that the WOWSERS of old have been reinvigorated and transformed into crusading moralists of language under the rubric of political correctness. Will political correctness dampen the characteristic excesses and vulgarity of Australian? Not only is the Lingo grammatically incorrect in vocabulary and usage, it is by its very casual, unofficial nature politically incorrect. As this book amply demonstrates, it is also the vehicle for much that is reprehensible in our society, especially in matters of race, ethnicity, gender, and other perceived differences. Yet at the same time the Lingo carries a powerful emotional charge of national identity, of belonging and shared meanings. These generally more positive aspects of the vernacular conflict directly with the tenets of political correctness increasingly enshrined in legislation, especially that relating to sexual harassment, equal opportunity and racial hatred.

Few would argue that the practices and prejudices these laws seek to deter are positive. But when those in power set themselves against everyday speech and effectively outlaw elements of that speech considered by so many Australians to be their national linguistic heritage, how representative can they be? And what will be the consequences of governments legislating against what people think and say? Is it possible to successfully do such a thing? Will these actions simply engender deep and widespread resentment, a linguistic Prohibition, forcing the attitudes carried in the Lingo underground where they will never be changed and, in the end, making the problems they were meant to solve even worse? Doing the wrong thing for the right reasons?

To a considerable extent, the support for Pauline Hanson (as distinct from that of her subsequent One Nation party) was a popular reaction to what was widely perceived as the constriction of colloquial expression. This seemed to be happening at the level of formal communication, such as anti-discriminatory language policies in government departments and elsewhere, but also informally in the moralistic grandstanding of individuals who purveyed these admirable practices in the context of convivial interaction. The imposition of official language strictures on the Lingo is still causing intense irritation and puzzlement among Australians used to the unfettered articulation of our speech. While the attempts of officialdom elsewhere to modify colloquial speech, and hence the attitudes it carries, may be controversial, in this culture they are seen by many as a direct attack on national identity. This attack comes at a time when larger shifts of economics and politics are bringing great change, disruption, and increasing hardship, furthering the feeling that those things considered to be — and valued as — Australian, are under serious threat. Whether these values are aspects of myth or not, or whether political correctness is a right-wing smokescreen are questions for intellectuals. For most speakers of the Lingo, and that is still most Australians, these values are TRUE BLUE.

Where to now? The only thing we can say with any confidence is that the Lingo will certainly live on in whatever forms are appropriate for changed times. The number of popular books on the vernacular, some of them extremely successful, that relentlessly appear in bookshops is testament to the profound hold that our informal language has on us. Other evidence can be gleaned from Letters to the Editor sections of our newspapers and just by listening to everyday speech. Lingo, warts and all, is the authentic expression of the popular mind. It has always cursed, blasphemed, vulgarised, and insulted everyone and everything. It will continue to do so, regardless of small things like the law. That is just words on paper. Lingo is words on the tongue. If the pen is mightier than the sword then Lingo is mightier still because it cannot be erased by edict, by burning books, by the WOWSERS, or the politically correct.

Of course Lingo can be changed. That is very much in its nature.

Social, political and economic forces have shaped the language and how we speak it, and will continue to influence its development. At the time of writing a number of new terms related to the issue of indigenous land rights have entered Australian English : MABO, WIK, 10-POINT PLAN, BUCKET-LOADS OF EXTINGUISHMENT (courtesy of Deputy Prime Minister Tim Fischer) and NATIVE TITLE. Already CLAIMED has developed as a verb meaning that one's leasehold land is UNDER CLAIM by one or more indigenous groups, a term used among those most affected by such matters, pastoralists and mining interests. More broadly, the term SECRET MEN'S/WOMEN'S BUSINESS is often heard when members of one sex wish to indicate that members of the other should mind their own business. This came into use as dispute about the building of the Hindmarsh Island (South Australia) bridge escalated to what, regardless of the rights or wrongs involved, many regarded as farcical proportions in the mid-1990s.

As late as 1997 there was evidence that the Americanism root is beginning to creep into our Lingo as a substitute for BARRACK. Root has been used a number of times on air by Australian football commentators. As it is inconceivable that football followers would not be acquainted with the Australian meaning of ROOT we can only assume that this is an example of the process through which Lingo can compartmentalise terms by context. As ROOT, with the meaning sexual intercourse and exhaustion or failure, hardly seems on the way to the *obs.* category in the dictionaries, it may be that the unremitting influence of the USA, especially through television, sport and youth culture, will lead to root being used here for sporting matters in the same way as it is used across the Pacific. This slightly crude term could be used simultaneously as a quite innocuous description of enthusiastic support for one's team, though it lacks the appeal of insulting the opposing team and the referee so essential to BARRACKING. We will not know for some time whether it will be a successful import.

It will be intriguing to listen to our Lingo in the next few decades. As Australia, in common with the rest of the world, moves away from 'nationalism' and towards the 'internation', how will our language change? The concerned letter-writers will certainly continue to express fear of a total takeover of our tongue by whatever culture happens to dominate the new world order. Another possibility is that a global Lingo will develop which is easily transportable, a kind of world pidgin that will not relate to any particular national group at all. Some early evidence of this came through a 1997 INTERNET survey of international youth lingo. Among other things, this revealed that the archetypal Australianism G'DAY is in use around the world. Further indicators of linguistic globalisation include the often-heard use of the phatic SORT OF, KIND OF and I MEAN by even highly articulate speakers of English. These are not Australianisms, but nor are they Britishisms or Americanisms. They are part of an evolving INTERLINGO that is beginning to be spoken wherever tongues wag, jaws CRACK and ears are BENT.

But even while these forces are creating a new kind of international English as the world stumbles towards some kind of a giant common market and, consequently, an increasingly common culture, regional and national stubbornness is asserting itself, as it has throughout Europe's agonised attempts to form an economic community. This assertion takes the form of a robust defence of local customs, traditions, and most of all, of local lingoes. For above everything else, Lingo is the carrier of national myth, and nowhere more so than in Australia. Regardless of whether or not we are a fiercely egalitarian, anti-authoritarian, no-nonsense people down here at the bottom of the world, many Australians still think we are and we like to portray ourselves in this way. Most of us still like to believe that we have a distinct and unique identity, a shared group of symbols, traditions, and language that defines us to ourselves and against all others. That mythic identity is carried most powerfully in our speech and we will even more fervently continue our colloquial commonwealth into the future world order, still a vernacular republic.

• • •

In 1996, a Queensland senator deserted the Labor Party of which he had been a representative for a good many years. His defection was, not surprisingly, greeted with outrage on the Left, especially as it gave the Federal Government a potential additional vote in the badly hung Senate. This event, and subsequent 1997 investigations into the senator's travel allowance claims and practices, generated some interesting examples of the Lingo in action The terms DOUBLE-DIPPING and RORTING were widely deployed in Federal parliament by ALP members. A National Party MP, Mr Jull, claimed that 'this government is not going to be part of any bit of spivery'; SPIVERY is a revival — or perhaps a continuation — of an item of World War II slang, once also used in Britain. But the most spectacular contribution was that of Labor Senator Robert Ray. During an impassioned attack on the senator, Ray pilloried his opponent, a large, ungainly man, as 'the Quisling Quasimodo from Queensland'. As long as Australians preserve this sensitivity for language and invective, the Great Australian Lingo is SAFE AS HOUSES.

SOURCES AND ACKNOWLEDGMENTS

Readers who have endured the EARBASHING to this point will be aware of the wide variety of sources that have been plundered. Some have been mentioned in the main text but there are other printed references that have helped in the putting together of this work. What follows is at best a very partial list of sources, inspirations, useful compilations and important signposts that I found along the way.

A Captain Grose produced a *Dictionary of the Vulgar Tongue* in 1785 (more usually known in its 1811 edition) which includes a good deal of cant and other terms that formed a large part of the lexicon of those transported here for their country's good. The earliest Australian Lingo dictionary is usually reckoned to be that of convictisms compiled by James Hardy Vaux in the very early 19th century and published in 1819. Vaux was followed by many other serious and less-so works. In the former category should be mentioned Edward E.Morris, *A Dictionary of Austral English* (1898), so serious that it includes hardly any slang and *The Sydney Slang Dictionary* (several editions, c. 1880s). In the latter category there was 'Turner O. Lingo' (in reality Mary Elizabeth Fullerton, perhaps the only woman to deal with 'Australian' until relatively recently) who produced *The Australian Comic Dictionary of Words and Phrases* (E.W. Cole, 1916).

More recently there have been many compilations and commentaries on various aspects of the Great Australian Lingo, including the ground-breaking G. Wilkes, *A Dictionary of Australian Colloquialisms* (various editions since 1978) and W. Hornadge, *The Australian Slanguage* (1980). Still the most impressive work of this kind is the corpus of Sidney Baker, of which *The Australian Language* (1945 and subsequent editions) is the crowning achievement. A recent and very comprehensive compilation of current (that is, late 1980s to early 1990s) colloquial speech obtained from mainly oral sources is M. Johansen, *The Dinkum Dictionary: A Ripper Guide to Aussie English*, reprinted and revised several times since 1988, most recently as *Aussie Slang* (Penguin, 1996). Nancy Keesing wrote an excellent survey of women's and family lingo in her *Lily on the Dustbin: Slang of Australian Women and Their Families* (Penguin, 1982).

There have been — and still are — many more ephemeral compilations of Australian colloquial speech. These are usually aimed at the humour market and so may be unnoticed by scholars. But these compilations often give an earful of what people are saying, leading up to and about the time of publication. They include: J. Ramsay, *Cop It Sweet* (Allegheney News Service, 1977); many works of 'Nino Culotta' (John O'Grady), such as *Aussie English: An Explanation of the Australian Idiom* (1965 and more than 30 reprints); the generally earlier works of Bill Beatty such as *A Treasury of Australian Folklore* (Rigby, 1980); Bill Wannan's *The Australian* (1954; rev. edn, 1963, and seldom out of print); the rhyming slang collection of John Meredith, originally published as *Learn to Talk the Old Jack Lang* (1984) and containing H.P. (Duke) Tritton's clever rhyming slang letter, written early in the 20th century and such amusing but informative fripperies as *The Australian Dictionary of Insults and Vulgarities*, compiled by 'Blind Freddy' (1988). There are others in this category too numerous to mention individually, as is the case with the frequent newspaper and magazine articles that provide examples of what people are saying at a particular time and place. This ongoing and extensive publishing activity is a good indication of our fascination for the Lingo.

The serious work of socio-linguists and like academic experts has, often over very long periods of painstaking research, helped us better understand some of the mysteries of Australian. A useful, though partial, selection includes: William Ramson's edited anthology of articles, *English Transported* (ANU Press, 1980) and his *Australian English: An Historical Study of the Vocabulary, 1788-1898* (1966); P. Collins and D. Blair (eds), *Australian English: The Language of a New Society* (University of Queensland Press, 1989); Pauline Bryant's 'The South-East lexical usage region of Australian English', *Australian Journal of Linguistics*, 9, 1989, and G. Simes, 'The language of homosexuality in Australia' in R. Aldrich and G. Wotherspoon (eds), *Gay Perspectives: Essays in Australian Gay Culture*, Department of Economic History, University of Sydney, 1992.

Michael Clyne has been a seminal influence in the field of community languages in many works, one of which provides a useful summary in G. Beed Davey and G. Seal (eds) *The Oxford Companion to Australian Folklore* (OUP, Melbourne, 1993). Eve Fesl has done extensive work on indigenous languages, also represented in the above-mentioned *Oxford Companion to Australian Folklore*. A number of linguistic and lexicographical articles have appeared in the journal *Australian Folklore*, a few of which have been mentioned in the text.

R. Dixon, W. Ramson & M. Thomas's *Australian Aboriginal Words in English* (OUP, 1990) and Jay Arthur's *Aboriginal English: A Cultural Study* (OUP, 1996) have confirmed that Aboriginal English is a number of regional dialect versions of Australian English.

In the dictionary line Karl Lentzner's *Dictionary of the Slang-English of Australia and of Some Mixed Languages* (Halle-Leipzig, 1892) is said to provide probably the first professional indication of the rise of a distinctive, new language that we now call Australian English. *The Macquarie Dictionary* (since 1981) and W. S. Ramson (ed.), *The Australian National Dictionary: A Dictionary of Australianisms on Historical Principles* (OUP,

Melbourne, 1988) are indispensable, as are the many offshoots of this ongoing research and publishing project headquartered at the Australian National Dictionary Centre, especially J. Hughes (ed.), *Australian Words and Their Origins* (OUP, Melbourne, 1989). Other valuable dictionaries of slang include that issued by *The Macquarie Dictionary* publishers under various titles, the most recent being J. Lambert, (ed.), *The Macquarie Book of Slang*, 1996, as well as *The Macquarie Dictionary* itself. The many, frequently mountainous works of Eric Partridge, especially *A Dictionary of Slang and Unconventional English* (Routledge & Kegan Paul, London, 1961–70) include a good deal of Australian slang, even if occasionally erratic in the accounts of its origins, meaning(s) and usage.

Specialised studies of the speech of social groups include material relating to soldiers, such as W.H. Downing, *Digger Dialects* (1919), recently revised by J. Arthur and W. Ramson, (OUP/AWM, Melbourne, 1990); B. Moore, *A Lexicon of Cadet Language: Royal Military College, Duntroon in the Period 1983 to 1985* (Australian National Dictionary Centre, Canberra, 1993); B. Cowham, *Lego Lingo: The Cadets' Language* (English Department, Australian Defence Force Academy, 1987). The Australian Language Research Centre at the University of Sydney has published a good deal of work on the speech of occupational groups, such as shearers, opal miners and also on Australian Rules football and historical Australianisms. In recent years Australian lexicography has extended to regionalisms, resulting in the publications of M. Brooks, *Words from the West ; A Glossary of Western Australian Terms* (OUP, Melbourne, 1994) and *Tassie Terms: A Glossary of Tasmanian Words* (OUP, Melbourne, 1995). Also important here is G. Simes, *A Dictionary of Australian Underworld Slang* (OUP, Melbourne, 1993).

Australian folklorists have long been involved in the collection of folk speech. Some notable contributors in this field include Bill Wannan whose classic work *The Australian* has been mentioned and who has also documented our Lingo in other works, including *Folklore of the Australian Pub* (1972). Others with an interest in this area include June Factor who has conducted extensive research into the language of children, soon to be published, while Gwenda Beed Davey has worked in this field and also in the area of familyspeak, some of which has appeared in her *Snug as a Bug: Scenes From Australian Family Life* (OUP, Melbourne, 1990). Many issues of the *Australian Children's Folklore Newsletter* have carried articles on and information about Australian folk speech. Other folklorists who have contributed to our knowledge and understanding of folk speech include Ron Edwards and Bill Scott in their many and various works, such as Edwards' *The Australian Yarn* (1st edn, Rigby, 1977), comparison of which with the University of Queensland Press, St Lucia (2nd edn, 1996) provides a salutary glimpse of politically correct editing bowdlerising the historical linguistic record) and W. Scott's *The Complete Book of Australian Folklore* (Summit Books, 1976). The *Australian Folklore Society Journal* carries items on folk speech from time to time. I have thrown in one or two contributions of my own, including *Soundings! A Collection of Contemporary Folk Speech* (Antipodes Press, 1990).

Primary historical sources for the Lingo are wildly diverse, including lit-

erary works, newspapers, diaries, letters, reminiscences, and the odd anonymous document containing lists of words and phrases that have sometimes
survived in prison notebooks, scraps of paper and other miscellaneous
sources, including the holdings of collections such as the Children's
Folklore Collection at the Australia Centre, the University of Melbourne
and the Western Australian Folklore Archive at Curtin University, Perth. For
more recent Lingo, as well as the Lingoists themselves, I have gained a good
deal of information from national, State and local newspapers, magazines
and other media — mass and specialised — publications and also from radio
and television. The Internet has also become an intriguingly chaotic source
of information about colloquial language, as well as a generator of its own
linguistic forms.

For comparative purposes I have depended on my own ears when trav-
elling, on a reasonably moderate consumption of imported film, television,
and popular song and on some non-specialist, but well-informed, works like
The Story of English by R. McCrum, W. Cran and R. MacNeil (Faber &
Faber/BBC, London, 1986), Bill Bryson's *Made in America* (Secker &
Warburg, London, 1994) and Stephen Burgen's *Your Mother's Tongue: A
Book of European Invective* (Victor Gollancz, London, 1996) and something
of an ear opener. Also useful for Americanisms is Robert L. Chapman,
Thesaurus of American Slang (Collins, New York, 1989) which I now
promise to return to the ABC producer who LOANED it ME in 1993.

The most important contemporary sources of the vernacular are the
mouths of Australians, and much of this book has been the result of long-
term collection — and practice — of the Lingo as spoken from about the
middle of the 20th century. I listened to what was being said in factories,
schools, warehouses, shops, offices, PUBS, garages, barbers' shops, homes,
radio stations, universities and on buses, trains, trams, planes, building sites,
stages, and wherever else I have been during the last 30 years. I wrote down
a lot, but not all, of what I heard. I have also benefited from many contributions, large and small. I would especially like to acknowledge and thank
folklorist Brad Tate for his interest in my work, together with my colleague
in Australian Studies at Curtin University, Don Grant, and socio-linguist
Pauline Bryant. These people — and many more, including a number of
anonymous publishers' readers — provided input to this work at different
times through the years. Also thanks to students in my Australian Studies
classes who have kept me reasonably up-to-date on the rapid changes in the
Lingo, especially in youthspeak, as have my daughters.

One or two sections of this book have appeared elsewhere, in one form
or another. The material on SEPTIC TANKS was first published in a slightly different version in *Overland* and some other SKERRICKS have appeared in journals such as *Australian Folklore*, the *Australian Studies Bulletin* and *The
Journal of Australian Studies* and the *Australian* newspaper.

The original draft of this work has been improved immeasurably by the
meticulous editing of Robin Appleton and Terry Johnston, and the attention of staff at UNSW Press. Any errors remaining are all my own work.

INDEX

THE SIXTH FORM COLLEGE
LIBRARY
COLCHESTER